The Future of Soviet Military Power

THE FUTURE

of Soviet Military

POWER

edited by

Lawrence L. Whetten

New York

Crane, Russak & Company, Inc.

The Future of Soviet Military Power

Published in the United States of America by

Crane, Russak & Company, Inc.

347 Madison Avenue

New York, New York 10017

ISBN 0-8448-0909-8

LC 75-39978

Printed in the United States of America

Contents

List of Participants
and Observers

PARTICIPANTS

Mr. Ray S. Cline
The Center for Strategic and International Studies
Formerly Director, Intelligence and Research, Department of State

*Professor John Erickson
Director, Defense Studies, University of Edinburgh

Mr. Fritz W. Ermarth
Senior Consultant, U.S. Government

*Colin S. Gray
Deputy Director, International Institute of Strategic Studies

Professor William Griffith
Director, Center for International Studies,
Massachusetts Institute of Technology

*Asterisk indicates author has contributed a part of this book.

Professor Pierre Hassner
Centre d'Etudes des Relations Internationales

Dr. Johan J. Holst
Director, Norwegian Institute of International Affairs

Professor Dr. Karl Kaiser
Director, Forschungsinstitut der Deutschen Gesellschaft
für Auswärtige Politik

Professor Dr. Werner Kaltefleiter
Director, Sozialwissenschaftliches Institute der Konrad-Adenauer-Stiftung

Professor Robert Legvold
The Russian Research Center, Harvard University

*Professor Dr. Richard Löwenthal
Osteuropa-Institut der Freien Universität Berlin

Professor Dr. Peter C. Ludz
Director of Research, Stiftung für Wissenschaft und
Politik and Universität München

Mr. Malcolm Mackintosh
British Cabinet Office

Mr. Uwe Nerlich
Stiftung für Wissenschaft und Politik

Mr. Andrew Pierre
Council on Foreign Relations, Inc.

Professor Dr. Klaus Ritter
Director, Stiftung für Wissenschaft und Politik

*Dr. Lothar Ruehl
Military Correspondent

*Colonel William F. Scott
Consultant, General Research Corporation

*Mr. Leon Sloss
The International Institute for Strategic Studies
Formerly Deputy Director, Political-Military Affairs, Department of State

Mr. Michel Tatu
Editor, *Le Monde*

Dr. Frank N. Trager
Professor of International Affairs, New York University, and Director of Studies,
National Strategy Information Center, Inc.

Konteradmiral Herbert Trebesch
Ministry of Defense, Federal Republic of Germany

*Professor W. R. Van Cleave
Director, Defense Studies, University of Southern California

*Professor Lawrence L. Whetten
Director, German Graduate Program, SIR, University of Southern California

OBSERVERS

VLR Dr. Helmut Alexy
Foreign Office, Federal Republic of Germany

Brigadegeneral Heinz zur Gathen
Ministry of Defense, Federal Republic of Germany

Colonel Mel Johnsrud
Deputy Director, Defense Nuclear Agency, U.S. Department of Defense

Ministerialdirigent Dr. Andreas Meyer-Landrut
Foreign Office, Federal Republic of Germany

VLR I Detlef Graf zu Rantzau
Bundeskanzleramt, Federal Republic of Germany

Mrs. Harriet Scott
Author of works on Soviet Military Affairs

Preface

On 1–2 May 1975 an international conference was convened at Ebenhausen, West Germany, under the aegis of the Stiftung für Wissenschaft und Politik and the University of Southern California. The seminar was generously funded by the Thyssen Stiftung, the Earhart Foundation, and the National Strategy Information Center. A total of twenty-nine participants and observers contributed to the overall theme of the Future Role of Soviet Military Power within the East-West Context.

The purpose of the seminar was to provide a forum for the exchange of views on the broad issues relating to the changing nature of Soviet power within the framework of the evolution of the Western alliance structure and the political relations of the great powers. It was considered relevant at that time to Western research and policy formation to convene an international gathering specifically designed to analyze the probable future of Soviet political and military power over the next two decades. It is now widely accepted among Western analysts that the era of détente and the level of arms control often associated with it have been less productive than expected. The initial stage of improving the East-West political climate and of identifying selected issues for greater cooperation and mutual benefit has contributed to a less hostile atmosphere. But the East-West multilateral dialogues presently underway in Vienna and recently concluded in Helsinki and the U.S.-USSR special relationship have not provided a common understanding about the nature and goals of "normalized" political relations, especially regarding the role of military power. Likewise, mutual perceptions of the military threat posed by the other side have not fundamentally changed. Both sides are improving the quality of their armed forces; indeed, the modernization of Soviet strategic forces has accelerated at such an unexpected rate that the United States is once again approaching major policy crossroads.

In addition, several new features in the Western political posture must now be incorporated into assessments of the utility of Soviet military power, including the U.S. retreat from Southeast Asia and the possible erosion of American interest in foreign affairs and leadership within the Western political system, the world energy, food, and monetary crises that seemingly elevate economic issues to higher national priorities than security matters, the changing thrust of European integration and Atlantic Alliance cohesion, and so on. While such unprecedented uncertainties introduce serious risk factors for Western planners, the Soviet Union is also subjected to persisting and new constraints—for example, the continuing problem of legitimacy and stability in Eastern Europe, its own vulnerability to the negative features of the modernization process, adverse seepage of selected European issues into broader Soviet interests in the Middle East, the Far East, and the Third World, the impact of NATO weapons-modernization programs, and the stake Moscow now has in preserving its special relationship with Washington. Thus, a variety of unexpected circumstances continue to underscore the relevance of the conference proceedings.

To facilitate the deliberations, four panels were created. Projections about the nature of soviet military power over the next two decades warrant detailed assessments of Western assumptions about Soviet military behavior over the previous two decades. A review of this topic from the West European viewpoint was made and the policy constraints experienced by the Soviet Union were then discussed before drawing conclusions about the implications for Western security and foreign policies.

Minor discrepancies in figures and doctrinal interpretations have been deliberately left in the papers presented in this volume. Slight redundancies stressing an author's individual emphasis have also not been deleted. These variations represent individual authors' viewpoints and reflect the multiplicity of views common in the field of strategy theory.

I wish to thank the contributing foundations whose financial support made possible the convening of the conference and the publication of its proceedings. I am also grateful to Professors Klaus Ritter and William R. Van Cleave who served on the organizing and editorial committees. Finally, the gathering could not have been a success without the thoughtful, professional, and efficient support provided by the Stiftung für Wissenchaft und Politik.

L. L. W.
1 August 1975
München

Introduction: Doctrine, Strategy, Capabilities— An Overview

Lawrence L. Whetten

The purpose of this introduction is to capture the intellectual essence of the international conference held at Ebenhausen, West Germany, on 1–2 May 1975, without attributing all of the salient comments to the respective participants and to introduce each paper by placing it within the context of the broader outline of the seminar's objectives. In both undertakings, I ask the indulgence of the participants, for my brief observations cannot match the lucidity of their treatment of a given topic. It will be noted from the list of participants, p. i, that a wide range of nationalities, political viewpoints, and technical expertise was represented, and this provided an uninhibited exchange of opinions that has been difficult to replicate in its entirety. I have also taken the liberty of interjecting some of my own thoughts.

SOURCES OF U.S. MISPERCEPTION OF SOVIET POWER

Over the past quarter century, estimates of Soviet military power and political intentions have probably been the most controversial aspect of the East-West conflict. At times it has been fashionable to draw sharp distinctions between these two attributes of Soviet policy: (1) the Soviets were politically hostile, but militarily contained, or (2) they were politically responsible, but were gaining military advantages. At present, it seems more accurate to minimize this seam and to aggregate all factors of Soviet power and its military and political applications into a single analytical framework. The use of a composite methodological tool reduces the impact of errors on policy predictions from any individual category. For example, in the late 1950s, the United States estimated that the USSR would construct rapidly a massive deployment of an ICBM missile force, which proved false. The Soviets turned instead to an M/IRBM force, targeted not against the United States but against Europe. On the political side, Washington failed to predict accurately Soviet intentions in any of the four uprisings in Eastern Europe, even though it had fairly precise tactical intelligence on troop dispositions. Presumably, the order of magnitude of improvements in national surveillance capabilities upon which SALT I and other agreements are based and the generally more circumspect Soviet behavior in recent years should provide more extensive and reliable information about Soviet weapons and political interests. But the United States was caught unaware politically by the October War and was surprised also by the performance of some of the Soviet-supplied equipment. Thus, the accuracy of perceptions of Soviet power and its utility is central to assessments of the stability of the international systems, relations between the great powers, and great power-small power problems.

At the outset, mention should be made of a general problem in military perceptions. It is not enough merely to identify and correct previous errors or misjudgments, and then to improve estimating techniques to preclude future inaccuracies. Changing analytical techniques must be compatible with the evolving nature of the political relationships among the great powers and with systemic dynamics to which the estimates are to be applied. For example, the détente process has been accompanied by an unprecedented expansion of Soviet strategic arms to the point that superiority has been achieved in some weapons categories. Likewise, the diminution in threat perceptions among the European public has been paralleled by the most rapid modernization of Soviet forces east of the Elbe River since World War II. Some observers explain such paradoxical developments with the capabilities-versus-intentions syndrome. But such comforting paradigms are inadequate for prudent national leaders and scholars of Soviet socialist development. New research techniques and analytical tools are necessary to place military forecasting within the proper perspective of a changing political environment.

Leon Sloss, Research Fellow from the International Institute of Strategic Studies, has underscored these and other problems in an informative overview of American estimates of the military balance over three decades. Sloss distinguishes five general factors that have influenced U.S. assumptions about Soviet power during this period. First, he alludes to Graham Allison's rational actor and bureaucratic politics models of decision making by stressing the importance of personalities as well as institutions. Although the various national agencies had "lives" of their own, often independent of each other and their leaders, their autarchy was best demonstrated in the application of policy, rather than in high policy formation where other factors assumed importance. One such factor was the domination of personalities over the defense communities: Dulles during the 1950s, McNamara in the 1960s, and Kissinger in the 1970s.

Technological improvement is the second factor highlighted by Sloss. On the one hand, it has complicated intelligence estimating by increasing the complexity of strategic technology; on the other, enhanced technical information collection capabilities have increased the risks of concealment or noncompliance to specified agreed objectives, for example, the SALT accords. A third element was the influence of the prevailing strategic doctrine at the time. Since the advent of the nuclear age, U.S. analysts have consistently claimed a monopoly on modern strategy thinking and defense planning. Both institutions and personalities often became mesmerized by prevailing views. A fourth factor was the influence of advocates of arms control. The United States has had a historical propensity for weapons reductions and for correlating arms stockpiles with political tensions. Many U.S. leaders have endorsed the proposition that normalization of political relations must be accompanied by some form of arms limitation. A final factor was the general understanding of the utility of military power. It was to be used defensively to protect U.S. and allied interests and to contain Soviet and Communist expansion and subversion—that is, military power was a stabilizing factor in a changing world. Political profits were expected from the discriminate, responsible use of power, especially in view of the risks of nuclear war.

In modifying these assumptions, the United States has introduced two new objectives over the past several years: (1) to use arms negotiations as a method of bargaining, communicating, and inducing restraints and (2) to focus more carefully on the perceptions of third parties about U.S. strategic power. Both the intensification of the Soviet dialogue and the concern with others' views of U.S. stature are a direct consequence of the loss of strategic superiority. They are a product of the U.S. desire to examine more accurately systemic change and the Soviet role in the new order without unduly damaging traditional U.S. principles and interests. The success of these new approaches is open to question.

In the final analysis, however, change of approach or emphasis cannot alter the fact that uncertainties remain so salient in threat forecasting that judgment must be introduced, in some cases resulting in highly subjective assessments. It is at this juncture that the five influential factors Sloss identifies become most significant. Because of the varying impacts of the five factors on decision makers and the variety of institutions and personalities, threat perceptions requiring judgment frequently become lowest-common-denominator compromises between contending agencies and vested interest groups.

Colin S. Gray, Deputy Director, International Institute for Strategic Studies, points out that this element of bureaucratic politics has been one of the most persistent sources of American misperceptions about Soviet military power, with the caveat that a dissenting minority is permitted. He offers other reservations that may, indeed, compound the case about misperceptions. First, it is difficult to be precise after the fact about the accuracy of perceptions or misperceptions. We can now trace fairly clearly both U.S. and Soviet military actions during the past three decades. But because there were few linear action-reaction developments and because each side often developed weapons systems and doctrines to compensate for disadvantages or to exploit favorable geostrategic assets, it is hard to decide who misperceived or deceived whom.

Second, the scale of the alleged U.S. misperception has been cast out of true proportion, probably as a result of the lessons of SALT I. The shock of the loss of strategic superiority and the failure to perceive that the Soviets were governed by their own interests and aims and not by universal military standards produced an unprecedented cathartic reaction among the formerly hubritic U.S. strategic analysts. The United States had attempted to negotiate its way out of its own strategic deficiencies through the process of educating the Soviets into accepting the notion that they and the United States faced common problems. The inability of the United States to introduce Western intellectual "scholasticism" or to use the SALT negotiations to halt the buildup of Soviet strategic weapons has minimized the importance of two U.S. innovations in threat perceptions, namely, conducting direct communications with Moscow and bolstering third-party estimates of U.S. power. The United States could not use direct contacts to preserve its advantages and has learned to live with its losses. Third parties have drawn the undesired, but not entirely unexpected, conclusions that the strategic procurement policies of the great powers follow a logic of their own. Nuclear war may be unlikely, but neither power can be assured of its impossibility. Therefore, both must plan defensively against such an occurrence. But nuclear strategic deterrence and parity are directed against the rival power and have almost no direct military consequences for third parties. True, there are political implications for the Soviets' new reinforcement of the cold war nuclear bipolarity, but they relate mainly to the U.S.-USSR adversary relationship and the exclusive status as superpower. The nexus between strategic nuclear power and political influence against lesser states is difficult to pin down. Thus, third parties are likely to attach as much importance to manifestations of American political determination as to acclaimed Soviet nuclear posture, especially in the wake of the Vietnam War and domestic pressures—factors irrelevant to the strategic arms competition. Thus, U.S. concern about third parties' estimations of its military power without demonstrable political will is likely to appear as merely "posturing." These two U.S. objectives to correct its own perspective through favorably altering perceptions of others will need further additives to produce the desired results.

A third reservation about American misperceptions centers on the U.S.

misconception of the nature of the U.S.-Soviet arms "race." The competition has been regarded often either as "keeping up with the Joneses," or as "keeping ahead of the bad guys," justifications that are largely irrelevant. Arms competition or force matching is natural to normal relations between rival powers. American rejection of arms competition as a normal property of the state of the present rivalry has led to false expectations about the nature of the balance of power and great power relations.

PROBLEMS ASSOCIATED WITH SOVIET MILITARY DOCTRINE

In discussing Soviet strategic doctrine, William Van Cleave, Director of Defense Studies at the University of Southern California, points out that for much of the period of U.S.-USSR rivalry there was surprisingly little effort devoted by American strategists to studying Soviet military options and doctrine. The U.S. perception of Soviet strategy was in reality a projection of American ideas. For example, the United States assumed that Soviet strategy included the American concept of firebreak between escalations in the incremental use of force, but there was no confirming evidence in the literature or in exercises—indeed the Soviets seem to stress the opposite, disregarding pauses or boundaries in applying force. In rejecting American doctrine, the Soviets seem to be developing their own for the attainment of the political goals of war.

Today there is a marked change in the U.S. attitude, a change brought about by the gap between expectations and actual developments witnessed at SALT. The existing genuine differences in objectives and resulting doctrines are now accepted by American analysts. According to Van Cleave, these analysts have reached several general preliminary conclusions about Soviet doctrine and capabilities: (1) there is a remarkable consistency between Soviet declaratory policy and debates in military literature and actual policy decisions; (2) the best method for analyzing technical capabilities is to determine the degree of confidence the Soviets have in the various systems; (3) Soviet doctrine is dominated by the nuclear weapons factor; (4) SALT has not induced any perceivable changes in Soviet doctrinal positions, negating the convergence theory in military intellectualism; and (5) because of technological improvement and the declining Western strength, the Soviets have adopted a counterforce and damage-limiting strategy (the new ICBM programs have three main objectives: expand target coverage, improve prelaunch survivability, and develop a hard-target kill capability).

Contrary to the expectations of many, the attainment of parity has not slowed down Soviet research-and-development efforts. They have now deployed a new intercontinental bomber at a time when the United States has phased out virtually all air-defense forces. It is bringing into production four new ICBMs to augment and/or replace the missiles about which the United States was negotiating in SALT I. Several of the new missiles are expected to have a multiple-independently-targeted-reentry-vehicle (MIRV) capability. They have now deployed the D-II-D-class submarine with sixteen 4,200-mile-range missiles and have apparently accelerated their antisubmarine warfare program. They are reportedly upgrading their antiballistic missile defense with new missiles and improved radars. Finally, they are apparently experimenting with exotic weapons: high-energy lasers (already installed as range finders in the T-70 tank), charged-particle beams, and the military use of space. These developments are very difficult to monitor and the intentions behind them are ambiguous. But it seems apparent that the Soviets are determined to maintain a quantitative force structure with sufficient technological sophistication to support a counterforce and damage-limiting strategic doctrine, plus a variety of conventional options.

Soviet military writings that are now being scrutinized in the reassessment of Soviet doctrinal thinking that Van Cleave refers to have several unique characteristics. They are pedantically precise in the use of terms. There are, for example, important distinctions between military thought, science, and doctrine. Experience indicates that what appears in public writings is an indirect, but fairly accurate, reflection of the thinking and doctrine that governs military policy behavior. Obviously, the entire body of Soviet military writings is not available in the West. But what is available is valuable for several reasons: it is fairly consistent with policy; it serves as a propaganda and ideological instrument and therefore as an indication of the state of morale; it is a vehicle for debate and discussion about future trends and development, as well as about existing problems and deficiencies; and finally, it is continuing evidence that the Soviets excel in the problems of living with nuclear power.

Constant scrutiny of Soviet military writings reveals that the doctrine is in the process of evolution. This evolution tends to be more progressional or linear than fundamental and is due to the expanding global responsibilities of the USSR, the creation of a viable overseas strategic capability, technological developments that affect such factors as command and control, and the types of wars and the nature of peace to be expected in a changing systemic political environment. Although there have been few basic changes or reversals, modest corners have been turned roughly every seven or eight years—1945–1953, 1953–1960, and 1960–1967—and a new milestone may emerge soon.

Doctrine at the theater level displays less singularity than on the strategic plane because of the important role assigned to conventional arms. Prior to 1967, strong emphasis was placed on the concept of the inevitability of theater war escalating rapidly to the strategic scale. At that time it was stressed that tactical nuclear weapons would play the dominating role at the outset of theater warfare. Early first use of tactical nuclear weapons was a consistent feature of the scenarios of Warsaw Pact exercises. The alteration in this pattern occurred in the annual 1967 fall exercises in which a genuine conventional phase preceded the release of nuclear weapons. This shift should not be interpreted as a diminution in the role of nuclear weapons and other weapons of mass destruction. Nor should it be seen as an adoption of the U.S. doctrine of flexible response or the use of minimal force. Rather it should be viewed as an attempt to provide dual capability and training for all units in order to ensure the maximal use of whatever forces are necessary to achieve the specified objective. Unlike the West, the Soviets seem to have developed a true doctrine for theater nuclear warfare that provides for early first use against NATO nuclear facilities. True, this shift adds flexibility to Soviet options by providing greater latitude for seizing the initiative and determining the level of violence, and in exercising discrimination and selectivity—factors that are likely to add confusion about intentions for Western political authorities who still tend to calibrate flexibility with minimal force.

Colonel William F. Scott examines Soviet tactical concepts; the organization and structure of the Soviet armed forces, including officer recruitment, training, and education; and tactical lessons learned from limited wars. He concludes that when construction troops, railway engineers, logistical support units, border security forces, and so on, are included, the total manpower figures for the Soviet armed forces should be increased by at least one million over the present official U.S. total. Scott also examines the Soviet military school system and concludes that the actual size of the trained reserves is substantially higher than officially estimated and that troop training has been demonstrated as highly proficient. This he attributes to the elaborate reservist organization and its complex training and equipment-maintenance responsibilities.

Soviet military education has been a long-neglected subject. Scott estimates that there are at least 141 highly specialized military schools in the USSR. They grant the equivalent of university degrees and have entrance requirements comparable to those of U.S. service academies. The chief difference is that the Soviets produce specialized officers for selected career fields, for example, engineers, artillery, and so on. Furthermore, normal universities have reserve-officer training programs for all physically qualified male students, adding to the number and cadre of the reserve formations. On balance there is solid evidence that the United States has miscalculated the total strength of the in-being and deployable manpower of the Soviet armed forces. These conclusions should not be regarded as alarmist views that the Soviets are suddenly twelve or even eight feet tall, but as indications of deficiencies in past research and as a suggestion for future work.

THEATER OPERATIONAL CAPABILITIES
OF SOVIET NAVAL, AIR, AND GROUND FORCES

The paper on Soviet naval operations reviews the history of Soviet naval policy and the construction of the world's largest navy. It briefly surveys the capabilities of the principal combat ships and presents an assessment of the worldwide naval exercises conducted in April 1970 and April 1975. It concludes that the Soviets have achieved a flexibility in operations somewhat short of the quantitative buildup, but that rough parity has been attained with the U.S. Navy for many contingencies.

For over seventy-five years Russia has maintained the world's third or fourth largest navy. But because of its exposure on four separate seas and its lack of direct access to strategic oceans, the Russian Navy remained largely a defensive weapon and conducted blue-water operations mainly as a demonstration of its stature as a great power. Twice under Stalin the Soviets planned to construct a truly offensive fleet capability, but higher priority programs curtailed its development. By 1962–1963 the Soviets had decided not to parallel Western naval concepts of constructing rival series of capital ships but had deployed a cruise missile on board submarines for strategic strikes and for long-range antiship purposes on surface combatants. It was primarily this innovation that within ten years contributed to a quantitative Soviet superiority over the United States (223 to 221 surface warships and nearly 200 more submarines). The capabilities of the individual vessels and the compositions of the respective fleets suggest that the Russian Navy has primarily political and deterrent peacetime missions and strategic nuclear delivery, sea-lane interdiction, and area defense wartime missions. The Soviet wartime threat is designed to force the Western navies to commit far greater resources for the protection of vital sea-lanes than posed by the actual Soviet threat, thereby reducing the overall potential danger to the USSR proper, while affording the Soviet Navy greater latitude on the high seas. It is mainly this discrepancy in missions that has brought Soviet naval expansion to rough parity with the United States, a level of parity marred by marked Soviet deficiencies.

The Soviet meteoric naval expansion has been paralleled by an increase in maritime and aerial lift capacity. Since the effective U.S. interdiction of Soviet military interests in the Congo and Cuba, the USSR has constructed the physical assets to support a genuine overseas strategy. It now has a modest intervention capability abroad that is expected to expand gradually. During the Mideast October War, for example, the USSR delivered nearly double the U.S. tonnage supplied to Israel by air and a total of nearly ten times as much by sea. During the crisis the Soviets doubled the number of surface combatants to forty and deployed them to protect sea-lanes into Syria and to counter the three U.S. carrier task groups in a manner that earned the respect of American naval officers.

When the Suez Canal was opened on 5 June 1975, the USSR became the closest naval power to the Indian Ocean (Odessa is less than 3,000 miles from the Persian Gulf, whereas Norfolk is more than 6,000 miles away). As a complement, the Soviets have reversed a long-standing aversion against foreign military bases and have constructed the most extensive basing complex of its kind in Somalia, giving staying power to its permanent naval presence in the Indian Ocean.

Thus the Soviets have constructed a true blue-water navy and the capacity to support an overseas strategy. The Soviet naval presence in the Mediterranean is likely to remain at the present level, roughly equal to that of the U.S. Sixth Fleet, but it is expected to increase in the Indian Ocean, West Pacific, and South Atlantic. It is this new dimension of Soviet military posture, as much as the increase in strategic nuclear strength, that has advanced the USSR into the category of a truly global power.

John Erickson, Director, Defense Studies, University of Edinburgh, has furnished a comprehensive assessment of Soviet tactical concepts and capabilities in the European theater. Since the end of World War II, the Soviet Union has insisted on maintaining a theater posture of relative superiority. Both conventional and nuclear capabilities have been modernized recently, indicating a determination to preserve the advantage Moscow considers essential. These increases include 30 percent in tank strength, 50 percent in artillery inventory, and 25 percent in tactical aircraft. These improvements suggest that the Soviets' concepts of operations envision a blitzkrieg-type assault against the West, using massed armored strike divisions along several main thrusts. The Soviets do not have a Western-style concept of the incremental use of force or even of escalation. Maximum power is to be employed to achieve victory with high confidence, whereas the nuclear option is to be used at any level or time required. The Soviets have demonstrated the least imagination in adapting tactical aircraft for the ground-support mission. Traditionally tactical air forces have been dedicated to air defense and short-range delivery of nuclear weapons. The recent introduction into the forward squadrons of the SU-19 marks the first instance that the USSR has developed and deployed an aircraft designed for close ground support, a deficiency that was frequently noted in the West.

These weapons improvements and percentage increases in order of battles, with a 20 percent increase in total manpower, have resulted in the strongest, most versatile theater-force structure the Soviets have yet constructed. The known high quality of the weapons and equipment leaves the training and morale of the fighting man the chief question mark about the proficiency of this posture. It is this component that is most difficult to assess. Since World War II, Soviet units have been used only for policing operations within their own security zone. Soviet troops train with chemical and nuclear weapons to a far greater extent than do their Western counterparts. But simulated exercises are only games, and the differences between them and a nuclear environment are almost impossible to comprehend.

How could a posture of relative superiority be used in military operations? Lothar Ruehl, West German Military Correspondent, outlines several options customarily cited: (1) a general attack on NATO's central region, with armored strike divisions forming the first several echelons, (2) blitzkriegs against the exposed and possibly isolated Northern or Southern Flanks, and (3) military probes or provocations. The aim of the first option would be to gain physical control over Central Europe in the event that political subordination failed on some crucial matter. A war of short duration would probably be confined to West Germany and possibly the Benelux countries. If the Rhine and the English Channel were reached, the remainder of Europe would probably accept neutrality in preference to Soviet troops. The objective of the second option would probably be to improve Soviet access to strategic oceans over the Norwegian Cape or through the Dardanelles. Unrestricted rights of egress have been traditional Russian goals, and Moscow may be willing to pay a relatively high price to attain them. An added incentive might be to encourage, through a military presence, the establishment of friendly neutral governments. The aim of the third option might be to use military contingencies against limited targets, for example, Berlin, to demonstrate Soviet military and political power and underscore Western weakness, divisiveness, or indecision. As a minimum, it would register the Soviet's continuing interest in the political future of the European continent.

Ruehl concludes that none of these options is feasible as long as NATO remains relatively coherent and strong. The purpose behind the major new increases, then, is largely to improve the long-standing discrepancies in the quality of some weapons, such as tactical nuclear systems and air-delivered munitions, and to augment force sizes in anticipation of negotiated reductions. Improving the Soviet posture on the short term (before limited reductions) could have important long-term effects. Introducing the most advanced systems before the cuts could permit greater latitude in maintaining relative superiority by providing a broader base for continued qualitative improvements. The use of the Soviet military buildup as a bargaining chip at the mutual force reduction (MFR) talks, however, requires qualification.

The overriding objective behind this dramatic expansion in military posture is the Soviet conviction that the European problem (its theater of paramount concern) must be solved to its satisfaction and that political influence can develop at the local level from strong military forces. The present Soviet security problem is that it does not dominate the military and political environment in Western Europe. The Soviets feel almost as threatened by Western Europe now as in the 1950s; tensions have been lowered somewhat, but the U.S. presence remains viable, and the ideological spillage from Western modernization is as dangerous as ever. The present situation must be superseded by a more attractive political disposition. With a high military profile, Moscow can conduct its diplomacy with the relative assurance that any political mistakes will have a minimal detrimental effect. Its commanding presence in Europe, therefore, has important military and political purposes, and if the security problem is not resolved to its minimum standard, Moscow will continue to remain vigilant, if not militarily assertive in Europe when conditions warrant.

MFR AND CSCE AND THE FUTURE
OF EUROPEAN SECURITY

It seems appropriate to consider the above arguments about the purposes of the increased Soviet military threat (direct application of force, a bargaining chip, or political influence) within the context of the multilateral negotiations concerning European security matters—the MFR talks in Vienna and the recently concluded Conference on Security and Cooperation in Europe (CSCE). Robert Legvold, Russian Research Center, Harvard University argues that the Soviets have maintained separate and distinct maximum and minimum negotiating goals for both conclaves. Moreover, both sets of aims have gone through identifiable evolutions.

In 1971—1972, the CSCE assumed the final dimensions of a major Soviet aim advocated intermittently since 1954—a European security conference that could codify the results of World War II. The Soviet maximum aims were to drop the twenty-year-old issue of reparations (subsequently paid by Bonn to Prague and Warsaw) in return for the shelving of the German reunification problem and the securing of international recognition of all European borders, as embodied in part in the treaties ratified by West Germany and four East European countries—a quasi peace treaty. The conference was to stimulate and buoy the détente process and promote Moscow's status as the dominant, but benevolent and restrained, regional great power. These aims were to be achieved by transforming the political and military structures in Europe along lines that would reinforce practically and psychologically the stability and security, and, therefore, legitimacy, of Eastern Europe. Finally, these structural changes were somehow to be incorporated into a continuous "security-review" process. This process was to prohibit unwanted alterations and promote desired changes, inhibit Western integration, and stimulate Eastern solidarity. Simply participating in the security process, according to Soviet thinking, invigorates self-awareness of defensive matters and enhances the stability of the entire process, provided, of course, that the process is properly oriented and controlled.

During the three-year CSCE negotiations, these maximum aims were diluted by several unanticipated developments. The rise of the various economic crises created unprecedented fissures among the industrial nations that deflected their attention from security matters. Higher priorities were attached to West-West and North-South problems than to East-West ones. Additionally, the CSCE had become an unwelcomed forum for the smaller states to voice opinions and indeed veto proceedings on a wide spectrum of regional issues. Indeed, the smaller states seemed to fill the vacuum left by the distracted major powers, but they lacked the authority to advance Soviet aims as desired.

The final compromise endorsed a nonlegally binding commitment to honor existing boundaries, but sanctioned peaceful alterations. The mechanism for controlling changes, primarily in the area of freer flow of information and people, was subject to essentially a dual standard. The document itself accepted the principle of freer exchanges across boundaries, but within specific limits. These limits were to be the subject of individual bilateral treaties negotiated separately between the interested parties. Thus, constraints on change in the East were likely to remain as rigid as ever, and the West's aim of promoting modernization would be subjected to precise parameters determined by Moscow. On the issue of the regularization of the multilateral review process, the USSR seemed to accept its vulnerability to attacks by the smaller states and agreed to the biennial reconvening of the forum as a surrogate for its own ill-defined concept.

The Soviets were consistently less interested in MFR than they were in the CSCE negotiations. Not until the United States tied the opening of the two conferences together did Moscow agree to a specific date for convening the talks. The Soviets' maximum aims at the MFR talks were understandably not too dissimilar from those at the CSCE, although they insisted on preserving the separate identity of the two negotiations. These objectives were basically to exercise constraints on the modernization and disposition of Western forces, while preserving their own desired advantages.

The Soviets have been dissuaded from these lofty ambitions by a variety of factors. First, the West has presented a cohesive position that the Soviets have not been able to fragment, calling for absolute ceilings and negotiated force symmetries (see Lothar Ruehl's discussion). Second, there are genuine difficulties in distinguishing between minimum and excessive force levels required to accomplish a political, as well as a military mission.

There is no facile formula for determining the number of in-place and deployable troops necessary to preclude unwanted political developments for both great powers in either Eastern or Western Europe. The Soviets reason, for example, that before they had stationed five divisions in Czechoslovakia a serious threat to the security and stability of Eastern Europe had emerged. Likewise, the United States acknowledges that its troop presence in the Federal Republic of Germany has a reassuring effect for many Europeans who fear renewed German assertiveness. Yet, neither side has complete confidence in the proposed correlations between the political missions and force postures. The Soviets do not accept an equality in the nature of the political missions and place greater emphasis on "worst-case" assumptions, reflecting a much higher risk factor to stability in Eastern Europe and their determination to maintain a force structure of relative superiority for both political and military reasons throughout Europe.

A third reason is circumstantial and similar to factors the Soviets encountered in the CSCE. After being denied their maximum aims at the CSCE, the Soviets modified their expectations about security conferences, and MFR has been relegated to the stature of a bow to détente. By its nature it is more difficult for it to serve as a step-by-step confidence-building process, separated as it is from the process of political détente. It must be seen, from the Soviet viewpoint, within the broader context of nuclear free zones, nuclear nonproliferation, prohibition against West European nuclear collaboration, and so on. The Soviet understanding of peace is the maximization of socialist class aims and of Soviet objectives in both security *and* foreign affairs. The MFR talks play a fairly innocuous role in this program because the time is not ripe, and the West's preoccupation with its own problems has relaxed pressure on the USSR for an early conclusion of the talks.

Yet the Soviet Union is curiously discontent. By the nature of its system, it cannot play a significant role in revolutionary changes in the economic systems and concepts that have governed world development for over a quarter century. Likewise, it recognizes that it has little influence as yet over the future of Western Europe. One suspects that the Soviets would prefer to wait until the West-West problems diminish and the relationship between multilateral bargaining and force postures becomes more distinct before becoming more heavily engaged in regional security matters. Thus, the Soviets may still have an incentive to seek a conclusion of the MFR talks.

If they wish to advance the presently deadlocked negotiations, they seem to have two rough choices: (1) they must concede something to the other side's principles or (2) seek only a token agreement that does not impinge on the values of either side. Either choice will probably be heralded as a measure of consolidation and reinforcement for the détente process and might be consummated by a proposal for some form of permanent follow-on consultation mechanism, minus the cantankerous neutral and "near-neutral" states. At this juncture it appears that the Soviets will opt for a token accord that can carry maximum political connotations and thereby reinforce the CSCE accord, but which cannot be regarded as permanent or immutable because the "aggregation of historic forces" precludes such rigidity.

One reason for the Western misperceptions of the strength of Soviet military power and its potential political utility in arms negotiations has been Western uncertainty about the nature of the adversary relationship. Defense Secretary Robert McNamara frequently stated that the tangible political clout gained against the Soviets from possession of strategic nuclear weapons was difficult to calculate. Such rationale was used to justify acceptance of the SALT I agreements and the loss of U.S. superiority. There was no threat in marginal increases in power, it was argued, because they could not be politically used. This was to be the basic concept for the stable structure of a generation of peace. Thus, American planners saw virtually no way to bring nuclear weapons to bear politically on the Soviet leadership, except by threatening the source of their power through the anticipated collapse of their political system.

The difficulty with such argumentation is that it has not been shared by the Soviets. The USSR attaches a high degree of political value to nuclear weapons, and it is not interested in marginal increases. McNamara announced in 1965 that the Soviets would not compete with the United States in strategic weaponry because they were overextended. But when technology and resources permitted, they invested in a program designed to gain parity and then visible superiority over the United States. The U.S. misperception was not only of Soviet technical and industrial capabilities, but, more importantly, of their attitudes on the political usefulness of Soviet strategic superiority, especially among the newly coveted third parties. Their sense of political reward is reminiscent of the U.S. notions in the 1960s: Political bonuses could be earned by exercising restraint against a rival while being in a position of manifest superiority. This has been a key premise for Soviet participation in the détente process. The Soviets expect to use this new strategic posture as a backdrop for the conduct of a more flexible foreign policy that may, when appropriate, include an increase in their willingness to accept risk in the face of challenge or to be more assertive under favorable circumstances.

Although in the technical sense, the Soviets have not achieved overall superiority, but rather parity with marked disparaties, they have gained political equality as encased in the Vladivostok communique. The attainment of military and political equality and the formal recognition of this fact by the opponent is one of the most significant accomplishments of the Brezhnev era. The Soviets probably now expect a relatively stable state to emerge in strategic competition that will persist for the next five to ten years. It will be characterized by a military standoff, lower levels of investment, and a refinement of the existing disparities. But because of their faith in the dialectic and the favorable "correlation of historic forces," they do not expect this stable state to become permanent. Western perceptions of future Soviet political designs must now be even sharper than in the eras of assured U.S. superiority or of arms-limitation accords.

The U.S.-Soviet Military Balance: Changing American Perceptions, 1945-1975

Leon Sloss

INTRODUCTION

This paper discusses American assumptions about Soviet strategic force postures during the 1950s and 1960s. No attempt has been made to write a comprehensive history. Rather the aim here is to identify the major factors influencing U.S. attitudes toward Soviet strategic programs. Soviet strategic forces are discussed largely in terms of the *balance* between U.S. and Soviet strategic forces because this is the way the matter is most usually viewed from Washington. Furthermore, this paper stresses *perceptions*, and at times varying perceptions, because there has never been "an American view" any more than there is a "European view" on such a complex and controversial issue as the strategic balance. The review begins in the mid-1940s after World War II and ends in the mid-1970s in order to provide some perspective on what came before and after the period in question.

TRENDS IN AMERICAN PERCEPTIONS—
THE ERA OF AMERICAN STRATEGIC SUPERIORITY

From the end of World War II until the late 1940s, American defense and foreign policies were heavily influenced by the assumption that Americans held

15

clear technical superiority over the Soviet Union in the nuclear weapons field, and although this condition was not permanent, it was likely to last for some considerable period of time. World War II ended with hope that the wartime alliance with the Soviet Union would persist. The overwhelming U.S. desire to "bring the boys home" resulted in swift demobilization of American forces except in Germany and Japan. Europe was preoccupied with recovery from the devastation of war; save for a few military leaders and technical experts, there was little concern about a Soviet nuclear threat that seemed but a distant and theoretical possibility in 1945. The prevailing assumption was that the Soviets would take a decade to develop nuclear weapons.

Hopes for a new era of peace soon were dashed, however, by Stalin's speech of 9 February 1946, which made clear that the Soviets would give top priority to building up their military power, and by the brutal Soviet occupation of Eastern Europe. In the spring of 1946, George Kennan, in his famous cables from Moscow, was warning the State Department that the Soviet objective was to "use every means to infiltrate, divide and weaken the West."[1] On the basis of Kennan's assessments, the foundation for a policy of containment was being laid. This culminated in 1949 with the establishment of NATO. The defense policy of NATO was based on the assumption that U.S. strategic nuclear power would be linked to the defense of Europe to offset and deter the use of superior Soviet conventional power. In short, the original concept of NATO was clearly designed for a period of U.S. nuclear superiority. American access to bomber bases in Europe gave U.S. technical and numerical superiority operational significance by bringing U.S. bombers within range of the Soviet Union. Although U.S. military-assistance programs began to build some nonnuclear capability in Europe beginning in 1949, and the accession of Western Germany to NATO in 1954 promised to add additional conventional strength, the strategy of the Atlantic Alliance remained heavily nuclear in the 1950s.

Also in 1949 the Soviets exploded their first nuclear weapon, and it was then clear that the U.S. nuclear monopoly would not last forever. However, the United States still retained a substantial lead in the nuclear field, and there seemed little doubt in 1949 that this advantage would persist for some time in view of presumed U.S. technological superiority.

As early as 1946, the initial efforts to bring nuclear arms under international control had taken place. The Lilienthal-Acheson Report, which led to the so-called Baruch Plan, proposed a scheme for international control over "dangerous activities" in the nuclear field.[2] The report recognized that the "extremely favourable position" enjoyed by the United States "is only temporary. It will not last." In describing the discussions that led to the report, Acheson makes

---

[1] Dean Acheson, *Present at the Creation* (New York: W. W. Norton, 1969), p. 151.
[2] Ibid., p. 153.

clear that the U.S. assumed even in 1946 that the Soviets were working rapidly to acquire nuclear weapons.[3] Yet well into the 1950s the development of a Soviet strategic capability equivalent to that of the United States was seen as a future problem rather than an immediate one.

Premonitions of Parity

One cannot define a precise date at which the United States began to consider Soviet strategic nuclear power as a serious military threat. As is usually the case, different people and institutions made differing assumptions. We have seen that as early as 1946 some American officials recognized that the Soviets would eventually become members of the "nuclear club." However, there was a tendency at that time to underestimate how rapidly this would occur, and thus there was a corresponding failure to think through the implications of a world in which the U.S. nuclear monopoly had disappeared. To most Americans, the first explosion of a nuclear weapon by the Soviet Union as early as 1949 came as a surprise. The explosion of a thermonuclear device only four years later and only a year after the United States came as an even greater surprise. Late in 1954 the concerns about the bomber gap had begun in Washington. A nuclear threat from Moscow began to be taken seriously. The launching of *Sputnik* in October 1957 culminated a decade in which the United States gradually came to accept the Soviet Union as a major nuclear power. This was followed by a brief period, 1957–1961, during which Soviet capabilities were exaggerated, and this led to the debates over the missile gap during the 1960 election campaign. Those who did perceive the implications of eventual nuclear parity had quite differing assumptions. Many scientists and politicians clung to the hope that international controls over nuclear weapons could be negotiated and, for example, urged that the United States not develop a hydrogen bomb. They argued, somewhat inconsistently (as many of the same people later argued with respect to the ABM), that a hydrogen bomb would have no military utility and that if the United States developed one, the Soviets would be forced to follow suit. As a result, they argued, all hope for arms control would evaporate. But there were others who maintained that the United States must take steps to retain superiority over the Soviet Union and that U.S. technological and industrial superiority made this possible. However, there were great differences over what the relative emphasis in U.S. strategic policy should be: offense versus defense; bombers versus missiles; ICBMs versus SLBMs. These differences, some strategic and some bureaucratic, tended to color each person's estimates of the threat.

The decision in 1953 by President Eisenhower to deploy U.S. tactical nuclear weapons to Europe resulted from several factors. First, these weapons now existed, and at least temporarily, the United States enjoyed superiority over

---

[3] Ibid., chap. 17.

the Soviets in this field. Second, there was the failure of NATO to meet the conventional-force goals established at the Lisbon ministerial meeting and the belief that tactical nuclear weapons might compensate for conventional inferiority. Third, the decision reflected a realization that U.S. strategic nuclear superiority by itself might not be adequate to deter aggression in Europe. This was one of the first concrete actions taken by U.S. authorities that recognized the fact that Soviet strategic power would eventually affect the balance of power in Europe. Yet the belief that the United States would retain numerical superiority in strategic weaponry persisted well into the 1960s. As Wohlstetter's recent studies of the "arms race" phenomenon show, many of the U.S. estimates of Soviet strategic capabilities in the early 1960s were based on the assumption that the Soviet Union had no intention of striving for numerical parity.[4]

The McNamara Era

The impact of Robert McNamara and his associates on U.S. strategic thinking during the 1960s cannot be overestimated. Soon after McNamara became secretary of defense, the United States achieved a powerful new tool for acquiring accurate intelligence on Soviet strategic capabilities—the intelligence satellites. Improved information acquired by satellite soon demonstrated that the intercontinental-missile gap favored the United States, not the Soviets. The new reconnaissance satellites permitted a very accurate identification of *current* missile and bomber inventories. But as Wohlstetter points out, this did not prevent gross misestimates of *future* capabilities.[5] Such estimates still depended on assumptions that frequently were in error. For example, the United States underestimated Soviet MRBM/IRBM deployment and overestimated ICBM deployments in the late 1950s and early 1960s because of mistaken assumptions of where the Soviets would place their priorities. Later the United States underestimated Soviet ICBM programs, at first because of a belief that the Soviet goal was less than numerical parity in ICBMs and later because of a belief that the Soviets sought no more than parity, assumptions that proved ill-founded. There were also some, including McNamara, who held the belief that the Soviets could be persuaded to accept parity if the United States exercised restraint in its statements and actions.

Using the highly accurate satellite intelligence data and the techniques of systematic analysis, McNamara attempted to systematize and quantify the process of strategic force planning. Systems analysis began with an assessment of the threat, and thus the technique of threat estimating was to be a central element in the force-planning process under McNamara and became a highly developed and

---

[4] Albert Wohlstetter, "Is There a Stragetic Arms Race?" *Foreign Policy*, nos. 15 and 16 (Summer and Fall 1974).
    [5] Ibid.

elaborate process in the U.S. intelligence community. The process tended to give a false concreteness to the estimates of Soviet strategic capabilities. The system forced McNamara to defend the scientific accuracy of his analyses and thus to exaggerate their reliability. One tended to forget that after all an estimate was an estimate was an estimate.

American assumptions about Soviet strategic power in the 1960s also were colored by the belief in the so-called "interacting spiral of the arms race." McNamara made a conscious effort to curb U.S. strategic programs in the hope that this would curb Soviet reactions. Having started the 1960s with a major effort to overcome what turned out to be a false missile gap, analysts and policy makers were by the middle of the decade again asking the question, "how much is enough?" McNamara attempted to pace limits on the size of U.S. strategic forces by quantifying the criteria for assured destruction and damage limitation, but increasingly he stressed the former objective because the latter seemed to lead to open-ended requirements.

Because of the central role played by threat estimates in the process of analysis, there was a tendency to manipulate estimates to prove a particular point about what U.S. forces were needed. In an effort to correct these tendencies, McNamara forced the system to develop alternative estimates based on differing assumptions. But as the Wohlstetter study shows, even the high estimates were, more frequently than not, too low. The persistent tendency after the early 1960s was to underestimate Soviet strategic capabilities even while the myth "that the Pentagon always exaggerates the threat" persisted.

Nixon and Kissinger

By the time the new administration took office in January 1969, strategic parity, if not a reality, was a foregone conclusion. One of the first tasks of the newly invigorated National Security Council (NSC) system, under Dr. Kissinger, was a thorough examination of the U.S. strategic posture and the options for the future. Faithful to the new Nixon/Kissinger approach, the system examined all relevant options (and some not so relevant ones) in excruciating detail. Added urgency was given to the study by two factors. First, increasing opposition was developing to the Sentinel antiballistic missile (ABM) program, which had been started under the Johnson Administration (with the very reluctant acquiesence of McNamara). The administration needed to decide whether to continue, modify, or abandon the program. Second, the Soviets were pressing for the initiation of SALT talks, which had been aborted by the Soviet invasion of Czechoslovakia in the fall of 1968. The administration was unwilling to enter into SALT before completing a thorough review of strategic options.

The essential outcome of the review, completed in the summer of 1969, was to settle for strategic parity, which was described by President Nixon as a strategy of sufficiency. By now the governing U.S. assumption (although there was some dissent) was that Soviet strategic programs had reached such a size and such a momentum that there was no feasible way to maintain superiority at an acceptable price. If the United States attempted to stay ahead, the Soviets were now in a position to prevent this. Indeed, the Soviets were then deploying the new SS-9 and SS-11 missiles at a rate of several hundred a year, whereas the United States had no plans to add to its forces. Still, it was assumed that the Russians would be likely to stop their deployments at about 1,000 ICBMs, the figure that had long been established as the U.S. plateau. The U.S. effort at this time was concentrated on qualitative improvements. This meant, in particular, the continuation of the multiple-independently-targeted-reentry-vehicle (MIRV) program, which had been initiated under the Johnson Administration. The ABM also was to be continued, although reconfigured to emphasize defense of missile fields, and with a new name—Safeguard.

The Nixon Administration soon faced a new problem in estimating Soviet strategic capabilities. By the early 1970s it became clear that future developments in strategic weaponry were to be primarily qualitative rather than quantitative. SALT I confirmed this situation by placing a limit on ICBM and SLBM forces, at least until 1977. The United States halted ICBM deployment in 1966–1967; by 1972 both sides ceased to add additional ICBM silo-launchers and the general limits of SLBM deployment had been established by SALT I. However, the United States had begun deployment of MIRVed missiles, and it was clear that the Soviet Union was striving to catch up in this area with a new generation of ICBMs then under development. The relevant factors in the strategic balance increasingly were becoming payload, accuracy, and reliability—factors that could not be estimated as readily as numbers of missiles and bombers. Once again, the U.S. intelligence community was operating, as in the 1950s, on the basis of imperfect estimates rather than hard intelligence, even for current Soviet capabilities.

Although the United States is now quite certain as to the numbers of Soviet strategic weapons, the deployment of mobile strategic missiles, which appears to be permitted by the Vladivostok Agreement, will create new uncertainties; and there remains much uncertainty today and much latitude for judgment about the qualitative factors that loom ever more important in assessing the strategic balance. For example, it is extremely difficult for the United States to estimate the accuracy of Soviet missiles with any degree of precision. Indeed, it is not possible to know the precise accuracy of any given U.S. missile, because accuracy can be sensitive to a number of transitory factors, such as weather.

Given this kind of estimating problem, there are bound to be differences in assessments of Soviet strategic capabilities. But these differences do not stem from technical estimating problems alone; other factors have influenced and continue to influence U.S. assumptions.

FACTORS THAT INFLUENCE U.S. ASSUMPTIONS—
PERSONALITIES AND INSTITUTIONS

Personalities always play an important role in political decisions. I believe that this is particularly true in an area that is as complex and esoteric as nuclear strategy. Only a handful of people really understand the problem in detail, and estimates of Soviet capabilities have remained highly classified, primarily to protect intelligence sources. Thus, the general public, and even the relevant congressional committees are extremely dependent on what the experts tell them. Although there are experts in and out of government, the government is in a position to control the flow of information to the public through classification. I do not suggest that the public and the Congress have been purposely misled as to Soviet capabilities, but in a relatively closed system (inevitably so, because of security considerations) it is easy for consistent biases to creep in. This seems to have been the case in the 1960s, as the Wohlstetter findings seem to indicate.

The personalities that were particularly influential were John Foster Dulles in the 1950s, Robert McNamara in the 1960s, and Henry Kissinger in the 1970s. Although Dulles was not concerned with the details of strategy and forces, his concept of massive retaliation was based initially on the assumption of U.S. superiority. However, by the end of the Eisenhower Administration, it was clear to Dulles and the president that U.S. superiority was waning, and even Dulles was talking about "selective retaliation."

The McNamara era must be divided into two phases. During the first year or so, McNamara was concerned with restoring a strategic balance that some believed was in danger of passing to the Soviets in 1960. It was during this period that additional funds were authorized to expand the ICBM and SLBM force, a program started under Eisenhower, and to increase the readiness of strategic bomber forces. However, after a brief flirtation with a counterforce strategy, marked by the Ann Arbor speech of June 1962, McNamara became increasingly influenced by the presumed dangers of the arms race. He also became convinced of the need to make major improvements in conventional forces and thus began to search for a rationale to limit expenditures on strategic forces. The result was a growing emphasis on "assured destruction" as the fundamental rationale for U.S. strategic forces. Underlying the assured-destruction strategy was the assumption that strategic parity was inevitable. McNamara probably made this assumption sooner than most, because of his conviction that a U.S. effort to retain superiority would lead to a spiraling arms race. By the end of 1963 it was clear that McNamara believed that the strategic forces then planned by the United States would be sufficient both for deterrence and for damage-limiting roles, and that they would remain superior to those of the

Soviet Union for at least the coming decade. In his speech to the Economic Club of New York on 18 November 1963, McNamara said:

> Deterrence of deliberate, calculated attack seems as well assured as it can be, and the damage-limiting capability of our numerically superior forces is, I believe, well worth its incremental cost. It is a capability to which the smaller forces of the Soviet Union could not realistically aspire. This is one reason, among others, why I would not trade our strategic posture for that of the Soviets at any point during the coming decade.[6]

At the same time, he went on to argue that "the damage which the Soviets could inflict on us and on our allies, no matter what we do to limit it, remains extremely high," and he concluded that "larger budgets for strategic forces would not change that fact."[7] Thus, while McNamara was assuring the American public that U.S. strategic forces were, and were likely to remain, superior, he was also pointing out that deterrence was mutual and was attempting to limit the pressures for major increases in strategic-force expenditures.

It remained for Nixon and Kissinger, less than a decade later, formally to accept "sufficiency," a concept that was already implicit in the McNamara statement of 1963. McNamara's major objective was to devise a rational system of force planning that would "quantify" the analysis of force requirements. Kissinger's search was for concepts that would order U.S. security policy and create a more stable relationship with the Soviet Union and China. Fundamental to the Kissinger approach was the identification of policy options so that the alternatives could be compared at the highest level, and not predetermined through bureaucratic bargaining. When the options were presented to Nixon and Kissinger in the summer of 1969, it seemed clear that parity was upon us and that Soviet superiority was a definite prospect for the future. There were two ways to meet the problem. One was to try to stay ahead, or at least even, through unilateral U.S. efforts. The other was to try to negotiate limits on strategic forces in SALT. The Nixon Administration chose the latter course while keeping open options to pursue the former, should negotiations fail. However, the momentum of Soviet programs gave them a distinct bargaining advantage. By 1972 it was clear that if there were to be negotiated limits on missile forces, the Soviets would have some numerical advantage. This situation was reflected in the Interim Agreement on Strategic Offensive Forces, which gave the Soviets numerical advantage in ICBMs and SLBMs. Kissinger argued that the differences were strategically insignificant and that what was important was to take a first step toward negotiating limits rather than to permit competition

---

[6] William W. Kaufmann, *The McNamara Strategy* (New York: Harper & Row, 1964), p. 305.
[7] Ibid.

to continue unchecked. Behind SALT I was the emerging Kissinger concept of an interlocking web of agreements that would give the Soviet Union a stake in maintaining stability. To Kissinger the numbers were less important than the fact that the first strand of the web had been woven.

There was one result that the McNamara and Kissinger approaches had in common. This was the detailed public exposure of U.S. intelligence estimates. For McNamara this was essential to explain the rationale for force and budget decisions. McNamara's Posture Statement became, during the 1960s, the major statement of U.S. security policy, and it contained a fairly detailed description of the threat assumptions on which U.S. strategic planning was based. As Wohlstetter has shown, these assumptions were often wrong, but they became the basis on which not only the United States but most of the world judged Soviet strategic capabilities. Kissinger found such assessments useful too in providing support for the policy options that the Nixon Administration had chosen. However, he found it intolerable that the major statement of U.S. security policy should emanate from the Department of Defense. As a result, in the early 1970s the President's Foreign Policy Report became the major vehicle for exposing U.S. assumptions on Soviet programs. (In the last two years, the Posture Statement and the statement of the chairman of the Joint Chiefs of Staff [JCS] have again become major vehicles for stating threat assessments because of the absence of a presidential report.) The result of these documents is to make official U.S. assumptions about strategy and Soviet capabilities publicly available in quite unprecedented detail.

TECHNOLOGY

Two important ways in which technology has affected U.S. assumptions have already been noted. The development of reconnaissance satellites revolutionized intelligence collection, whereas the development of MIRV further complicated intelligence estimating.

In the 1950s it was necessary to estimate current Soviet programs on the basis of very limited evidence. Estimates were based on what little was known of Soviet scientific and industrial capabilities and on a few detectable events such as nuclear explosions and missile firings. These were later supplemented by limited U-2 photography. Projections were based on U.S. experience, which often proved to be a faulty analogue. Satellite photography has permitted quite accurate assumptions to be made about current strategic missile and bomber deployments and has made possible the SALT agreements based on "national technical means" of verification. As we have also seen, however, accurate current assumptions do not assure accurate future projections.

Technology also is complicating estimates today. Assessments of the strategic balance are becoming more dependent on qualitative factors and more difficult to estimate. Thus, there will inevitably be greater uncertainty in the future about key elements in the Soviet strategic capability than there has been in the past fifteen years. This may not be an unmixed blessing. When it is certain that intelligence is uncertain, there may be less of a tendency to rely too heavily on the accuracy of intelligence estimates as a guide to planning. On the other hand, the uncertainties facing planners in the future, which can only be partially alleviated by arms-control agreements, are an incentive to planning on the basis of "worst-case" assumptions. Wohlstetter has shown that the widespread dependence on worst-case assumptions was largely a myth in the 1960s, but it could still become a reality in the 1970s.

STRATEGIC THEORIES

We also have seen that the dominant personalities who influenced U.S. assumptions in the 1950s, 1960s, and 1970s were, in turn, strongly motivated by their own strategic theories. Dulles, drawing heavily on the advice of the JCS, was convinced that deterrence could be based on massive retaliation, although the image that often is conjured up by that term does not do full justice to the subtlety of Dulles's thinking. McNamara was influenced by his theories of the arms race to adopt mutual assured destruction as his governing strategy. The McNamara strategy also was heavily influenced by the assumption that the Soviets would plan their strategic forces for the same objectives and in the same way as did the United States. Kissinger's approach has been dominated by his concept of an interlocking web of relationships and by the conviction that the assured-destruction strategy did not provide the flexibility necessary for an era of negotiation. Hence the development of flexible options, an idea initiated by McNamara in 1960, revived by Kissinger in 1970, and articulated by Schlesinger in 1974. Strategic concepts influenced views of Soviet capabilities. Dulles was slow to anticipate strategic parity. McNamara anticipated it, but underestimated how rapidly it would be achieved. Kissinger has had to live with it and has devised a political strategy to accommodate an era of parity.

THE INFLUENCE OF ARMS CONTROL

Throughout the period in question, the influence of the arms-control community on strategy and on U.S. assumptions has been growing. The effort to control nuclear weapons began with Hiroshima and with the scientists who felt a sense of guilt at the vast destructive power they had created. The failure of the Baruch Plan was followed by efforts to ban the hydrogen bomb and then by the campaign to end nuclear testing. However, it was not until the 1960s that arms-control considerations became a central element in U.S. force planning. Today, many believe that arms control has become the dominant factor in U.S. strategic force planning.

Arms control has not had a consistent effect on U.S. assumptions with respect to Soviet strategic forces. The general tendency of arms control is to generate pressures for restraint on strategic programs, but arms control also has generated the "bargaining-chip" argument, which, for example, was a major rationale for support of the Safeguard ABM program in 1969 and 1970. At times, arms-control advocates have tended to underestimate Soviet strategic capabilities in an effort to demonstrate that the United States did not need to do as much. For example, many of those who argued that the Soviet Union was not aiming for parity in the 1960s did so in order to convince the U.S. government that it was the United States that was stimulating the arms race. At other times, arms-control advocates have exaggerated Soviet strategic capabilities to demonstrate that the United States ought to accept limits that would halt the Soviet Union short of the assumed capabilities. Many who supported the SALT I agreement argued that Soviet strategic forces were destined to go far higher if there were not an agreement. The point is that advocacy of arms control has had a tendency to color estimates of Soviet capabilities even though the bias has not been consistent.

VIEWS ON THE ROLE OF MILITARY POWER

At one extreme is the theory of convergence—namely, that the U.S. and Soviet systems are converging and are destined to become even more compatible in the years ahead. Convergence theorists hold that military power has less and less relevance, and large strategic forces stand in the way of accommodation. This view tends to place little importance on relative military capabilities and asserts that detailed estimates of Soviet strategic capabilities are largely irrelevant.

A somewhat different view holds that in a period of rough strategic parity, differences in the details of strategic forces matter very little, so long as there is a rough balance of power, a term that is almost never precisely defined. Those adhering to this position feel that the United States should not attempt to match Soviet strategic power item by item, and thus the precise details of Soviet strategic capabilities are not critically important. A frequent corollary of this view is that the United States should restrain expenditures on strategic programs in order to devote more resources to conventional forces, which is where the balance really counts.

A third view concentrates heavily on the negotiation process as a means for reducing tensions and the risks of nuclear conflict. Those taking this position view U.S. strategic power in relation to that process. They assert that a balance must be maintained in order to negotiate from strength, but the aim is negotiation, and a strategic balance is only a means to that end. They also tend to view the details of Soviet strategic capabilities as less important than the overall balance.

A fourth view, which has recently been expressed most forcefully by

Secretary of Defense Schlesinger, is concerned with the perceptions of the military balance by third parties. The point here is that perceptions of the strategic balance can influence political attitudes and actions of those nations whose policies must, to a greater or lesser degree, be responsive to pressures from the superpowers. Thus, the details of the strategic balance, such as relative throw-weight, assume considerable importance.

Finally, there is a view that continues to see the strategic balance primarily in military terms. Those taking this position assert that the risk that the Soviets could achieve strategic military superiority in the years ahead is real. They are most inclined to be concerned with detailed threat estimates and to project the Soviets as achieving usable military superiority over the United States during the next decade.

CONCLUSIONS

From this review of changing, and often contradictory, U.S. assumptions about the strategic balance, the following conclusions may be drawn: First, the task of estimating Soviet strategic capabilities, particularly future capabilities, remains an uncertain game; there is much latitude for judgment. Second, judgments are heavily influenced by political and strategic preconceptions. Particularly important are assumptions about the risks of nuclear war, about the possibilities of convergence, about the value of arms-control agreements in stabilizing international relations, and about the political value of military power.

The current official U.S. view appears to make the following assumptions:

1. The risks of nuclear war are low, but not zero. The United States must make every effort to keep these risks low.

2. While convergence of the U.S. and Soviet social systems is unlikely in the foreseeable future, and many issues will continue to divide the two superpowers, both have a common interest in avoiding situations that could lead to a nuclear conflict.

3. Arms control and other agreements can create a climate of cooperation in which the risks of nuclear war are reduced and the incentives for stability are enhanced.

4. In an era of nuclear parity, it is doubtful that nuclear forces can be used to advantage by any nation beyond their role in deterring the use of nuclear weapons by others.

Although these assumptions do not lead to any necessary set of conclusions about Soviet strategic power and the resultant military balance, they have led the U.S. government to concentrate heavily on two aspects of strategic power in recent years. One is to stress the role of strategic forces in negotiations. Strategic programs have been used increasingly as signals in the negotiation process. The other is to consider the importance of the perceptions that third parties may have of the strategic balance. Both of these factors can account for the recent U.S. emphasis on counterforce matching. On the one hand, potential counterforce capabilities are seen as exercising leverage in negotiations with the Soviet Union. On the other hand, they are seen as an increasingly important element in perceptions of the strategic balance. Thus, when one reads U.S. estimates of Soviet strategic capabilities and assessments of the strategic balance, one needs to consider what audience this particular statement is attempting to reach and what are the strategic assumptions on which it is based.

The "Racing Syndrome" and the Strategic Balance

Colin S. Gray

THE "SYNDROME" MYTH

A vague term borrowed from a very inexact science (psychology) is more likely to mislead than to instruct when it is imported uncritically into the study of international politics. A "syndrome" is a set of mutually reinforcing symptoms that indicate a particular abnormal state. In this paper it is suggested that the only "arms-race syndrome" worthy of note is that characterizing those commentators who believe that a protracted arms competition between the superpowers is in some way "abnormal." Lest my principal *general* contentions should be obscured by the detail that follows, they are stated here:

1. A relationship of "armored watchfulness" possibly of a character worthy of ascription as an "arms crawl" or an "arms race" is entirely normal between great powers.

2. Although certain features of Soviet-American relations have been abnormal, what is remarkable about the so-called *nuclear age* is the degree to which classical statecraft has not been repudiated. Proof of this can be seen from a brief study of the relations between other great-power conflict sets in international history, especially with respect to the degree of the nations' preeminence in the interstate pecking order, the ideological drives that have molded

their psycho-milieus, and the lethality of the military currency of their competition.

3. Although Soviet and American arms-race behavior has been distinctively Soviet (and Russian) and American, this behavior is in most important respects fully congruent with the activities of past, prenuclear, arms-racing principles.

In short, Soviet-American arms-race behavior is not a proper subject for analytical dissection by those addicted to the deployment of the conceptual and methodological tools of abnormal psychology. The nuclear arms race is an example of "international politics as usual": one may not approve, but the striking of moral postures is analytically as debilitating as it is irrelevant.

COMMENTARY

Leon Sloss[1] and I are in broad agreement as to the factors that have combined to structure American perceptions of Soviet strategic policy. Hence, this paper is meant to complement the views of Sloss, rather than to present an alternative view. There are some differences between us as to historical interpretation, particularly as regards events of the 1950s, but these do not constitute any philosophical divide. Because I intend to discuss the themes raised by Sloss, rather than offer a detailed exercise in counterpoint, it is useful that a few specific disagreements and addenda be noted at this juncture.

First, I do not think it is accurate to say that the decision in 1953 to deploy tactical nuclear weapons in Europe "was perhaps the first concrete action taken in recognition by U.S. authorities that Soviet strategic power would eventually affect the balance in Europe." A great deal of what is known as "the Korean Rearmament" comprised "concrete" recognition that an age of nuclear stalemate was imminent. During the spring of 1950, the year 1954 was identified as "the year of maximum danger," for it was thought that in 1954 Soviet nuclear capability would for the first time effect a standoff with respect to the deterrent efficacy of strategic power. A joint State-Defense paper, filed as NSC-68 on 12 April 1950, called for an unspecified, but across-the-board, increase in the American defense effort, so as to compensate for the anticipated reduction in the extended deterrent value of the Strategic Air Command (SAC). Following the North Korean invasion, the supplementary request for new obligational authority for FY 1951 and the crucial guideline papers for FY 1952—NSC-68/1, 2, 3, and 4—to the very considerable extent to which they related to concerns

---

[1] This paper is a discussion of, and expansion upon, the themes raised by Leon Sloss in the preceding paper, "The U.S.-Soviet Military Balance: Changing American Perceptions, 1945–1975."

other than the war in Korea, all reflected the belief that there was no adequate substitute for local stopping power.[2]

Second, Sloss refers to the decision by the Nixon Administration to continue with the MIRV program-testing having begun in August 1968. On 3 December 1974, Henry Kissinger said, "I would say in retrospect that I wish I had thought through the implications of a MIRV*ed* world more thoughtfully in 1969 and 1970 than I did."[3] While the Nixon Administration was sensible in its decision to continue with MIRV, it is a little difficult to see what has been revealed since 1969 concerning the implications of MIRV that was not fully apparent at the time.

Third, it is misleading to state that "by the end of the Eisenhower Administration . . . it was clear to Dulles and the president that U.S. superiority was waning, and even Dulles was talking about 'selective retaliation.' " Dulles thought that he was talking about "selective retaliation" at all times. For example, in a paper written on 18 July 1956, in preparation for a NATO meeting, Dulles wrote: "U.S. Military Policy. That is essentially a policy of deterring war by a capacity for selective retaliation."[4] However, on 29 November 1954, Dulles denied that a local conflict "would be turned into a general war with atomic bombs being dropped all over the map."[5] This is not to say that SAC could have performed in any very selective fashion in the mid-1950s.

Fourth, it is worth noting that although President Nixon sought to make the notion of sufficiency his own, President Eisenhower accepted this idea as early as 1955. By way of illustration, on 2 March 1955 Eisenhower said, "There comes a time, possibly, when a lead is not significant in the defensive arrangements of a country. If you get enough of a particular type of weapon, I doubt that it is particularly important to have a lot more of it."[6]

Fifth, Sloss argues that in 1969 the United States confronted "two ways to meet the problem" of maintaining parity and precluding the emergence of a measure of Soviet strategic superiority: These were through "unilateral U.S. efforts" or through an attempt "to negotiate limits on strategic forces in SALT."

---

[2] NSC-68 is examined in Paul Hammond, "NSC-68: Prologue to Rearmament," in *Strategy Politics, and Defense Budgets,* ed. Warner R. Schilling, Paul Y. Hammond, and Glenn H. Snyder (New York: Columbia University Press, 1962), pp. 267–378.

[3] Henry Kissinger, "Background Briefing on the Vladivostok Accords," 3 December 1974, pp. c-2-3.

[4] John Foster Dulles, Document, NATO, Untitled, Draft no. 1, 18 July 1956, Dulles Papers, File IX, July–December 1956, "NATO Meeting 8–15 December 1956" (Princeton, N.J.: Princeton University Library).

[5] John Foster Dulles, "Results of the Strategy," in *Documents on American Foreign Relations, 1954,* ed. Peter Curl (New York: Harper, 1955), p. 18.

[6] Dwight D. Eisenhower, cited in *Public Papers of the Presidents of the United States, 1955* (Washington, D.C.: Government Printing Office, 1959), p. 303.

These were not alternatives. Attempts to negotiate one's way out of strategic postural inadequacies are doomed to disappointment.

Sixth, it is unconvincing to assert that "Dulles was slow to anticipate strategic parity." If anything, it could be argued that the Eisenhower Administration endowed Soviet strategic power with a greater degree of deterrent efficacy than was warranted by the state of the strategic balance.

Seventh, Sloss states that "Many who supported the SALT I agreement argued that Soviet strategic forces were destined to go far higher if there were not an agreement." As an addendum, Sloss could have proceeded to observe that this argument has reappeared with respect to the Vladivostok ceilings. In "background briefings" on 25 November and 3 December 1974, Henry Kissinger stated that the intelligence community predicted that a SALT II-less world would see Soviet offensive forces and MIRV launcher numbers far in excess of 2,400 and 1,320, respectively, by 1985.[7]

THE SOURCES OF PERCEPTION AND MISPERCEPTION

It is easy to be a critic. After the event, faulty assumptions may be identified with a degree of confidence that even the academic commentator did not feel at the time. Elsewhere, I have argued that the sources of American arms-race predictive error would seem to stem from combinations of the following (slightly amended) factors: cultural-technological *hubris;* a disinclination to recognize the distinctive, specifically national characteristics of arms-race behavior; an inattention to bureaucratic and political systemic behavior; and an unwillingness to recognize the implications of the strong possibility that an arms race may be waged, not because of a technological imperative, nor as a product of bureaucratic inertia, but rather as a purposive instrument of foreign policy.[8]

This focus upon the United States betrays nothing more sinister than the limited mandate accorded this paper, my own limited competence, and the gross imbalance in our knowledge concerning the strategic behavior of each super-power. Although the United States is, necessarily, uniquely prone to make distinctively American assumptions about the arms race and the strategic balance, the propensity to err is not uniquely an American characteristic. Faulty American projections of Soviet strategic capabilities are reasonably well-known,[9] but it does behoove the commentator to remember that (1) many predictive errors were by no means shared by all or even a majority of the defense

[7] Henry Kissinger, "Background Briefing on the Vladivostok Accords," pp. A-11-131.

[8] Colin S. Gray, "Predicting Arms Race Behaviour," *Futures,* vol. 6, no. 5 (October 1974), pp. 380–388.

[9] Particularly well-known thanks to the dissemination of declassified American intelligence estimates by Albert Wohlstetter. See "Legends of the Arms Race," *USSI Report 95-1* (Washington D.C.: U.S. Strategic Institute, 1975).

community, and that (2) a listing of Soviet errors in prediction concerning future American strategic programs would probably be just as substantial. Also, even some gross mistakes in prediction—however easily attributable to distinctively home-grown American traits—rested upon reasoning that was not at all crude or implausible at the time. By way of illustration of this last point, one of the most forthright advocates of the "missile-gap" thesis was that supremely political analyst, Henry Kissinger. *The Necessity for Choice* makes interesting reading in 1975.[10]

In detail, American arms-race performance may be criticized in a thoroughgoing fashion. But, until recently—for which a different judgment is in order—the assumptions that have moved policy have been fully adequate to meet political needs. The United States recognized that it was committed to a qualitative and quantitative arms competition with the Soviet Union. This recognition should, in policy-action terms, be attributed to the summer of 1950. The United States has been *fairly* consistent in its attention to the second-strike survivability of an adequate deterrent force. (There are a few arguable exceptions—for example, SAC-base vulnerability in the early and mid-1950s.) However, until recent years at least, the United States has acknowledged by her postural actions that a measure of strategic superiority was both desirable for the relative freedom of foreign policy action that it allowed and was *probably* necessary given the vast asymmetry of extended deterrent tasks that each superpower imposed upon its strategic forces. The intuitive character of stalwart adherence to the assumptions that (1) strategic forces must be invulnerable, and that (2) strategic forces have political meaning, has given rise to much misunderstanding. Those strategic analysts who have consistently stressed vulnerability dangers, real or imagined, invite the criticism that they ignore "the inhibitory political and psychological imponderables"[11] that must discipline any leader's predelictions for nuclear adventure. This criticism has been leveled at the RAND team who sought to argue in the 1950s for the delicacy of the "balance of terror," just as it is leveled today at those who worry about the hard-target counterforce potential of 1,320 Soviet MIRV launchers.

The basis for such apparent strategic paranoia is not a fixation upon the technical aspects of that underanalyzed and overused concept, *strategic stability*; rather it is a sensible recognition that we cannot know the details of Soviet strategic arithmetic any more than we can predict with confidence what Soviet risk-taking propensities will prove to be in a particular crisis (in circumstances

[10] Henry Kissinger, *The Necessity for Choice: Prospects of American Foreign Policy* (New York: Anchor, 1962, first published in 1960), particularly pp. 15–16. "For all the heat of controversy, it is important to note that there is no dispute about the missile gap as such. It is generally admitted that from 1961 until at least the end of 1964 the Soviet Union will possess more missiles than the United States."

[11] Bernard Brodie, *War and Politics* (New York: Macmillan, 1973), p. 380.

and with individuals unknown and unknowable today). Strategic force posture should be designed so as to minimize the chance that Soviet strategic analysts could present to a desperate Politburo a game plan for strategic assault that offered even a fair prospect of success. If this be paranoia or worst-case analysis, then I am in favor of paranoia and such analysis.

The second fundamental assumption concerning strategic force design has been that such forces *probably* cast a political shadow that may be related but tenuously to their predicted efficacy in war. This assumption may be quite false, but the basis for its endorsement lies, not in intellectual conviction, but in the realization that it could prove to be extremely dangerous to act as though it were false. Despite the "premonitions of parity" discussed by Sloss, it was a fact that optical, "bifocal" and even militarily meaningful American strategic superiority characterized the strategic balance until the very late 1960s. If one inquires as to the political mileage recorded as the payoff from this protracted condition of American advantage, no very confident replies are to be expected. One cannot write an alternative history for the 1950s and 1960s—one wherein the Soviet Union clearly led the United States in both the quality and quantity of its strategic forces. While accepting the strong possibility that men have been deterred by the prospect of *nuclear war,* not by premonitions of *defeat in nuclear war,* it would still be a bold step (or leap of faith) to assert that a bilateral consciousness of strategic superiority/inferiority, as one prominent component in the overall balance of forces, has no, or no significant, impact upon the propensity to assume risks.

Save for an aberrational period in the mid- and late 1960s, the American defense community has always tended to endorse the notions that (1) the Soviet Union equates "a good deterrent" with "a good war-fighting capability" (the two ideas are not logically opposed)[12] and that (2) the Soviet Union seeks to derive whatever political advantage is attainable from her strategic arms-racing efforts. To accept these two notions as "working hypotheses" need not imply a mindlessly hawkish approach to matters strategic; such acceptance may rest upon the agnostic thought that relative safety lies in acting *as* though these notions were true.

One of the most dangerous streams of thought about the strategic balance in the United States is what may be termed "the myth of insular strategic voluntarism," the idea that a particular perception of strategic truth will make us free. This approach to strategic problems holds that the world is a fit subject for conceptual manipulation; I believe *X*, I repeat *X*, therefore *X* is so. Ignorant Russians seem to believe that a favorable ICBM throw-weight imbalance on the order of 6:1 by 1985 will be of political significance. They can be *dissuaded* of

---

[12] See John Erickson, "Soviet Military Policy: Priorities and Perspectives," *The Round Table,* no. 256 (October 1974), pp. 373–374.

this heresy, so the argument goes, by strategic conceptual education by Western scholars and officials. A putative hard-target counterforce nonequivalence is politically significant almost solely because irresponsible Western analysts keep telling themselves, the American public, Soviet officials, and anyone else who will listen, that such possible nonequivalence is significant. Strategic "problems" of a hypothetical character will go away if we do not talk about them. More generally, there are voices to be heard today that advocate a "benign neglect" of strategic and arms-control issues. Great debates on strategy and on SALT outcomes focus attention on issues that are best ignored—or at least treated in very minor key. This theme of conceptual education/manipulation contains a good idea that is struggling to emerge. However, when overstated—as generally is the case—it betrays a denial of the possibility that Soviet analysts may prefer their own ideas, and a denial of the inevitable debating features of democratic political cultures.

Particular errors in prediction concerning Soviet strategic force posture may be laid at the door of the factors mentioned above: *hubris,* distinctive domestic roots; bureaucratic and political systemic insensitivities; and, particularly of late, a disinclination to believe that the arms race may be waged as an instrument of foreign policy.

Hubris

Running through the arms-race performance of the United States has been a persisting overweening confidence in the superiority of American ideas, of American technology, and of American purposes. This measure of *hubris* reflects a long-standing faith in the *uniqueness* of the United States that has not, alas, spilled over into a due appreciation of the uniqueness of other polities. Very many American analysts, politicians, and officials have confused the American way of arms racing and (in aspiration only) arms controlling with *the* way of conducting these activities. If it is believed that "the American way" is also, necessarily, "the best way," it should follow that the arms-race rival will follow in the American path. To the extent that Soviet strategic practice appears to deviate from "the American way," this may be explained, not in terms of an alternative vision of strategic truth, but rather as the product of technical incapacity and/or conceptual and defense-analytical backwardness. The "false dawns," for the Soviet Union, of the short-lived bomber and missile gap prognoses in the United States tended to reinforce to a dangerous degree the confidence of Americans in their way of conducting strategic business. The long-term effect of these misprojected "gaps" was to discredit all "gap-mongering." Fifteen years on from the *apogee* of the missile-gap debate, one finds the impermeable credo that (1) "gaps" will not occur, but (2) if they do, they will not matter.

Under some circumstances American self-confidence is a strategic asset. But such *hubris* may also lead to the under valuation of ideas that were "not made here," may promote a dangerous contempt for the strategic potential of rival states, and will certainly encourage a misleading appraisal of the degree of correlation between American objectives and American resources. As the United States attempted too much in Indochina, so it seems bent upon making too little of the political consequences of her total defeat in that theater.

The Domestic Roots of Strategic Behavior

Despite the scholarship of a handful of industrious and empathetic Soviet-area specialists, American arms-race performance has been, and continues to be, bedeviled by the implicit assumption that the race is being conducted against an errant "country cousin." From arms-race issue to arms-race issue, the notion that the race fundamentally is being run against a symmetrical opponent continues to mislead. The effect of this belief may be located with respect to predictions of Soviet procurement of long-range bombers; of early generation ICBMs—as opposed to Europe-related IRBMs and MRBMs; of only a modest force of second-generation ICBMs; and, on a different though parallel track, of Soviet conduct in SALT.[13] This is not to suggest that the Soviet Union has pursued an idiosyncratic arms-race path, impervious to non-Soviet examination. It means only that the USSR has tended to "cut her own trail," borrowing some technical solutions and ideas, but rejecting many others.

Bureaucratic Politics and the Political System

Until very recently, and possibly even to this day, American analysts have tended to be far more impressed with the (their!) alleged logic of new technologies—and with the perceived postural and doctrinal implications of those technologies—than they have been with the unique bureaucratic and political systemic settings within which strategic force decisions are forged. Bureaucracy may be bureaucracy, whether it be housed in Washington or in Moscow, but the rules of accountability, the distribution of influence, the degree of superior political direction, the scale of lateral communication, and so forth, differ enormously. A "common logic" of technology may have led each superpower down paths of similar strategic capabilities, but these paths have not been cut simultaneously, nor have they proceeded—even in lagged fashion—closely in parallel.

Assumptions concerning future Soviet strategic behavior that compromise a projection of American strategic desiderata, or that are believed to express a strategic reasoning that is culture-neutral, are almost certain to be confounded. Although it should be the case that an improved understanding of the politics of

---

[13] I pursue this last point at length in "Détente, Arms Control, and Strategy: Perspectives on SALT," *The American Political Science Review* (forthcoming).

defense policy making in Moscow will enable the United States to race more intelligently, it is very far from certain that such improved understanding will yield an arms-control, let alone an arms-reduction dividend. Because weapon systems are deployed for a variety of reasons, strategic and extrastrategic, answers to the question "why" may be of academic interest compared with answers to the question "what." Naturally, high-confidence understanding of Soviet decision processes should facilitate improved prediction of weapon deployment. The analytical dissection of Soviet bureaucracy is an exercise necessarily flawed by the presuppositions brought to the task by the analyst. In short, there is a tendency for people to find that for which they are looking—just as there is, on occasion, a tendency for the Soviet authorities to provide "evidence" in support of the prior convictions of foreign analysts. Visiting Westerners, depending upon their policy tendencies, discover (1) "young modernizers," men familiar with, and apparently sympathetic toward, Western arms control concepts, or (2) "young Stalinists," men familiar with the Western literature yet vigorously competitive in their approach to the arms relationship and to arms-control negotiations. (Sometimes the modernizers and Stalinists are the *same* men.) In other words, one sometimes feels that our professional Moscow-watchers reveal as much of themselves as they do of their subject.

The Arms Race as an Instrument of Foreign Policy

Since the mid-1960s, on a wide scale in the American defense and arms-control community, though prior to that period in the case of some individuals, actual Soviet strategic capabilities and projections of Soviet deployment have been interpreted in the distorting mirror of the conviction that the nuclear arms race is fueled by forces that transcend political purpose. It is important to recognize the "level-of-analysis" confusion that has reduced the value of some of the arms-race theory that has been purveyed over the past decade. Virtually every explanation of arms-race dynamics that has been provided is true—*to a limited extent.*

It is now academically *chic,* and sensible, to emphasize the interplay of domestic forces that, in shifting conjunction, move interstate competitive arms behavior. If one inquires, in academic circles, as to "what drives the arms race?" some mix of the following candidates is likely to be advanced: interstate action-reaction processes (a fairly mindless view); action-reaction processes between *and* within armed services; bureaucratic politics (something of a portmanteau candidate); the character of political/social systems; electoral politics (in the United States, of course!); organizational momentum; technological innovation; industrial production-line follow-on imperatives; the military-industrial-complex; and the nature of the capitalist economic system.[14]

[14] See Colin S. Gray, *The Soviet-American Arms Race: Interactive Patterns and New Technologies,* WN-8719-ARPA (Santa Monica, Calif.: RAND, August 1974), chap. 2.

Whatever the mix of explanations preferred, the message is unequivocal—there are "bad" and/or "foolish guys" locked into a system of competition that is bereft of foreign-policy meaning. Virtually every extant and putative Soviet strategic force activity can be explained away strictly in terms of the dynamics of domestic forces. The SS-18 and SS-19 may *appear* to pose threats to American fixed-based ICBMs, but *really* these missiles show the bureaucratic politics; but such analysis tends to play down the strong possibility that most, if not all, relevant Soviet bureaucrats were agreed that they needed a good hard-target killing ICBM to succeed the SS-9 and SS-11. From the American point of view, dissection of the bureaucratic politics of the SS-18 and SS-19 versus their rivals is strictly small change. This is not to deny that the resource-allocation debate in Moscow may be cast more broadly: more theater capability *or* a new generation of ICBMs now. It is my inclination to believe in the obvious implications of posture. A very high throw-weight ICBM, enjoying the services of an on-board computer, that is capable of dispensing multimegaton MIRVs from a post–boost-phase vehicle must be presumed to be intended as a high-confidence silo killer—unless, that is, one chooses to believe that Soviet officials are unaware of the military implications of their forces.

THE "RACING SYNDROME" AND POLITICAL RELATIONS

By virtue of their joint preeminence in international politics, the superpowers cannot help but be rivals. The fact that the Soviet Union adheres to an ideology of conflict, of unremitting struggle, should not blind us to the fact that political (and hence military) competition would characterize Soviet-American relations, whatever were the character of their political systems. A condition approximating one of *arms race* is endemic to their relationship. Through agreement, mutual exhaustion, or the pressure of competing resource demands, the pace of the arms competition may periodically slacken to the point where one can write convincing articles to the effect that really there is not *a race* on at all, but such a demonstration would be a trivializing exercise. In the same way that the U.S. Army Air Force selected the Soviet Union as its postwar foreign threat referent,[15] so each superpower could not help but be suspicious of the intentions of the other, based solely on the logic of latent insecurity potential ("who can do me most harm?").

The impact of "the racing syndrome" on superpower political relations has been zero, because there is no such thing as a "racing syndrome." But belief in the existence of a "racing syndrome" has had a considerable effect. If you

---

[15] See Perry McCoy Smith, *The Air Force Plans for Peace, 1943–1945* (Baltimore: Johns Hopkins University Press, 1970), p. 69.

scratch the surface of a dedicated American arms controller, you will probably discover an old-fashioned, and high-minded, idealist. Such a man believes that conflict, arms race, crisis, and war are abnormal features on the landscape of history. Somewhere around the corner, is *the* agreement that will terminate the disease of arms competition. This belief, let it be proclaimed, is false. Limited arms-control agreements, for limited political ends, can and often should be signed. But the transnational arms-control community cannot, by its endeavors, devise agreement packages that effectively will write *finis* to the competitive character of international politics. One is reminded of the well-known American strategist who believed, in all innocence, that the solution (one among many possible) to the defense problems of South Vietnam was to provide a good rural police force.

Advocates of the notion that there is an arms race syndrome, a set of abnormal characteristics of behavior, would—unwittingly, one is to presume— have the United States (alone—since Soviet writers have not been strongly represented among the analysts of arms-race dynamics) ignore the elementary precept of prudence. To repeat points registered above: to indulge in "bad-case" analysis and to assume that relative strategic power could have foreign policy meaning *is not to believe* that (1) the "bad case" is a probable future, or that (2) strategic forces are easily translatable into political influence. The stakes are potentially so high in strategic force analysis that the prudent official accepts the possible costs of overdesigning his strategic posture. Because one cannot know what "might have been," it can never be certain that a strategic posture was excessive in scale and sophistication for the policy tasks that it supported.

Soviet Doctrine and Strategy: A Developing American View

William R. Van Cleave

Our views on the essence of war and the views accepted in the capitalist states' doctrines are diametrically opposed.

Lieutenant General I. Zavyalov
Krasnaya Zvezda, 19 April 1973

It is particularly important to keep in mind that the question of the essence of nuclear missile warfare is not correctly treated in works of bourgeois military theorists.

Lieutenant General S. Lototskiy
Voenno-Istoricheskii Zhurnal, September 1973

Innovative search and original solutions were convincingly manifested at troop maneuvers in recent years, which constituted a new stage in the training of troops to conduct modern combat operations.

Major General A. S. Milovidov
Problems of Contemporary War, 1972

One must have the ability to change methods of combatting the enemy when circumstances change.

V. I. Lenin
Polnoye Sobraniye Sochineniy (Complete Works)

The above epigraphs, from prominent Soviet sources, indicate both clearly and paradoxically the situation that faces a person who is trying to interpret Soviet strategy. For a long time in the United States, little effort was devoted to the interpretation and understanding of Soviet military doctrine, concepts, and objectives. The U.S. official and intellectual communities, to the extent that they were involved in such matters, projected Soviet strategy and force planning primarily on the basis of American assumptions about preferred concepts and strategies. These assumptions, rooted ethnocentrically in formal models and mechanical theories of strategic stability (and, at the theater level, in a "firebreak" philosophy), were not derived from a study of *Soviet* views. Soviet strategic thought was generally considered to be rather backward and, therefore, not to be taken seriously so much as to be enlightened. At the time, Soviet military capabilities were sufficiently limited that capability analysis tended to support the American approach. The logic that was followed in U.S. strategic planning, therefore, was attributed in mirror-image fashion to the Soviets and the broad disdain for Soviet doctrine continued through the 1960s.

As one former Department of Defense (DOD) planner observed, during the 1960s it was assumed in the DOD that the "rational" U.S. technological strategy and approach to force planning and procurement were also followed by the USSR: "DOD was planning for both sides. . . . If policy-makers had assumed the more rational premise that there was some underlying motivation for Soviet weapons programs they would have encouraged analysis of the motivation."[1]

When it was occasionally noticed that Soviet doctrinal literature not only revealed no functional equivalent to mutual assured destruction or conventional emphasis concepts, but seemed to express resolute opposition to them, it was argued that it was only a matter of time until it would change. Western analysts remained reluctant to give up the notion of Soviet backwardness. Some argued that Soviet doctrine "lagged" behind the more up-to-date doctrine of the United States by five to seven years.[2] In time, a convergence or "sympathetic parallelism" of views, it was argued, was inexorable.

In fact, there has been *some* convergence, but hardly as expected, and then

---

[1] Francis X. Kane, "Criteria for Strategic Weapons," *Strategic Review,* vol. 2, no. 2 (Spring 1974), p. 45.
[2] Roman Kolkowicz, "Strategic Elites and Politics of Superpower," *Journal of International Affairs,* vol. 26, no. 1 (1972).

only fragmentarily. In some respects there has been a convergence of American thought on strategic matters and arms control with the Soviet approach, rather than vice versa. In most respects, however, there remain important national differences—but at least now there is more inclination in the United States to try to understand the differences and to appreciate that they are real.

The problem that has partially refocused American thinking is that an enormous gap appeared between the premises and expectations of dominant American strategic and arms-control thought of a decade—or for that matter half a decade ago—and the results obtained during those years.

What we have experienced in SALT and observed in Soviet strategic force planning have forced a reassessment of Soviet concepts and objectives—and of our own basic premises. There has been some thoughtful shaking of the foundation of MAD (mutual assured destruction) logic and a growing dissatisfaction with many premises of U.S. arms-interaction theory; and there have been some changes in the American approach (at least rhetorically), but it is too early to say that major changes have been made. Concurrently, a new interest in studying the Soviet side of the equation has emerged in America.

This leads to the problem of how one studies Soviet military thought and planning. In general, there are two ways to assess Soviet doctrine, concepts, and objectives: (1) analyze the capabilities they have and are developing, in short, where and how they spend their rubles; and (2) study their thinking as revealed in writings, military exercises, or force dispositions. If the two assessments are inconsistent, we have problems. If they seem to be consistent, we are entitled to draw conclusions—and, insofar as can be determined, there seems to be a remarkable consistency between what we see the Soviets doing militarily and what they say they are doing. (Even suggesting this, however, is subject to a caveat. Exegesis of a substantial body of literature, even assuming it to be reasonably trustworthy, is risky and subjective. It is possible to find isolated statements to support predetermined cases. Few analyses are entirely free from this weakness. It must simply be recognized.)

Some maintain that there is little to be gained from reading open Soviet military writing and assert that it is largely propagandistic—both for the Soviets and for the West—rather than revealing. Certain writings may indeed be aimed at influencing Western thinking, at deceiving the Russian people, or at raising the morale of Soviet troops. On the other hand, even with the well-known internal Soviet compartmentalism, it is necessary to inform, indoctrinate, and instruct the Soviet military, and with the size of that military it is not possible to keep such activities on a very closely held classified level:

> Members of the ruling hierarchy provide through their public utterances a substantially accurate picture of what they are up to and why, at least in a strategic sense. This is due to the requirement for uniformity that is so vital

to the Soviet political system. Not only must those at the top speak with a single voice, but the entire hierarchy must echo that voice.[3]

Or, as another observer put it:

> . . . there are sharp limits beyond which the Soviets cannot go in their efforts to structure foreign audience perceptions simply through rhetorical fiat. It is important to bear in mind in this regard that Soviet military doctrine is not primarily a set of carefully contrived external propaganda poses but an important body of functional operating principles for internal consumption by the Soviet military. Since the Soviet military leadership can scarcely afford to lie to its own officer corps about its strategic intentions and objectives merely to deceive the West, and since the size and complexity of the Soviet political-military infrastructure preclude the communication of policy guidelines solely through secret channels, it should only stand to reason that the bulk of declared Soviet military doctrine should reflect a reasonably faithful image of actual Soviet strategic thinking.[4]

Soviet literature on professional military doctrine, therefore, is quite important in determining Soviet military doctrine, concepts, and strategy. Perhaps no greater testimony to this can be found than the recent official citation of Sidorenko's *The Offensive*[5] in support of Secretary of Defense Schlesinger's interpretation of Soviet doctrine and strategy as reported to Congress in April 1975.[6]

However, a problem inherent in studying Soviet military writings, if they are to be used to project or predict the nature of any future military conflict between the USSR and the West, is that the writings are indeed of, by, and for the military. Although they reflect military doctrine and planning, doctrine and planning do not necessarily determine the course that the highest political authority will pursue at any given time. Consequently, it may be argued, there are distinct limitations in the use of such literature. On the other hand, in the USSR, military doctrine receives the highest political imprimatur, publications on such doctrine must have political approval, and the Soviet military occupies a central institutional role in Soviet political-military affairs unparalleled in the West. That such doctrinal military writing does not necessarily dictate political

---

[3] Foy D. Kohler et al., *Soviet Strategy for the Seventies* (Miami: Center for Advanced International Studies, University of Miami, 1973), p. 5.

[4] Benjamin A. Lambeth, "The Sources of Soviet Military Doctrine," in *Comparative Defense Policy,* ed. by F. B. Horton II, A. C. Rogerson, and E. L. Warner III. (Baltimore: Johns Hopkins University Press, 1974), p. 214.

[5] A. A. Sidorenko, *The Offensive (A Soviet View)* (Moscow: Voyenizdat, 1970). Translated and published by the U.S. Air Force in *Soviet Military Thought* (Washington, D.C.: Government Printing Office, 1974).

[6] James R. Schlesinger, *The Theater Nuclear Force Posture in Europe, A Report to the U.S. Congress in Compliance with Public Law 93–365,* April 1975.

decision making does not warrant belittling it. Moreover, as observed by the Secretary of Defense Schlesinger, there is consistency among doctrinal writing, exercises, and posture:

> National leaders are not, of course, constrained to follow the doctrine their military forces use. . . . Nevertheless, Warsaw Pact forces are postured primarily for the type of theater-wide nuclear strikes pictured in doctrine and exercises.[7]

Greater limitations, perhaps, in the use of professional military writings are the following: (1) they seem generally to apply more to large-scale military operations than to significantly more limited ones; (2) within fundamental doctrinal guidelines, operations and tactics are evolving, so that what has been written may in important respects not be conclusive; and (3) earlier writings may not convey the nuances that have subsequently evolved (although, again, general doctrine has remained remarkably consistent).

Finally, firm analysis of Soviet strategic thought is difficult not only because of the uncertainty of the information about how and why Soviet leadership makes military decisions, but also because of differences in terminology and the Soviet way of employing Western terms but with subtly different meanings. Even when the same or similar phrases are used, it is not clear that we are thinking and talking about the same thing—equivalence, equal security, strategic forces, conventional war, nuclear war.

Analyzing capabilities is not much more exact. Under the best of conditions, we have varying degrees of confidence in our ability to analyze Soviet weapons under development, and even after deployment. We may know more about long-range strategic offensive forces, due to our ability to observe flight testing, than we do about the performance of defensive systems and shorter-range offensive systems. We have inadequate knowledge of Soviet philosophy and objectives regarding the design and development of nuclear warheads. There are, in short, many gaps in our knowledge.

Still, it is possible to reach reasonable conclusions. Many elements of Soviet doctrine are too obvious. (Roger W. Barnett has written a recent interesting analysis based upon Soviet literature.)[8] In this respect, it is possible to conclude as did the Center for Advanced International Studies at the University of Miami:

> Soviet military theory, doctrine, strategy, war planning, force structure and organization, instruction and training programs, battle exercises, resource allocation, research and development programs and activities, civil defense efforts, indoctrination programs for the troops and for the population, war readiness measures, and so on, are all keyed to and dominated by the nuclear

---

[7] Ibid., p. 11.

[8] Roger W. Barnett, "Trans-SALT: Soviet Strategic Doctrine," *Orbis,* vol. xix, no. 2 (Summer, 1975).

weapons factor. . . . Neither SALT I nor on-going negotiations for SALT II have any discernible impact on overall Soviet postures, activities, or plans relative to the further development and possible utilization of nuclear weapons.[9]

Whatever fragmentary "convergence" may seem to exist, Soviet military literature is most uncomfortable reading for Western supporters of the convergence theory. The disassociation of Soviet views from Western doctrine has been a consistent and categorical theme. The theme has been particularly pronounced in the writings of Lieutenant General Zavyalov, Major General Milovidov, Marshal V. D. Sokolovskiy, and others, including Minister of Defense Marshal Grechko, in *Krasnaya Zvezda (Red Star)* and *Kommunist Vooruzhennykh Sil (Communist of the Armed Forces).* These articles have stressed repeatedly the idea that "our views on the essence of war and the views accepted in the capitalist states' doctrines are diametrically opposed."[10] Soviet writers who in the past reflected some aspects of Western strategic or arms-control thought have been explicitly renounced:

> In some works by Soviet authors there are errors, for example, in the question of the essence and consequences of a nuclear missile war. The authors of these works have absolutized the quantitative analysis and arithmetical calculation of the destructive power of nuclear weapons. Whereas the dialectical approach to research into the nature of war and the question of victory in it presupposes not only a quantitative but also a qualitative analysis of economic, scientific, technical, moral, and political factors, and also the military factor proper.[11]

In this respect, the Soviet military hierarchy has rejected the notion of convergence with the West, as have the national political leaders in the political respect.[12]

While the SALT I agreements, for example, were regarded by many in the West as mutual agreement on basic concepts of stability and interaction, there is nothing in Soviet literature and interaction that lends much encouragement that the Soviets espouse that view.

It might also be kept in mind that the Soviets demand less measurability and modeling predictability in their approach to planning military forces than is the U.S. analytical wont. Even though certain objectives and doctrinal elements,

---

[9] Leon Goure et al., *The Role of Nuclear Forces in Current Soviet Strategy* (Center for Advanced International Studies, University of Miami, 1974), p. ix.

[10] Lieutenant General I. Zavyalov, *Krasnaya Zvezda*, 19 April 1973 (FBIS, III, 79, M–2).

[11] Major General A. Milovidov, *Krasnaya Zvezda*, 17 May 1973 (FBIS-SOV-73-100, 23 May 1973, M–2).

[12] Leon Goure et al., *Convergence of Communism and Capitalism: The Soviet View*, Center for Advanced International Studies (University of Miami, 1973).

such as war-fighting capability, counterforce, and damage limiting, are strong and enduring, the Soviet approach to strategic programs might be seen not alone in terms of specific, identifiable objectives. The Soviets are probably governed as well by a general faith in strength and superiority over the West wherever possible, strength to draw upon (as one might money from a savings account) for whatever opportunities, contingencies, or challenges may occur, and strength to create opportunities as the "objective conditions" or "correlation of forces" change.

Military strength and superiority also have a very strong ideological value, which shapes the perceptions and goals of Soviet leaders. Thomas Wolfe has observed that "Soviet strategic philosophy appears functionally incompatible with finding any clear stopping points. . . . Soviet doctrine represents a mandate for endless competition without defined standards of what constitutes enough."[13]

STRATEGIC DOCTRINE, GOALS, AND PROGRAMS

The explicit renunciation in Soviet military writing of the basic concepts of both American strategic theory and the Western view of arms interaction and arms control is matched by a shunning of American notions of strategic stability and parity. ("Bewitched by the magic of the 'omniscient' mathematics of systems analysis, the U.S. 'strategic community' led by the then U.S. Defense Secretary R. McNamara began regarding the two opposite socioeconomic systems solely as two giant weapons systems.)[14] Soviet writers do not share the U.S. faith in "parity" (or, in recent rhetoric, "essential equivalence"[15]); nor do they hold either the view that parity can be equated with stability, or that attempts to limit damage in the event of war and to maximize counterforce capability promote instability.

This is in contrast to the dominant American approach. It might be recalled that President Nixon reported that the U.S. government viewed the Soviets drawing abreast of the United States in strategic nuclear forces in 1969 as an "opportunity."[16] Professor Pipes has commented on this American faith in parity:

> The most striking illustration of America's faith in the Balance of Power [that is, parity] principle was the decision to allow the Soviet Union to

[13] Thomas W. Wolfe, *Worldwide Soviet Military Strategy and Policy*, RAND P-5008 (Santa Monica, Calif.: The RAND Corporation, April 1973), p. 17.

[14] G. Trofimenko, "The USSR and the United States: Peaceful Coexistence," *SShA: Ekonomika, Politika, Ideologiya*, 2 January 1974 (FBIS-SOV-74-30, 12 February 1974, B-6).

[15] William R. Van Cleave and Roger W. Barnett, "Strategic Adaptability," *Orbis*, vol. xviii, no. 3 (Fall 1974).

[16] Richard Nixon, *U.S. Foreign Policy for the 1970's: II, A Report to Congress*, 1971.

attain parity in nuclear weapons. . . . It would be difficult to find, in the whole history of international relations, another instance of a country deliberately reducing its advantage over a rival for the sake of attaining an equilibrium.[17]

Soviet writings particularly reject the idea that there would be no victor in a nuclear missile war and—in contrast to mutual assured destruction views that would eschew superiority and try to assure that both sides would lose in a nuclear missile war—link superiority and war-fighting capability to victory. In obvious agreement, Soviet forces are designed for fighting and winning a nuclear war.

This does not mean that the Soviets are unconcerned with deterrence (although, as a separate concept, the term enjoys much less vogue than it does in U.S. intellectualizing); rather it means that they are unwilling to separate deterrence and war-fighting, as has been the Western tendency. Because war-fighting and winning are such key elements in Soviet strategic doctrine, and because neither parity nor assured-destruction capabilities provide acceptable promise of either objective, such Western concepts must again be rejected. This approach is buttressed as well by the Soviet concept that military force confers meaningful political power and thus that inferiority is a political liability and superiority an important political asset. Consequently, despite what some in the West maintain, Soviet literature, force programs, and arms-control (SALT) agreements do not reflect Soviet acceptance of what have for some time been prevailing American strategic and arms-control concepts.

In this respect, it should be noted in passing that some change in these American concepts is in evidence,[18] and to the extent that this change is away from a rigidly interpreted assured-destruction philosophy there begins to be some of the "reverse convergence" noted above. The matter is a complicated one, however, because there are elements in recent American strategic thought— for example, the concepts of very limited and selective strategic nuclear op-tions—for which there is as yet very little evidence in Soviet writing and exercises. There is a controversy today as to whether or not the Soviets do or would embody within their strategic doctrine such concepts. On the one hand, they do not seem to have included them in the past (although that may have been due to absolute and relative limitations in capability), and there has been some explicit renunciation of the "Schlesinger doctrine" in Soviet media, along the lines of that which met Secretary McNamara's 1962 Ann Arbor speech.[19]

---

[17] Richard Pipes, "Russia's Mission, America's Destiny," *Encounter,* October 1970.

[18] Van Cleave and Barnett, "Strategic Adaptability."

[19] M. A. Milshteyn and L. S. Semeyko, "The Problem of the Inadmissability of a Nuclear Conflict," *SShA: Ekonomika, Politika, Ideologiya.* Translated and reprinted in *Strategic Review,* vol. 3, no. 2 (Spring 1975).

On the other hand, the very emphasis of Soviet doctrine on military targeting, improvement of war-fighting capabilities, and damage limiting connote selectivity of targeting, although not necessarily limited strategic options, and an appreciation of *strategic goals* as opposed to indiscriminate mass destruction. Moreover, some attention is being given in Soviet military writings to military flexibility and to controlled conflict, as will be discussed and documented below in the section on theater warfare. And Soviet military capabilities certainly evidence a flexibility conducive to controlled operations, even on the strategic-exchange level. The commitment reflected in past Soviet political-military writing to massive nuclear strikes in the event of nuclear exchanges may be undergoing some change.

Examining for the moment specifically the question of strategic arms control, it is again clear that the Soviets depart from conceptual Western views. Although he was discussing Soviet writing prior to the SALT agreements, Thomas Wolfe's conclusions summarize subsequent writing as well:

> . . . the articles hinted that it was "illusory" to seek Soviet security via arms agreements; they reiterated the familiar theme that Soviet military policy should aim at the attainment of superiority; and they cited Lenin's advice about the inevitability of war between the rival systems as a better guideline for Soviet military preparations than banking on the possibility of preventing war.[20]

In addition to the fact that the SALT agreements served to acknowledge politically Soviet strategic gains and advantages, from another vantage point one can suggest that the USSR satisfied in SALT its major strategic-arms-limitation objective by choking off the U.S. ABM. The Kremlin probably perceived that U.S. ABM technology was superior to that of the USSR, and that this disparity would spoil the image of U.S.-USSR strategic parity (or USSR superiority), would have asymmetrical international political effects advantageous to the United States, and would have an adverse impact on Soviet strategic counterforce objectives. As regards the last effect of U.S. ABM superiority, it must be recognized that it was not defense of population that concerned the Soviet leaders (the MAD interpretation wherein damage reduction vis-à-vis a civil assured-destruction capability is "destabilizing"). By 1970–1971, when Soviet efforts intensified in SALT to limit to minimum levels any U.S. ABM, it was clear that the United States would in all likelihood not deploy the nationwide area-defense component of Safeguard. The four sites of retaliatory-force defense were another matter. This remained alive, and with the May 1971 SALT

[20] Thomas Wolfe, *Soviet Interests in SALT: Political, Economic, Bureaucratic and Strategic Contributions and Impediments to Arms Control* (Santa Monica, Calif.: The RAND Corporation, September 1971).

understanding, which effectively rechanneled SALT from the direction of the U.S. proposal of 4 August 1970, the United States based its ABM limitation position on those ICBM defense sites. The Soviet concern, not over population defense, but rather over defense of U.S. ICBM forces, was a direct manifestation of a counterforce doctrine. The Soviets clearly viewed the potential effectiveness of U.S. ABM defense of Minuteman differently than did many commentators in the United States.

The willingness of the Kremlin *apparently* (a necessary qualification in view of Soviet ABM efforts since 1972) to forego their own ABM system was to them a highly advantageous trade-off in view of the superiority of U.S. ABM technology and the potential defense of U.S. strategic offensive forces. A probable result of the SALT treaty, in addition, would be a slowing U.S. ABM (RDT&E), which would allow the Soviets to close any gaps and perhaps move ahead technologically. This did not reflect a deemphasis on strategic war-fighting and damage limitation in Soviet doctrine and concepts. That was merely shifted to a more heavy emphasis and reliance on the counterforce capabilities of Soviet strategic offensive forces, particularly the ICBM force, and to an upgrading of civil defense (symbolized by raising the post of civil defense chief to the level of deputy minister of defense). One caveat: This reasoning implies that the Soviets did, in fact, however temporarily, agree to forego ABM deployment. With the rich radar base throughout the USSR, the existence of 10,000–12,000 SAM launchers, and the recent SAM/ABM (it is becoming more difficult to distinguish) testing program, that implication is not quite a comfortable one.

There is no doubt that Soviet military doctrine and objectives are counterforce based. This emphasis is heavy on, but not confined to, strategic or hard-target counterforce;[21] it is broadly based in terms of important military targets in the West, hard or soft, in an order of priority that, according to Soviet

---

[21] It may be useful to point out that the term counterforce is not synonymous with hard-target kill. Some military targets have been hardened to nuclear and blast effects, some have not, and some cannot be. To use counterforce to describe only destruction of missile silos is to impoverish the term. Counterforce (military) targets may be soft, hard, harder, hardest, from an ability to withstand only a few pounds per square inch (psi) of additional overpressure to perhaps a couple thousand psi, with only silos and some command facilities in the last category. Moreover, even for hard-target capability, the significance of counterforce resides in the degree to which it exists. There is some degree of hard-target counterforce capabilities in all ICBM forces statistically. The measurement of accuracy (CEP) is a statistical expression of where we may expect 50 percent of the weapons to detonate relative to the target, and hard-target kill probability is a function statistically of the number of weapons that one is willing to dedicate to a single target, as well as the accuracy and the yields of those weapons. If one were willing to dedicate a large number to a single target, high kill probabilities may be achieved, but it may not be an efficient use of that number of weapons, it may not result in anything close to a favorable exchange ratio, and it certainly may be far from a first-strike capability.

The differences in the hard-target potentials of different warheads, or MIRVs, must be understood also. Accuracy is the most important single factor. An improvement in accuracy by a factor of two has the same effect against a hardened target as increasing yield by a factor of eight; or, 100 KT at 0.25 nm gives the same psi overpressure and single-shot kill

literature, runs something like this: strategic missile forces, strategic bomber and submarine bases, nuclear arsenals, major military bases and concentrations worldwide, C^3 (command, control, and communications) centers, and finally political-administrative centers and war-supporting industry. Coverage of military targets probably expands both categorically and geographically as Soviet targeting capabilities grow.

The consistent emphasis in Soviet doctrinal literature on military targeting and on means of limiting damage to the USSR, and on the ability to fight, survive, and win a war fought with nuclear missiles, is underlined by Soviet strategic force programs and by the continuing attention devoted to air defense and civil defense. The Soviet ICBM program has "three main objectives— expanded target coverage (particularly military) with MIRVs, improved pre-launched survivability with new silo designs, and the attainment of a significant hard-target kill capability."[22]

The U.S. secretary of defense and the chairman of the Joint Chiefs of Staff (JCS) have recently described and projected Soviet strategic force programs in some detail. The effort continues in unprecedented magnitude, "a truly massive effort," as Secretary of Defense Schlesinger termed it; "we are now beginning to witness in the Soviet Union the largest initial deployment of improved strategic capabilities in the history of the nuclear competition."[23] General George S. Brown reported to Congress:

> The Soviet Union is pressing forward vigorously with massive programs for near-term deployments involving every facet of offensive strategic power. At

---

probability as 800 KT at 0.5 nm (neither very good against hardened targets: about 0.10 probability against a 1,000 psi target and about 0.16 against a 500 psi target, which demonstrates the difficulty of attaining even high single-shot kill probabilities against such targets). However, yield is also important, particularly where there are large differences. The following chart gives some examples of variable combination of accuracy, yield, and numbers of (reliably arriving) RVs in terms of kill probability against a target hardened to 1,000 psi, and also demonstrates clearly the differences in hard-target counterforce capability between U.S.-type MIRVs and Soviet-type MIRVs:

Yield:	0.04 MT		0.15 MT		2 MT	
Number of RVs:	1	3	1	3	1	3
0.3 nm	0.04	0.08	0.10	0.27	0.45	0.83
0.2 nm	0.10	0.25	0.20	0.50	0.73	0.98

First strike or significant hard-targeting of even fixed land-based forces is much more complicated than this simplified chart would suggest because there are major problems of timing and coordination, degradations to be expected in accuracy and systems performance, and possibly detrimental effects of the nuclear detonations of some warheads on other arriving warheads (that is, "fratricide").

[22] James R. Schlesinger, *Annual Defense Department Report,* FY 1976 and 1976T, February 1975, II-14.

[23] Ibid., I-5.

the time, it is improving appreciably, at a more gradual rate, capabilities for strategic defense and pursuing with firm determination development of advanced technology appropriate to the *entire* strategic equation.[24]

I emphasize *entire* for the reasons noted below.

This "massive program," if not constrained by SALT and/or balanced by major U.S. counterforce, "will result in serious superiority over the United States in the years ahead."[25] It is by no means clear that Soviet restraint or failure, or SALT, will result in a brake upon this momentum. The Soviets seem to feel no obligation to promote U.S. security interests or to contribute to the U.S. sense of security—factors deeply ingrained in U.S. arms-control thinking. Our experience with strategic arms limitation to date makes it unlikely that constraints sufficient to reduce the expected strain from Soviet force developments on the U.S. strategic posture will come from that quarter. The Soviets appear to perceive themselves as being on the verge of significant strategic superiority, and of a decisive war-fighting and war-winning capability in the event strategic deterrence breaks down. Former SALT negotiator Paul Nitze has written:

> Soviet officials took the view that the correlation of forces had been and would continue to move in their favor. . . . On balance, they have reason for their stated belief that the net correlation of forces has been, and is, changing in their favor. Until this trend changes, the prospects for obtaining arms control agreements, which would significantly relieve the strain upon the U.S. defense posture, are less than good.[26]

In terms of specific strategic force programs, without going into detail, the most dramatically obvious is the ICBM program that is producing four new ICBMs for possible near-term deployment (the SS-17, SS-18, and SS-19 are now being deployed according to ex-Secretary of Defense Schlesinger's press conference of 20 June 1975), all of greater throw-weight and accuracy than their predecessors, all MIRV*ed* or MIRV*able,* one of which (SS-16) is a probable mobile ICBM. And the Soviets may be developing yet another ICBM generation yet to be flight-tested. One recent source refers to "at least ten additional strategic systems that have not yet reached flight-test."[27] The secretary of defense has estimated that, if deployed fully, within SALT limitations, these

---

[24] George S. Brown, chairman of the Joint Chiefs of Staff, hearing before the Committee on Armed Services, U.S. Senate, 94th Cong., 1st sess. 5 February 1975, on S.920 (DOD Appropriations), *Part I: Authorizations,* p. 207.

[25] Schlesinger, *Annual Defense Department Report,* FY1976 and 1976T.

[26] Paul Nitze, speech at Los Alamos Scientific Laboratory, October 1974. Reprinted in *Foreign Policy,* vol. 17 (Winter 1974–1975), pp. 146–147.

[27] Edgar Ulsamer, "The Soviet Drive for Aerospace Superiority," *Air Force Magazine,* vol. 58, no. 3 (March 1975), p. 44. Subsequently, the Secretary of Defense confirmed this

systems will represent ten to twelve million pounds of throw-weight and over 7,000 warheads in the megaton range, or 15,000 in the Mark-12 Minuteman III warhead range, compared to a programmed two million pounds and 2,000 ICBM MIRVs for the United States.[28]

These forces can no longer be regarded merely as a "brute force" compensating in quantity and yield for U.S. qualitative advantages. The reliability of these systems has been improved and seems good. Their expected accuracies (at least for the SS-18 and SS-19) at initial and full operating capability (IOC and FOC) may approach those of the United States, certainly enough for the yields to be effective against hardened targets.

> Many in the United States assume that our missiles have greater accuracy and reliability while the Soviets have greater payload. Based on Soviet technological performance in the past, there is no reason to believe that any Soviet lag cannot be corrected, and probably more rapidly than our estimates now show.[29]

This statement seems consistent with the recent annual reports of the secretary of defense and the chairman of the JCS.

The SS-18, with large MIRVs and a 0.25 nm CEP is described by the secretary of defense as an "excellent hard-target killer."[30] Despite the greater throw-weight of the SS-18 and its potential for a large number of RVs, the SS-19—deployed in large numbers in the SS-11 silo-launchers—could become the main MIRVed Soviet hard-target counterforce system. With four, six, or eight MIRVs on a roughly 7,000-pound throw-weight missile,[31] and with CEPs of 0.15–0.25 nm, a force of several hundred to a thousand SS-19s would be an awesome hard-target threat.

As to the thrust of Soviet research and development (R & D) in these programs, the secretary of defense has referred to improvements in the reentry vehicles of all these systems that improve accuracy for (hard) counterforce purposes: "The development by the Soviets of much higher betas [that is,

report of Soviet development of yet another generation of ICRMS. Donald H. Rumsfeld, *Annual Defense Department Report,* FY1977, 27 January 1976, pp. 65 and 67.

[28] James R. Schlesinger, hearing before the Subcommittee on Arms Control, International Law and Organization, Committee on Foreign Relations, U.S. Senate, 93rd Cong., 2nd sess., on *U.S.-U.S.S.R. Strategic Policies,* 4 March 1974, made public 4 April 1974, pp. 5–7.

[29] William F. Scott, "Soviet Aerospace Forces and Doctrine," *Air Force Magazine,* vol. 58, no. 3 (March 1975).

[30] Schlesinger, *U.S.-USSR Strategic Policies* and *Briefing on Counterforce Attacks,* hearing before the Subcommittee on Armed Services, International Law and Organization, Committee on Foreign Relations, U.S. Senate, 93rd Cong., 2nd sess., 11 September 1974. Released January 1975.

[31] Brown, hearing before the Committee on Armed Services, U.S. Senate, 5 February 1975, p. 207, and Schlesinger, *U.S.-U.S.S.R. Strategic Policies.*

ballistic coefficients] in their reentry bodies is clearly intended as a movement toward accuracy." He went on to judge that: "Continued deployment of this new force, even with the terms of the Vladivostok Agreement, will give the Soviets the capability to threaten the survivability of the Minuteman force."[32]

Another major Soviet strategic offensive force development, which might have been expected with the phasing out of North American air defenses, is the Backfire strategic bomber. Backfire is now a major issue in the SALT negotiations following the Vladivostok Agreement. If the Backfire is not included in the 2,400 ceiling set at Vladivostok, despite the fact that its weight is two and a half times that of the FB-111 and its size four-fifths or so that of the B-1, and even though it can deliver a sizable payload on CONUS (Continental United States) targets without refueling ("On one-way missions, recovering in friendly or neutral territory, the Backfire is capable of delivering weapons anywhere in the United States without refueling."),[33] the USSR may exhaust the 2,400 ceiling with strategic ballistic missiles alone, and still have a modern intercontinental strategic bomber force.

There are in addition to the ICBM, SLBM, and strategic bomber programs, three areas of apparently extensive Soviet R & D that should be mentioned before leaving the strategic force category. First, in March 1975, Dr. Malcolm Currie, director of Defense Research and Engineering, told the Senate Committee of Aeronautical and Space Sciences that the Department of Defense is concerned over what seems to be Soviet development of military space capabilities, including manned military space missions. He described an aggressive space program with "major emphasis on support of military operations."[34] This was supported by another recent report that concluded that "without a doubt the bulk of the Soviet [space] program . . . is made up of a series of operational military missions."[35] From 1970 through 1974, according to the same source, the Soviets successfully launched 405 missions to earth orbit or escape, compared to 136 for the United States, and increased this pace during the first six months of 1975 with 74 percent of those launches being of a military nature.[36] The nature and purposes of this program will be known only with time; it may be mainly for surveillance, battle assessment, and C^3, or for antisatellite purposes, or for the testing of offensive or defensive space-based weapons systems.

The other two areas of Soviet R & D are ABM and ASW (antisubmarine warfare), where massive and apparently mounting programs are in existence.

---

[32] Schlesinger, *Briefing on Counterforce Attacks,* pp. 311–312.

[33] James R. Schlesinger, hearing before the Committee on Armed Services, U.S. Senate, 94th Cong., 1st sess., 5 February 1975, on S.920 (DOD Appropriations), *Part I: Authorizations,* p. 218.

[34] Malcolm Currie, in *Soviet Aerospace,* vol. 12, no. 11 (17 March 1975).

[35] Charles S. Sheldon, II, "The Soviet Space Program," *Air Force Magazine,* vol. 58, no. 3 (March 1975), p. 54.

[36] Charles S. Sheldon, II, "Soviets Set New Launch Record for First Six Months 1975," *Soviet Aerospace,* vol. 13, no. 10 (7 July 1975), p. 71.

Little is known about ASW capabilities, but a "senior defense analyst" was publicly quoted recently as saying there is "considerable evidence to question assumptions about the alleged invulnerability of the sea-based deterrent."[37] Increased effort on the ABM program since SALT I has produced advanced interceptor missiles and all-purpose ABM radars, both of which may be movable and rapidly deployable, according to congressional testimony of Major General Robert C. Marshall, manager of the U.S. ABM program.[38] For possible future ABM technology, it is noteworthy that: "high-energy laser weapons and even more advanced charged-particle-beam weapons technology are among the most lavishly funded areas of Soviet military R & D."[39]

Both the FY 1975 and FY 1976 Defense Department reports emphasize the amount of money and effort being devoted in the Soviet Union not only to the military in general, but to military industry and R & D in particular. The Soviets outspend the United States by some 20 percent or more in military R & D, and by over 60 percent in strategic offensive forces.[40] Colonel William Scott has summarized the situation well in the following observation:

> The military sector of the Soviet economy absorbs the best scientific, technical, and management brains in the Soviet Union, and receives first priority on resources. The Soviet Party-military-industrial complex has no counterpart in Western nations. . . . Emphasis on the development of nuclear weapons, missiles, and other advanced weaponry probably comes from top Party leaders as well as from military leaders and the aerospace industries.[41]

This is made amply clear in Soviet writings where the devotion of science to the development of military strength, including, for that matter, even the utilization of the social sciences to improve the morale and thinking of the fighting man, is stressed; for example:

> There is taking place a vigorous erosion of the boundaries between theoretical and applied knowledge; the *entire* scientific knowledge front is being applied to the development of military affairs. Today one cannot specify with assurance a single branch of science in which the military aspect would

[37] Ulsamer, "The Soviet Drive for Aerospace Superiority," p. 48.

[38] Major General Robert C. Marshall, testimony before the Senate Armed Services Committee, March 1975, quoted in *Soviet Aerospace,* vol. 12, no. 13 (31 March 1975); also see *Aviation Week and Space Technology,* vol. 102, no. 5 (3 February 1975), p. 71.

[39] Ulsamer, "The Soviet Drive for Aerospace Superiority," p. 49; also "Soviet Press Laser ABM Development," *Aviation Week and Space Technology,* vol. 102., no. 16 (21 April 1975).

[40] Schlesinger, *Annual Defense Department Report,* FY1976 and 1976T, II-14. These estimates were revised upward in 1976 with reports by the former Director of the Defense Intelligence Agency, Lt. Gen. Daniel Graham, that the USSR is spending over 20 percent of Gross National Product on military programs, and by Secretary of Defense Rumsfeld that the USSR is spending better than $50 billion more annually in the military than is the U.S. *Soviet Aerospace,* vol. 15, no. 9 (1 March 1976) and vol. 15, no. 10 (8 March 1976) respectively.

[41] Scott, "Soviet Aerospace Forces and Doctrine," p. 34.

be neutral. Every scientific field is either being utilized for the military or there exists a potential for such utilization. An example of this is the field of zoology, which studies the structure and functions of various animal organs. This knowledge can be applied to the design of technical devices. In recent years a new science has arisen—bionics, which studies mechanisms of self-regulation and adaption to environmental conditions as existing in nature for application in technology. Knowledge of the entire complex of sciences dealing with human higher nervous activity, pharmacology, medicine and chemistry is being extensively utilized. . . .

Comprehensive preparation of our fighting men for combat operations under the conditions of modern war demands mobilization of a broad scientific knowledge front. First of all, it is essential to condition them from a moral-political and psychological respect. The social sciences are extremely important in forming moral-political qualities in fighting men. They confirm Marxist-Leninist ideology and sociopolitical ideals, which become the basis of the fighting man's ideological conviction. . . .

Supported by the advantages of socialism, the Communist Party and the Soviet government are doing everything possible to secure the nation's defense capability. One area of this activity includes the establishment and *continuous improvement* of a *qualitatively new* technological base for the Soviet Armed Forces—the principal material element of their fighting strength. In dealing with these problems the CPSU has proceeded and does proceed from Lenin's important thesis which states that economic potential should be directly embodied in the material foundation of an army's combat power. . . .

The development, production and mass arming with new weapons have defined the military technological revolution, a *most profound, radical change* in the entire material-technological base of the Soviet Armed Forces.[42]

Many aspects of the Soviet Union's military R & D program are unclear to us, but we know that its priorities are the highest in the Soviet economy and that its guidance and control come directly from the Politburo. As the Director of Defense Research and Engineering, Dr. Malcolm Currie told Congress in February 1975:

Soviet priorities, trends and accomplishments show that there was no hollow rhetoric in the Communist Party Central Committee Resolution on December 1973, which said: "The development of Soviet science has special significance when the scientific-technological revolution has become the most important area in the competition of the two opposed world systems." The U.S.S.R. has deliberately emphasized the greatest possible rate of

[42] General Major A. S. Milovidov et al., *The Philosophical Heritage of V. I. Lenin and Problems of Contemporary War* (Moscow: Voenizdat, 1972). Translated and published by the U.S. Air Force in *Soviet Military Thought*, no. 5 (Washington, D.C.: Government Printing Office, 1974), pp. 145–147 (italics added).

advance in military technological programs at the expense of improvement in the civilian standard of living.

The foremost—and unquestionably the most important—conclusion from our assessments in this area is that the Soviet Union shows every sign of continuing to concentrate a major portion of its military RDT & E on strategic weapons, both offensive and defensive. Soviet success in enhancing their strategic forces and in creating a base for further improvements is more pronounced than for any other area of military R & D specialization.[43]

The Soviets have sustained a major military technological offensive across the board designed to "overtake and surpass" the United States, which is now appearing in much new and more sophisticated hardware:

> The final measure in security terms of the overall effectiveness of the Soviet R&D establishment is the impressive output of advanced military products. The deployment of major strategic and general purpose weapons systems, along with sophisticated munitions, radar systems and electronic systems, vividly illustrate the progress the Soviet Union has made during the past decade.[44]

In addition to the recently visible manifestations of this program, there are major aspects of it hidden to our observation. Some of these, as with the possible application of laser and charged-particle-beam technology to ABM noted above, we obtain only hints about. We can frequently guess pretty well their direction, but we cannot know where they will actually go until sometime in the future:

> There are gaps and unknowns in our understanding of Soviet military RDT & E activities and intents. Our concern for these enigmas is profound. Can the Soviets develop some exotic technology for application to actual weapons systems, and—if so—will our own technological resources be adequate to counter or offset them? These enigmas in toto may represent a significant percentage of the Soviet military RDT & E budget. Furthermore, many of them have an apparent or possible relationship to vital mission areas of our own forces. Some of the enigmas appear to be related to strategic missiles; others may be oriented toward new approaches to ballistic missile defense, and some may be directed against our fleet ballistic missile submarine. Still others seem to represent possible threats to our general purpose forces.[45]

But we do know that, however impressive the Soviet R & D program that produced those forces that were recognized in the 1972 SALT agreements, since

[43] Malcolm Currie, in *Soviet Aerospace*, vol. 12, no. 8 (24 February 1975).

[44] Brown, hearing before the Committee on Armed Services, U.S. Senate, 5 February 1975.

[45] Currie, in *Soviet Aerospace*, 24 February 1975.

those agreements were signed there has been—in the words of ex-Secretary of Defense Schlesinger—"an explosion of R & D activity" in the strategic area. One direction of this explosion, according to the secretary of defense, is amply clear:

> The Soviets are plowing ahead toward the acquisition of major counterforce capabilities and if you study Soviet doctrine there is no inhibition whatsoever on going after U.S. strategic capability. That inhibition is something that one sees in U.S. arms controllers; but in Soviet-military doctrine they indicate that they are going first and immediately after U.S. strategic forces, silos and the rest.[46]

THEATER AND TACTICAL DOCTRINE

I have chosen to interpret my topic—American assessment of Soviet doctrine and strategy—broadly enough to include the theater operational and tactical realm, because this is currently a matter of great interest in the United States. While it is not yet reflected very much in U.S. or Atlantic Alliance planning, there is some change in the American view of Soviet theater doctrine and capabilities. Similar to our new interest in closer attention to what the Soviets are doing and saying related to strategic forces, Americans are looking with more interest on such things as Soviet military literature and exercises in the theater.

It is noteworthy that, in his FY1976 annual report to Congress, ex-Secretary of Defense Schlesinger saw fit to emphasize the Soviet theater nuclear capability and interest in a rather unprecedented statement: "But however much the original initiative lay with us, the Soviet Union has shown the liveliest possible interest in the concept of theater nuclear warfare. As a consequence, *it is now the Soviets who set the pace here,* as they do in so many other respects."[47]

This remark, and the entire section, is in interesting contrast to last year's report in which no such hint was given and theater nuclear warfare was dismissed in less than one page that left considerable doubt about the entire matter and about American attention. And following and expanding on this year's report in the same vein was the April report of the Department of Defense to Congress in compliance with last year's amendment by Senator Nunn to the Defense Appropriation bill.[48]

Until recently in discussions of NATO defense, there has been but a modicum of discussion of Soviet tactical nuclear weapons and doctrine, and the "lip service" that has been given to Soviet theater nuclear force capabilities has been cast, not so much in the light of Soviet doctrine and its possible military significance, but rather in terms of the additional mass destruction that would result from nuclear employment. It appears to have been tacitly assumed that

---

[46] Schlesinger, cited in *Soviet Aerospace,* vol. 13, no. 11 (14 July 1975), p. 79.
[47] Schlesinger, *Annual Defense Department Report,* FY1976 and FY1976T, III-1 (italics added).
[48] Schlesinger, *The Theater Nuclear Force Posture in Europe.*

the Soviets do not understand any better than Western strategists the relationship between tactical nuclear forces and possible future theater conflicts.

Although there is now new attention to the Soviet side of the theater nuclear
equation, the United States has yet a long way to go to incorporate Soviet
doctrine into theater defense planning. The major U.S. planning assumption is
that a Soviet/Pact attack, however determined, will be nonnuclear and will be
countered by nonnuclear means until a stalemate is reached and the situation is
"stabilized." (Although the FY1977 Defense Department Report for the first time
explicitly identified "two main cases that concern us in Central Europe," including
surprise attack with the usual planning scenario of noticeable Pact mobilization
prior to attack, both were non-nuclear in description. That was in spite of earlier
remarks in the same Report that emphasized Soviet/Pact theater nuclear orientation.)* Officially, Western use of tactical nuclear weapons is "not pre-
cluded," and some sort of use is envisaged should the nonnuclear defense clearly
fail—such use presumably retrieving the loss and stopping conflict, by its politi-
cal-psychological impact if not its military. In this approach, first use then will in
all planning-assumption likelihood rest with the West. (In July 1975 the American press carried reports and editorials concerning statements by ex-Secretary of
Defense Schlesinger reaffirming this. See, for example, a *Washington Post* editorial of 8 July.)

Is this the way the Soviets see it? Not according to Marshal Grechko and the
authoritative Soviet work, *The Offensive:*

> The operational and tactical missile units comprise the basis for the fire-
> power of the Ground Troops. This is a qualitatively new branch of arms
> which is the *basic means for employing nuclear weapons* in combat and
> operations.[49]
>
> "Troops attacking in a different way will overcome the enemy's defense, not
> by 'gnawing through' on narrow sectors and a solid front as was the case in past
> wars, but simultaneously across a broad front from the march, at high tempos,
> right after nuclear strikes . . ."[50]

Based upon what can be determined from available evidence, it would seem
that the basis for NATO's planning is questionable in its virtual denial of the
obvious nuclear orientation of Soviet doctrine regarding theater war. Although
the Soviets naturally deny in their writings that they are the initiators of the
conflict, their doctrine strongly emphasizes an offensive based upon surprise,
initiative, and speed, and preemption upon sensing that an enemy attack is about
to be launched. As the Department of Defense now recognizes, "Warsaw Pact
forces are generally structured for offensive rather than defensive operations."[51]

*Secretary of Defense Donald H. Rumsfeld *Annual Defense Department Report,
FY1977,* 27 January 1976, pp. 117 and 101 respectively.
    [49] Marshal Andrei A. Grechko, *On Guard for Peace and the Building of Communism,*
Joint Publication Research Service, 54602, 2 December 1971, p. 33 (italics added).
    [50] A. A. Sidorenko, *The Offensive (A Soviet View)* in *Soviet Military Thought,* p. 221.
    [51] Schlesinger, *The Theater Nuclear Force Posture in Europe,* p. 13.

Rapid "counterstrikes," seizure of the initiative, and a "counteroffensive" that fully expects to employ nuclear weapons at the earliest propitious moment seem ingrained in Soviet doctrine. The traditional Soviet emphasis on the offensive in combat has been developed into a modern blitzkrieg strategy oriented around rapid territorial advance exploiting the use of nuclear weapons and operations in a nuclear environment.[52] Statements in the Soviet literature on the importance and expected use of nuclear weapons in the offensive are replete and consistent; the following are random examples:

> This weapon [nuclear] . . . is expected to insure the rapid achievement of strategic results at the very start of combat actions. . . . What is more, the use of nuclear weapons sharply increases the combat capability of ground forces and offers them extensive new opportunities for waging actual offensive operations.[53]

> To attain the greatest effectiveness, it is recommended that the nuclear strike be launched at the start of the firepower preparation unexpectedly for the enemy. Preemption in launching a nuclear strike is expected to be the decisive condition for the attainment of superiority over him and the seizure and retention of the initiative.[54]

> . . . use of nuclear weapons has further emphasized the role of the offensive as a decisive form of military action, even giving rise to the necessity to solve defensive tasks by means of active offensive operations.[55]

> The employment of nuclear weapons has greatly increased the role and significance of surprise in combat and has raised the requirement for its attainment.[56]

An in apparent contrast to the Western planning assumptions of a protracted period of Soviet mobilization prior to combat, Marshal Grechko admonished his forces:

> The time factor has particular significance in combat readiness. . . . At present, the enormous speed of the missiles and aircraft requires that troops be brought into a state of full readiness in literally a few minutes. . . . The Armed Forces should be ready under any situation to thwart a sudden attack by an aggressor both involving the use of nuclear and conventional weapons.[57]

There is every evidence that the Soviet military planning for theater warfare is based primarily upon operations in a nuclear environment, based upon their

[52] Ibid.

[53] Marshal of Armored Troops P. A. Ropmistrov, *Vremya i Tanki* (Moscow: Voyenizdat, 1972), JPRS 969.

[54] Sidorenko, *The Offensive (A Soviet View)*, p. 115.

[55] Lieutenant General I. Zavyalov, "Nuclear Weapons and War," *Krasnaya Zvezda*, 30 October 1970.

[56] Major General I. Kupchenko et al., *Voennaia Istoriia (Military History)* (Moscow: Voyenizdat, 1971).

[57] Grechko, "On Guard for Peace and the Building of Communism," p. 52.

own application of nuclear firepower—their doctrinal writings focus on it, their training is oriented to it, as are their major exercises, and their organization and equipment reflect it. Standard Soviet military equipment provided in the Middle East, such as armored personnel carriers and trucks were equipped with nuclear effects sensors and instructions for a nuclear environment. The keen Soviet interest in tanks and tank warfare is based not alone on Soviet blitzkrieg operations but also on a perceived advantage of tanks in nuclear warfare:

> As postwar exercises have shown, tanks are more suited than other types of military equipment to combat actions where nuclear weapons are used. In particular they are suited to enduring powerful dynamic loads. The advantage of the tank is that its armor protects the crew against light radiation [that is, thermal effects] and decreases the effects of penetrating radiation, while the tank's actual weight gives it stability which protects it against the shock wave. As a result of this, the use of tanks under conditions where nuclear weapons have been employed makes it possible to wage combat action immediately after the nuclear explosion, on contaminated terrain.
>
> Thus the conclusion can be drawn that the appearance of nuclear weapons not only failed to diminish, but on the contrary only strengthened the role of the tank in battle.[58]

Not so curiously, as indications of Soviet interest in limited or controlled warfare increased, many in the West argued in mirror-image fashion that Soviet interest was in nonnuclear war and that the Soviets were changing to the Western conventional-force emphasis.

Soviet doctrine does assign a vital role to conventional weapons; considering the very substantial Soviet conventional capability, this certainly makes sense. And nonnuclear conflict, even against the U.S. forces in Europe, is seemingly not ruled out. As Colonel Sidorenko states in *The Offensive*:

> In spite of the fact that nuclear weapons will become the chief means of defeating the enemy, their role and capabilities cannot be made absolute. . . . In a number of cases, regimental-size units or smaller will have to perform various combat actions, including the attack, without use of nuclear weapons, using only conventional organic "classic" means of armament.[59]

However, this is clearly a far cry from a conventional-emphasis doctrine. References to nonnuclear conflict in Soviet doctrinal writings are generally confined explicitly, as in the Sidorenko quote, to small-unit actions and/or are coupled with statements about the decisiveness of nuclear strikes, the importance of *combined* nuclear arms operations, and the need to conduct conven-

---

[58] Ropmistrov, *Vremya i Tanki.*
[59] Sidorenko, *The Offensive (A Soviet View).*

tional operations with a view to possible nuclear strikes. It is in this context that most statements on the use of conventional forces are couched; for example:

> Nuclear warhead missiles will constitute the decisive means of warfare. Conventional weapons will also be employed; and under certain conditions combat operations by units and elements may involve only conventional weapons. . . .*
>
> The development of nuclear weapons caused qualitative changes in the methods and forms of combat operations and introduced many new factors into the principle of concentration. In the past, massing was expressed in a physical concentration of men and weapons along narrow axes. This created the requisite superiority over the enemy and ensured successful execution of the combat mission in the selected sector. Now it has become very dangerous to effect a large concentration of men and equipment in a small area. At the same time it has become possible to apply the massed efforts of heavy firepower scattered over a large area.
>
> The massed employment of nuclear weapons and other firepower, as well as the high density of tanks and other combat vehicles in combined-arms major units produce sharp changes in the situation. Troops should be able to concentrate rapidly in order to launch a powerful attack on the enemy, and they must be able to disperse just as swiftly, in order not to present a convenient target for a nuclear strike. . . . The conflict between concentration and dispersal of forces is resolved by increasing force mobility.[60]

The main thing that will influence the mode of operation of the troops will be the continual threat of nuclear weapons. From this fact derives the most important task—to teach the troops to operate either with or without the use of nuclear weapons—to achieve a rapid changeover from one form of operations to the other, from fighting with conventional weapons to conditions of nuclear weapons.

> The art of conducting military operations with the use of nuclear weapons and that of employing conventional forces have many fundamental differences. But they are not in opposition, they are not mutually exclusive, and are not isolated one from the other; on the contrary, they are closely correlated and are developing as a single body.[61]

. . . the path for the advance of the troops will be cleared by nuclear weapons.[62]

Modern motorized rifle troops equipped with armored vehicles of high trafficability are capable of accomplishing marches over great distance quickly, entering the battle from the march and conducting it without

---

*Grechko, *On Guard for Peace*, p. 43.
[60] Milovidov et al., *The Philosophical Heritage of V. I. Lenin and Problems of Contemporary War*, pp. 150, 104-5.
[61] Zavyalov, "Nuclear Weapons and War."
[62] Krupchenko et al., *Voennaia Istoriia (Military History)*.

dismounting in close coordination with the tanks, . . . forcing water obstacles . . . and developing the offensive at high rates after nuclear bursts.[63]

As these quotations imply, Soviet doctrine for major use of conventional weapons (such as in a NATO-Warsaw Pact conflict) views their use primarily in the context of nuclear conflict, actual or potential, where they play a complementary role to the primary nuclear role. In fact, it begins to appear as if the Soviets may conceptually include battlefield employment of nuclear weapons as part of "conventional" operations, whereas "nuclear missile war" tends to connote theater employment of nuclear weapons in some depth against main enemy military targets. (Soviet doctrine calls for theater-wide countermilitary attacks when NATO is believed about to launch a massive theater nuclear attack.)

This has been recently acknowledged officially by the Department of Defense:

> The Warsaw Pact does not think of conventional and nuclear war as separate entities. Despite a recent trend to improve the conventional forces . . . the Warsaw Pact strategy, doctrine, and forces are still strongly oriented toward nuclear operations.[64]

It should be considered that a major Soviet nonnuclear offensive, particularly if it did require approximately a month of mobilization as U.S./NATO planning would have it, would maximize NATO's ability to mobilize for its defense and would permit it to disperse its nuclear warheads and delivery systems, which are normally stored at a relatively small number of sites vulnerable to nuclear attack. By such a strategy, the Soviets—in a remarkable demonstration of military cooperation and fairplay—would be promoting NATO's defensive capability and placing the Soviet offensive in jeopardy.

Thus, unlike the Western ambivalence toward the use of nuclear weapons in the theater, the Soviets seem to have developed the basic elements of a true nuclear doctrine and strategy for theater warfare.

Their views on theater warfare are in contrast to those prevailing in the West, where conventional forces in NATO are held to be the primary instrument for defense and for resisting an anticipated conventional-only assault, whereas tactical nuclear weapons use should be avoided ("raise the nuclear threshold"); but, if used, their use per se will bring hostilities to an end by the threat of nuclear escalation.

Although the Soviets revere and expect to exploit the military revolution wrought by nuclear weapons, they do not apparently attach the same political-

---

[63] Sidorenko, *The Offensive (A Soviet View)*, p. 49.
[64] Schlesinger, *The Theater Nuclear Force Posture in Europe*, p. 10.

psychological distinction to nuclear versus nonnuclear conflict that the West does. "Escalation" is not *defined* as the use of nuclear weapons as it tends to be in the West. (Nuclear escalation, of course, may occur, and it is discussed in Soviet writings, but escalation is not by definition the use of nuclear weapons.) To the Soviet way of thinking, the nature of a war is determined and distinguished first and foremost by the political objectives involved, not by the use or nonuse of nuclear weapons. This was clearly expressed last year in *Red Star:*

> Of course, all this does not mean that there is no qualitative difference between nuclear-missile warfare and warfare waged by conventional means. But the objective scholar is obliged to follow general moral criteria for assessing war depending not on the technical means with which it is waged but on the political aims which it serves.[65]

The writers of *The Philosophical Heritage of V. I. Lenin and Problems of Contemporary War* take great issue with those Western writers who regard the nature of war to be determined by the use or nonuse of nuclear weapons, and who allege that nuclear usage by itself changes the basic political essence of warfare:

> Techniques and methods of falsification of the essence of war, couched in "nuclear" terms, have become quite widespread. They are permeated with the spirit of relativism and sophistry, a pseudo-innovative approach to this problem. Manifested in them is a nihilistic attitude toward theory and past experience, an anarchistic rejection of theses and conclusions reached in the pre-nuclear age, as well as an inability to interpret new phenomena from the standpoint of genuine science.
>
> Referring to the development of nuclear missile weapons, the ideologues of imperialism are attempting to torpedo Marxist-Leninist theses which reveal the link between politics and war, to belittle their cognitive value for the "nuclear-age." They declare that the new weapon has radically and fundamentally altered the relationship between politics and war, has disrupted the correlation between them which has developed over many centuries, and has made obsolete the formula of war as a continuation of politics by violent means.
>
> Although the development of this new weapon does introduce substantial changes into the correlation between politics and war, it does not eliminate the relationship between them. . . . Thus the relationship between politics and war, thoroughly revealed in the writings of Lenin, not only remains valid in the Nuclear Age, but acquires even greater significance.[66]

[65] Rear Admiral Professor V. Shelyag, "Two World Outlooks—Two Views on War," *Krasnaya Zvezda,* 7 February 1974 (FBIS-74-30).

[66] Milovidov et al., *The Philosophical Heritage of V. I. Lenin and Problems of Contemporary War,* pp. 45–47.

In summing up an evaluation of Soviet doctrine and strategy for ground forces, Professor John Erickson concluded:

> The orientation was, and is, basically nuclear: certainly the notion of conflict at any level of weapons employment has been admitted, but there has been little, if any change in the broad-based Soviet feeling that any conflict seriously joined in Europe could scarcely be kept within the kind of "limits" which American theorists tended to purvey. The Soviet view of "flexible response" *as enunciated by NATO* was one of ill-concealed skepticism, either about the feasibility of holding on at the conventional level or the employment of tactical nuclear weapons in "selective" fashion. As for the elaborations of the basic principles underlying likely Soviet practice, these have been subject to a number of sophisticated glosses, but no basic revision.[67]

Erickson's remarks, in my view, require some elaboration. They should not be taken to suggest that the Soviets have and recognize *no* options short of massive theater-wide employment of nuclear weapons, nor that Soviet doctrine excludes entirely selective use or limited use of nuclear weapons in operations or tactics. It is true that Soviet military literature was at one time dominated by writing to the effect that nuclear warfare would not be limited or selective, but would, rather, assume widespread, even indiscriminate, general-war characteristics as a matter of course. The weight of evidence from Soviet open literature indicated that concepts of limiting nuclear warfare to levels meaningfully distinguishable from massive employment had little place in Soviet military thinking. Even then, however, Soviet literature conveyed the impression that escalation to general nuclear war could be avoided by quick military victory, even when nuclear weapons were used to produce the victory. This is what one Western observer termed the *"fait accompli"* approach.[68] As NATO shifted in the 1960s to "flexible response," and as Soviet military capabilities and strategies evolved, there seemed to appear more willingness to contemplate various limitations and to plan for tactical warfare as a separate problem, even while massive nuclear strikes against the enemy's nuclear means were still viewed as decisive. It seems fairly clear that Soviet targeting is directed at military targets, and probably those military targets crucial at the time to their objectives. This implies selectivity, however widespread.

In more recent years, references to the inevitable escalation of nuclear war, to the impossibility or improbability of keeping nuclear war within definable bounds, have begun to be replaced in Soviet military literature and exercises

---

[67] John Erickson, *Soviet Military Power* (London: Royal United Services Institute, 1971), p. 77.

[68] John R. Thomas, "Limited Nuclear War in Soviet Strategic Thinking," *Orbis* (Spring 1966), p. 203.

either by silence on the subject (in the case of exercises, perhaps because they end short of strategic or massive theater-wide nuclear strikes), or by suggestions of limited and selective nuclear weapons employment. Ex-Secretary of Defense Schlesinger has reported:

> In their exercises the Soviets have indicated far greater interest in the notions of controlled nuclear war and non-nuclear war than has even before been reflected in Soviet doctrine.[69]

The view has been advanced that wars on various levels are possible, that Soviet forces must be prepared for them, and that warfare remains, even when nuclear, an act or instrument of politics. One would hesitate to label this "flexible response," because of the Western connotation of the term, which, is not that of the Soviets. However, the increased capability and flexibility of Soviet Ground Forces and Frontal Aviation may have something to do with a somewhat more flexible approach to viewing nuclear combat. The Soviets appear to have a new confidence in their ability to prosecute war at various levels successfully without escalation beyond bounds consistent with Soviet political and strategic objectives. After all, if pragmatism alone were not enough, escalation serving neither political nor strategic objectives would be a direct contradiction and refutation of Marxist-Leninist principles.

Marxism-Leninism stresses flexible orchestration of political and military actions to suit the situation and the best interests of the Soviet Union. There are many conceivable situations in which the Soviet leadership might well believe their best interests to be served through distinguishable limitations on the use of nuclear weapons; and Soviet forces now appear to have the capability for limited nuclear operations that can be adapted to the objectives and the conditions at hand.

While remaining strongly nuclear oriented and retaining an emphasis on the decisiveness of timely nuclear strikes against the most lucrative and critical enemy military targets, Soviet thought on nuclear warfare may be undergoing some refinement. Soviet policy with regard to nuclear warfare in Europe appears to be moving away from emphasis on inexorable escalation in any direct war between the United States and the USSR, and toward the working out of various boundaries.

It is necessary to be cautious rather than dogmatic in advancing this suggestion. Our information is not only incomplete, but it is far from satisfactory. Moreover, matters of degree are involved. It is true, as the University of Miami study group concluded, that in open Soviet military literature:

---

[69] James R. Schlesinger, *Nuclear Weapons and Foreign Policy,* hearing before the Subcommittee on U.S. Security Agreements and Commitments Abroad, Committee on Foreign Relations, U.S. Senate, 93rd Cong., 2nd sess., March–April 1974, p. 183.

Current Soviet theater war concepts, like its strategic concepts, pay greatest attention to the nuclear war case in which nuclear weapons would be used to destroy the enemy's nuclear capability, his large troop formations, fleets and weapons storage sites, and to "pave the way" for the rapid advance of Soviet troops.[70]

But the statement properly says "greatest attention," not exclusive attention. Moreover, that the objectives cited *must* be accomplished, as the study group also concludes, "by the combined use of the Strategic Rocket Forces and Air Forces against distant targets" is not clear. The nuclear capability and flexibility of Soviet Ground Forces and Tactical (Frontal) Aviation Forces have improved, some reports have the Soviets stationing more nuclear weapons forward in the theater—Professor Erickson has even estimated recently that the number forward in the theater has doubled in the last few years to approach the 7,000 ascribed to NATO[71] —and USSR-based long-range nuclear forces may not be needed for theater objectives. Frog and Scud capability in the theater continue to be improved; Scud reaches most critical military targets in Western and Central Europe (save those in the United Kingdom); and there seems some recent emphasis on tactical nuclear air strikes, at least insofar as the Soviets seem to be changing that aviation from a fighter-interceptor orientation to include strong strike elements.[72] That distinction would be consistent with the conclusion reached by a recent study that, "In the more recent Soviet material there is a very clear and explicit treatment of theater nuclear war as a separate and distinct engagement. References to 'strategic' are hard to find."[73]

In both doctrine and capability, the assessment of distinctive limitations *within* theater nuclear warfare—for example, restricting nuclear usage to the immediate battlefield, or to a relatively few controlled strikes to "pave the way," or to employment of very low yield or tailored effects—is more difficult. Here, information is particularly uncertain and fragmentary. Still, it is difficult to maintain dogmatically either case without some doubt. That is to say, those who would insist, along with Enthoven and Smith,[74] that there is *no* discriminate capability or inclination, and essentially no interest in limited tactical nuclear combat, are on at least as shaky ground as those who would read some limited and

[70] Leon Goure et al., *The Role of Nuclear Forces in Current Soviet Strategy*, p. 19.

[71] John Erickson, "Soviet Military Capabilities in Europe," *Journal of the Royal United Services Institute*, March 1975, p. 67.

[72] Brown, hearing before the Committee on Armed Services, U.S. Senate, 5 February 1975, p. 244.

[73] Joseph D. Douglass, Jr., *The Soviet Theater Nuclear Offensive*, System Planning Corporation, Arlington, Va., Research Note 201, 6 February 1975. Sponsored by Office of Net Technical Assessment, Office, Director, Defense Research and Engineering, Department of Defense.

[74] Alain Enthoven and K. Wayne Smith, *How Much Is Enough? Shaping the Defense Program, 1961–1969* (New York: Harper & Row, 1971).

discriminate tactical nuclear capability in Soviet military options. This is one of those areas mentioned at the outset where it is possible to be subjectively selective in what one sees.

The book *The Offensive,* it is true, in discussing nuclear employment in the theater, tends to emphasize large-scale introduction of nuclear weapons on the operational level. In this regard, it is also somewhat supported by the Soviet doctrinal manual, *Tactics,* which states:

> Nuclear strikes are not included in the usual concept of fire. They are decisive means of destruction of the enemy, a new element for construction of the defense, and should be applied primarily for the destruction of enemy means of nuclear attack, destruction of major groupings of his troops, and the solution of other most important problems.[75]

Yet, *The Offensive* also treats tactical use of nuclear weapons. And, as has been noted, Soviet literature seems to hold out the possibility of both small-scale and large-scale use of nuclear weapons and to distinguish battlefield (tactical), theater-wide (operational), and strategic levels of warfare. Limits suggested pertain both to geography and to targets (as well, of course, as to political objectives). There are substantial differences between the West and the Soviets in thinking about nuclear weapons, as indicated, which emphasize the Soviet war-fighting view as compared with the Western tendency to regard the nuclear weapon primarily as a punitive-retaliatory or politically demonstrative weapon, whose use should be avoided except as a last resort. Soviet studies of the uses of nuclear weapons in *combat* operations involving different conditions of warfare have been mentioned at the highest level:

> Work has begun on a broad complex of questions concerning the conduct of combat operations under conditions involving the use of both nuclear and improved types of conventional weapons. The equipping of all the branches of the armed forces with nuclear missile weapons brought forth the need for thoroughly reviewing the various concepts regarding the nature of a possible war.[76]

Although firm evidence indicating established Soviet requirements for low yield and discriminate tactical nuclear weapons is lacking, there are suggestions. Yields on the order of 5 KT are publicly estimated in congressional sources, with an average Soviet tactical (theater, not including MR/IRBM) yield suggested at 20 KT, both of which suggest low-yield weapons, however much the figures may

---

[75] V. G. Reznichenko, *Tactics* (Moscow, 1966). Translated by the Officer's Library. Foreign Technology Division, Wright-Patterson AFB, October 1967.

[76] Marshal Grechko, "On Guard Over Peace and Socialism," *Kommunist,* no. 7 (8 May 1973).

be spun out of whole cloth.[77] And there are references in Soviet military literature to both low-yield tactical weapons and the use of prompt nuclear radiation as a primary kill mechanism on the battlefield (for the attack of armored units):

> Nuclear weapons are still being improved. There are two trends in the further development of these weapons. One of them consists in the creation of nuclear charges of smaller power intended for operation-tactical purposes. . . . The Soviet Union has large stockpiles of charges of small and colossal power.[78]

> Through the efforts of scientists, designers, engineers, workers, and military specialists, nuclear warheads of various power levels . . . have been created.[79]

It may be that characteristics generally ascribed to Soviet theater nuclear forces—poor accuracy, high yields—were accurate characterizations of past-generation weapons, but inaccurate for future, or perhaps even some present, weapons. The Soviets undoubtedly have the technology for the development of various types of nuclear weapons, including discriminate battlefield weapons; and our evidence that they have limited this development, voluntarily, is not very good. As a former Assistant to the Secretary of Defense for Atomic Energy testified:

> We have little knowledge of the Soviet warhead designs, of their vulnerability, or of Soviet testing or development philosophy. . . . We do not know what the Soviets have accomplished in their test program since 1963, but unless their program was a very sterile one, the Soviets would almost certainly be in a far more favorable position to upgrade their future stockpile with even more effective tactical and strategic weapons.[80]

As to the employment of radiation on the battlefield, it is clear that the Soviets have well known the basic nature of radiation and even enhanced radiation weapons for some time; and a recent military manual on antitank warfare dwells at some length on the advantages of radiation over blast kill:

[77] *Nuclear Weapons and Foreign Policy*, pp. 133, 216.

[78] *Marxism and Leninism on War and the Army* (Moscow: 1972). Reprinted in *Strategic Review*, vol. 1 (Fall 1973), p. 80.

[79] Marshal of Artillery K. Kazakov, *Pod Znamenem Lenninizma*, no. 19 (October 1972), JPRS 57799, 19 December 1972.

[80] Testimony of Carl Walske, Assistant to the Secretary of Defense for Atomic Energy, *Prospects for a Comprehensive Nuclear Test Ban*, hearing before the Subcommittee on Arms Control, International Law and Organization, Committee on Foreign Relations, U.S. Senate, 92nd Cong. 1st sess., 1971, pp. 132–133.

However, in performing the mission of destroying armored troops on the field of battle it is expedient to destroy such a basic element as the tank crews in and outside the tanks. This makes it possible to deprive the enemy armored troops of their combat power with a greater economy of ammunition, in shorter periods and with a high destructive probability.

The point is that the effective radius of a nuclear explosion is one and a half to twice as great against a tank crew [using radiation] as it is against a tank [using blast] (3–4 times as great in the case of low-yield explosions).[81]

To confirm the relation of radiation kill to blast kill radii, the book presents a tabulation of kill radii for different yields beginning at *0.02 KT.* The implication of the discussion is not only that radiation kill of personnel would make tanks softer targets, but that quite low yields are most effective and suitable.

In addition, Soviet military writings on tactical combat note the necessity for offensive operations in areas where nuclear bursts have taken place, discussing radiological contamination, tree blowdown, and rubble as problems that make passage difficult (all problems that would be exacerbated by high-yield fission weapons).

The meaning of such suggestions for Soviet doctrine remains inconclusive. But it is conclusive that Soviet military capabilities are developing and becoming more flexible, and that Soviet operations and tactics are being studied, tested, and possibly refined in a variety of means and conditions. This is hardly surprising given the Soviet emphasis on flexibility and adaptability to changed conditions, a Leninist injunction that has appeared in much recent military literature. It is said, for example, that "Lenin's dialectically flexible approach" is the foundation of Soviet comprehension of the dynamics of warfare and of Soviet strategy where the goal—within the framework of overall doctrine—is "*to make a specific analysis of a specific situation.*"[82]

> Flexibility and definiteness of thinking, as a synthetic expression of the demands of dialectical logic, are extremely important in the area of military theory and practice. . . . A flexibility is needed which could adequately reflect the maneuverable nature and dynamism of the course of combat operations. Levin provided examples of flexible and precise considerations of the concrete situation and enemy tactics, examples of employment of diversified forms and methods of class struggle, their skilled combination and substitution, and selection of the most effective one at each moment.
>
> Flexibility and definiteness in a commander's activities presumes the courage to innovate. *Innovative search and original solutions were convinc-*

---

[81] Major General G. Biryukov and Colonel G. Melnikov, *Antitank Warfare* (Moscow, 1972). Published in English by Progress Publishers, p. 69.

[82] Milovidov et al., *The Philosophical Heritage of V. I. Lenin and Problems of Contemporary War,* p. 275 (italics added).

ingly manifested at troop maneuvers in recent years, which constituted a new stage in the training of troops to conduct modern combat operations.[83]

Perhaps some developments along the lines suggested are part of these innovative applications of the basically nuclear-oriented Soviet doctrine. In any case, this area deserves our closest attention.

[83] Ibid., pp. 277–278 (italics added).

Changes in Tactical Concepts within the Soviet Forces

William F. Scott

INTRODUCTION

There seems to be little agreement among Western analysts on what changes, if any, have taken place in tactical concepts within the Warsaw Pact forces between 1955 and 1975—the first two decades of their existence. Some assume that these forces are turning more and more toward reliance on conventional weapons, rejecting the earlier nuclear emphasis that had characterized Khrushchev's regime. Others appear to feel that the Soviet Union has accepted the concept of limited nuclear war, as understood in the West. According to proponents of this view, should nuclear weapons be introduced into a NATO-Warsaw Pact conflict, there would be little danger of the Soviet leadership permitting the war to escalate to general nuclear war.

There are also variations on these themes. For example, some feel that Soviet forces, in a NATO-Warsaw Pact conflict in which only conventional weapons were used, would be limited to a blitzkrieg-type strategy. Soviet armed forces, according to this school of thought, do not have sufficient logistical-support forces to permit the continuation of nonnuclear war in the NATO area for more than a few weeks.

Assumptions about the Warsaw Pact military forces, and changes believed to be taking place within them, affect our perceptions of the military strength needed by the NATO nations. These assumptions also are a major basis of our negotiations at international conferences such as MFR (mutual force reduction) and SALT (strategic-arms-limitation talks).

With the benefit of hindsight, what have been the basic tactical concepts of the Warsaw Pact forces since the early 1960s and have these forces been structured organizationally to wage the type of war indicated by these tactics? Answers to these questions are necessary if we are to discover what military concepts Soviet military forces have adopted in the mid-1970s and what changes might be under way that will be implemented by the 1980s. This paper examines Soviet tactical concepts, the organization and structure of the armed forces, officer recruitment, and tactical lessons learned from limited wars.

FUNDAMENTALS OF SOVIET TACTICAL THOUGHT

In 1955, when the Warsaw Pact was formed, Soviet political-military leaders already had tested both nuclear and thermonuclear weapons. By 1957 they had achieved successes in the development and testing of ballistic missiles. While these tests were in progress, extensive research was under way within the Ministry of Defense to determine what impact the marriage of the nuclear weapon and missile would have on strategy, operational art, and tactics. This research exercise extended into the military districts, fleets, and schools. A number of studies resulting from this research, known as the "Special Collection," were transmitted to the West by Oleg Penkovskiy.[1]

Influenced by these studies, the Soviet leadership announced the doctrinal decision that the nuclear weapon would be the decisive factor in any future world war.[2] This decision required a reevaluation of the entire Soviet military structure. One result of the reevaluation was the formation of the Strategic Rocket Forces as an independent service in 1959. These forces subsequently were declared to be the primary Soviet service, a rating retained to this day.

This new doctrine, based on the primacy of the nuclear weapon, was first announced by Khrushchev in January 1960.[3] Doctrine, according to Soviet definition, is a system of scientifically based views, accepted by the government, on the nature of modern war.[4] Doctrine looks only to the future. And most

---

[1] Oleg Penkovskiy, *The Penkovskiy Papers* (Garden City, N.Y.: Doubleday, 1965), pp. 251–260.

[2] Marshal M. V. Zakharov, ed. *50 Let Vooruzhennykh Sil SSR (50 Years of the Armed Forces of the USSR)* (Moscow: Voyenizdat, 1968), pp. 520–521.

[3] N. S. Khrushchev, "Disarmament for Durable Peace and Friendship," address delivered at the Fourth Session of the Supreme Soviet, USSR, 14 January 1960, published in *On Peaceful Coexistence* (Moscow: Foreign Languages Publishing House, 1960), pp. 126–182.

[4] *Slovar' Osnovnykh Voyennykh Terminov (Dictionary of Basic Military Terms)* (Moscow, Voenizdat 1965), p. 41.

importantly, "in the content of Soviet military doctrine the main place is occupied by the proposition which pertains to the problem of the preparation and conduct of a nuclear rocket war."[5]

In the Soviet armed forces, military strategy works out and investigates the concrete questions concerning the character of a future war, the preparation of the country for war, the organization of the armed forces and the methods of waging war. Strategy is subordinate to doctrine. Therefore, the new doctrine required a new strategy, which had to be understood and applied throughout the Soviet armed forces. A group of officers, headed by the former Chief of the General Staff, Marshal V. D. Sokolovskiy, took the basic documents concerning the new doctrine, unified them into a logical whole, and then presented them in an unclassified form for the study and indoctrination of all officers. The result was *Military Strategy* edited in 1962 by Marshal Sokolovskiy;[6] in December 1962 another publication appeared, written by Defense Minister Marshal Mal inovskiy and entitled *Vigilantly Stand Guard Over the Peace*.[7] In these two publications are found the basic tenets of Soviet military thought, which remain essentially valid even today.

IMPACT OF DOCTRINE AND STRATEGY
ON THE SOVIET ARMED FORCES

All the Soviet services were affected by the introduction of nuclear weapons, although initial priority was given to the Strategic Rocket Forces. As weapons became more numerous, with widely varying yields, they were allocated for specific purposes to the Ground Forces, Troops of National Air Defense, Air Forces, and Navy.

In the early 1960s, Khrushchev tended to emphasize the superiority of the nuclear weapon over other types of armaments. One reason for this was the serious Soviet military manpower problem at that time. Few babies had been conceived in the Soviet Union between 1941 and 1945. The number of youth reaching military service each year declined from over 2,380,000 in 1957 to a low of 917,000 in 1962. It was not until *1973* that the annual number of new recruits reached the same level as the late 1950s.[8]

For a brief period, therefore, Khrushchev stressed in his public utterances

[5] General Major S. N. Kozkov, ed., *Spravochnik Ofitsera (Officer's Handbook)* (Moscow: Voyenizdat, 1971), pp. 74–75.

[6] Marshal V. D. Sokolovskiy, ed., *Voyennaya Strategiya (Military Strategy)* (Moscow: Voyenizdat, 1962).

[7] Marshal R. Ya. Malinovskiy, *Bditel'no Stoyat Na Strazhe Mira (Vigilantly Stand Guard Over the Peace)* (Moscow: Voyenizdat, 1962). For a discussion of doctrine, see pp. 16–29.

[8] Murray Feshbach, "Population," *Economic Performance and the Military Burden of the Soviet Union,* Joint Economic Committee of the Congress of the United States (Washington, D.C.: Government Printing Office, 1970), p. 68.

the savings in military manpower that could be affected through the use of nuclear weapons. This was done primarily for propaganda purposes, but also because military manpower problems were real. There was no basic dispute between Khrushchev and his marshals on this subject, nor within the military itself.

By 1964, students at the Malinovskiy Tank Academy in Moscow were being taught tank tactics in a nuclear war environment. The use of nuclear weapons on the battlefield, it was felt, should not necessarily cause the tank to lose its combat capability. Provisions had been made to protect the tank crew from nuclear, chemical, and biological agents. Armored personnel carriers also were equipped so that personnel in the vehicles would survive on a chemical-biological-nuclear battlefield. In fact, occupants of these vehicles, without disembarking, could even carry on combat actions.

Soviet military doctrine and strategy, as stated by Marshal Sokolovskiy, Marshal Malinovskiy, and all other Soviet spokesmen, including those in the 1970s, specify that any future world war will demand multimillion-man armies and that troops must be prepared to fight with both nuclear and conventional weapons. Nuclear programs, as well as the basic tenets of military doctrine and strategy formulated under Khrushchev's tenure, have continued in force through more than a decade of Soviet leadership under Leonid Brezhnev. Modifications that have taken place have not invalidated the basic premises.

MODIFICATION OF SOVIET MILITARY DOCTRINE

When NATO adopted the concept of flexible response as its official policy, the previous position that a Soviet attack automatically would be met with nuclear weapons was altered. Subsequently, in 1967, the Soviets adapted their own policy. It would be stressed, however, that this was only a modification of Soviet doctrine and did not invalidate the basic doctrinal tenets that had been adopted while Khrushchev was in power. As explained by a Soviet spokesman in 1968, "In our times conditions may arise when in individual instances combat operations may be carried out using conventional weapons. Under these conditions, the role of conventional means and the traditional services of the armed forces are greatly increased."[9]

In 1969 Marshal Grechko, the Soviet Minister of Defense, further explained:

Much attention is being devoted to the reasonable combination of nuclear rocket weapons with perfected conventional classic armaments, to the cap-

[9] Lieutenant Colonel V. M. Bondarenko, "The Modern Revolution in Military Affairs and the Combat Readiness of the Armed Forces," *Kommunist Vooruzhennykh Sil (Communist of the Armed Forces)*, no. 24 (December 1968), p. 69.

ability of *units and subunits* to conduct combat actions under nuclear as well as nonnuclear conditions.[10]

The following year Marshal Grechko restated the same thought:

> The main and decisive means of conducting battle will be the nuclear rocket weapon. In it, "classical" kinds of weapons will find application. In certain circumstances, the possibility is admitted of conducting combat actions by *units and subunits* armed with conventional weapons.[11]

Since 1969 the expression "units and subunits may fight with or without the use of the nuclear weapon" has become a standard reference in numerous articles, pamphlets, and books. "Units and subunits" in the Soviet military lexicon refer to military organizations no larger than regiments and battalions, respectively.

Soviet exercises and large-scale maneuvers, in general, appear to have followed the stated doctrine. Vlatava, in 1965, was nuclear throughout the course of the maneuver. Dnieper, in 1967—the year in which the doctrinal modification was made—started with a nonnuclear phase and at a later time went nuclear. The same pattern has been repeated in maneuvers since that time—Dvina, Bug, and Sever.[12] They began with a nonnuclear phase, and then, according to the scenario, the opponent launched a nuclear strike.

Soviet doctrine considers that a war beginning with a nonnuclear phase may go nuclear at any time. This is one of the reasons that the initial objectives in any conflict remain the same—to seize, destroy, or neutralize the nuclear means of the opponent.

Should a war begin between Warsaw Pact and NATO forces utilizing nonnuclear weapons only, initial strikes would be directed at missile launch pads and at airfields from which nuclear strikes might be launched. Strikes would be conducted by elements of long-range aviation, as well as by tactical aircraft. Tactical ballistic missiles using conventional warheads, such as Scuds and Frogs, might also be targeted against known nuclear facilities. Paratroopers complete with tanks would be dropped in an attempt to seize nuclear stockpiles, with other tanks driving forward to make contact. Every possible means would be used to seize or to destroy NATO's nuclear capability.

This poses some questions. What would happen if NATO forces had the same initial objectives with respect to destroying the Warsaw Pact's nuclear capability

[10] Marshal A. A. Grechko, *Red Star,* 27 November 1969 (italics added).
[11] Marshal A. A. Grechko, *Kommunist,* February 1970 (italics added).
[12] See, for example, V. Gol'tsev, *Bol'shiye Manevry (The Great Maneuvers)* (Moscow: DOSAAF Publishing House, 1974).

at the beginning of a nonnuclear conflict? Would either side permit its nuclear weapons, delivery capability, and command facilities to be eliminated by the other, while restricting the actual fighting to conventional weapons? These are questions the Soviet defense intellectuals will not discuss.

According to Soviet views, there is a firebreak between conventional and nuclear weapons. However, once nuclear weapons are introduced, there can be no further firebreaks based on size of weapons or restrictions of their use to a given area. This is not to suggest that Soviet leaders do not understand concepts that distinguish between tactical and strategic nuclear weapons, theater versus general nuclear warfare, and so forth. Their discussion of these concepts denotes an awareness and sophistication that probably exceeds Western discussions of the same doctrine.[13] Soviet spokesmen rather simply do not appear to feel that artificial restrictions are feasible.

The signing of SALT I and subsequent agreements have not changed these basic Soviet concepts. The first major Soviet military publication following President Nixon's visit to Moscow in May 1972 was Marshal Rotmistrov's *Time and the Tank*.[14] In mid-1973 General Lomov's *Scientific-Technical Progress and the Revolution in Military Affairs*[15] restated the doctrinal tenets of the early 1960s. Both the 1974 and 1975 editions of Marshal Grechko's *The Armed Forces of the Soviet State*[16] are cautiously worded as befitting a member of Brezhnev's Politburo. However, no major change is reflected from previous writings, despite the ongoing negotiations concerning SALT, MBFR, and the European Security Conference.

ORGANIZATION AND MANPOWER

The basic structure of the Soviet armed forces is described in the 1974 issue of the *Yezhegodnik (Yearbook)* of the *Bolshoi Soviet Encyclopedia:*

> The Armed Forces of the USSR consist of the Ground Forces, Strategic Rocket Forces, Troops of National Air Defense, Air Forces and Navy, comprising the services of the Armed Forces, and also the *tyl of the Armed Forces, Troops of Civil Defense* and border and internal troops.[17]

[13] Marshal V. D. Sokolovskiy, *Voyennaya Strategiya (Military Strategy)*, 3d ed. (Moscow, 1968). For an English translation see, *Third Edition, Soviet Military Strategy*, edited, with analysis and commentary by Harriet Fast Scott (New York: Crane, Russak, 1975).

[14] Chief Marshal of Armored Troops P. A. Rotmistrov, *Vremya i Tanki (Time and the Tank)* (Moscow: Voyenizdat, 1972), especially pp. 248–283.

[15] N. A. Lomov, *Nauchno-Tekhnicheskiy Progress i Revolyutsiya v Voyennom Dele (Scientific-Technical Progress and the Revolution in Military Affairs)* (Moscow: Voyenizdat, 1973).

[16] Marshal A. A. Grechko, *Vooruzhennyye Sily Sovetskovo Gosudarstva (The Armed Forces of the Soviet State)* (Moscow: Voyenizdat, 1974, 2d ed. 1975).

[17] *Yezhegodnik (Yearbook)* (Moscow: "Soviet Encyclopedic" Publishing House, 1974), p. 73 (italics added).

This organizational structure has a significant impact on the type of conflict the Soviet Union is best suited to wage, the command and control procedures and methods that would be utilized, and the research-and-development priorities for weapons systems it will more likely seek. There is a tendency in the West to mirror-image the Soviet military structure with the conventional army, navy, and air forces found in NATO nations. Assumptions *about* the Soviet organizational structure may have blinded some Western military and political planners to the capability of Warsaw Pact forces to wage a protracted war, both nuclear and nonnuclear. In particular, recognition of the *tyl* (rear or logistical services) seldom is found in Western writings about Soviet military forces. Because of these different perceptions, the basic Soviet military structure is reviewed here.

The Strategic Rocket Forces control all Soviet land-based missiles with ranges greater than 1,000 kilometers. These forces figure in the NATO-Warsaw Pact equation in a very definite manner. Soviet IRBMs (intermediate-range ballistic missiles) and MRBMs (medium-range ballistic missiles) cover all Western Europe as well as most of Asia.

Soviet Ground Forces generally are considered to be the primary factor in any possible NATO-Warsaw Pact conflict. This service is composed of four basic branches: motorized rifle, rockets and artillery, armor, and troop air defense. Troop air defense of the Ground Forces often is confused with the Troops of National Air Defense. Each of the four Ground Force branches has its own school system (see below). Generally NATO and Warsaw Pact forces are compared on the basis of the number of divisions of motorized infantry and tanks. It might be well to pay more attention to the other two branches, troop air defense and rocket troops and artillery. Frogs and Scuds—Soviet operational-tactical missiles with ranges less than 1,000 kilometers—are part of the rocket troops and artillery branch. Troop air defense has its own antiaircraft artillery and surface-to-air mobile missiles, such as the SA-4 and SA-6.

Troops of National Air Defense (PVO Strany) comprise the third service. Some analysts confuse PVO fighter aircraft with elements of frontal aviation of the Soviet Air Forces. Troops of National Air Defense have their own officer procurement, as well as their own flying, radar, and missile schools. There does not appear to be any closer relation between a pilot in PVO Strany and the Soviet Air Forces than there would be between a navy pilot, and an air force pilot in the United States.

Since 1971, air-defense forces of the East European nations have been under the control of the commander-in-chief of the Soviet Troops of National Air Defense.[18] This extends the area of Soviet PVO Strany to the borders of West Germany. In the event of a NATO-Warsaw Pact conflict, be it nuclear or

---

[18] Vice Admiral Z. Studzinskiy, "Our Unbreakable Combat Union," *Red Star,* 28 March 1975.

nonnuclear, air defense of the Warsaw Pact nations would be controlled from Moscow. Interceptor aircraft of Marshal Batitskiy, commander-in-chief of PVO Strany, therefore, could have a sanctuary in the USSR, complete with repair facilities, safe from attack by both aircraft and missiles, hardly the equivalent of NATO interceptors having a sanctuary in the United States.

Soviet Air Forces, the fourth Soviet service, are divided into three primary components: long-range aviation, frontal aviation, and transport. All these would be engaged in any NATO-Warsaw Pact conflict, in either nuclear or nonnuclear conditions. Elements of long-range aviation would be assigned targets such as NATO missile-launch areas of airfields, attacking with conventional or nuclear weapons. They probably would operate under direct assignment of the Supreme High Command, through the commander-in-chief, Soviet Air Forces. Frontal aviation, formed into air armies both in time of peace and war, is assigned to military districts and to the groups of forces abroad. The commander of aviation of the military district or group of forces sits on the military council of the district and is responsible to the staff of the Soviet Air Forces for his actions. Soviet military districts and groups of forces abroad are the approximate equivalents of joint commands in the United States. Transport aviation, the third component of the Soviet Air Forces, also includes helicopters. Operational tasks of these components probably are directed by the General Staff, through the staff of the Soviet Air Forces.

The Soviet Navy, the fifth Soviet service, is also a major factor in any NATO-Warsaw Pact balance. Keeping the forces of NATO supplied through sea-lanes in the event of a conflict may determine success or failure. Disruption of sea-lanes would be the task of portions of both the Soviet Navy's surface force and submarine fleet, supported by the hundreds of bomber and long-range reconnaissance aircraft now assigned to this service.

SUPPORT ELEMENTS

As has already been noted, conventional wisdom in the West generally has failed to take into account Soviet support forces. Those forces not only include the *tyl*, but also other departments and agencies directly under the Soviet Ministry of Defense. In many cases the subordination and assignment of support elements within the Soviet armed forces are blurred and difficult to identify.

Building and construction troops, who are commanded by a Deputy Minister of Defense, may number between 100,000 and 300,000. We know them best by their work in civilian construction and rebuilding activities. When Tashkent was partly destroyed by an earthquake in 1965, most of the rebuilding of the city was accomplished by military construction troops. In Moscow many of the most modern buildings, such as the new international terminal at Moscow's Sheremetyevo Airport, Star City (home of the Soviet cosmonauts), and a number of the apartment and office buildings on the new Kalinin Street were the work of this military construction force.[19] Lieutenants are provided to this branch through four higher military schools, three of which offer four-year courses and the fourth a five-year course for military builders. Officer output of these four schools is probably between 1,200 and 1,400 lieutenants each year.

Railway troops are an important factor when considering the ability of the Warsaw Pact forces to wage a protracted conventional war against NATO. In the fall and winter of 1974–1975, items appeared almost daily in the Soviet press about the work of these troops in the construction of BAM—the new section of the Trans-Siberian Railroad north of Lake Baikal. Railway troops are found throughout the USSR.

Pipeline troops are another sizable support force element. Marshal Sokolovskiy, in all three editions of *Military Strategy,* specifically notes their importance in military operations. Attention given to pipelines within the USSR as a whole is shown by the fact that in 1955, fourteen billion ton-kilometers of fuel were pumped by this means, and for 1965 the projected figure was 200 billion ton-kilometers.[20] Such pipelines, designed for military purposes, probably extend to the western borders of the Soviet Union.

Military kolkhozes supply many of the fresh vegetables and other food products to all the Soviet armed forces. Their numbers appear to have increased significantly since 1967. They are manned by military personnel, with some assistance from civilian workers. Like practically everything in the Soviet Union even remotely associated with defense matters, their locations and exact numbers are a military secret.[21]

Troops of the tyl (rear services) perform general quartermaster tasks for the Soviet armed forces. They are responsible for providing food, clothing, fuel, medical support, ammunition, repair facilities, and other services. The commander of the *tyl* maintains five military schools, graduating lieutenants in various specialties after courses varying from three to five years.

The elements noted above are but a portion of the Soviet support units. When the numbers of these troops are taken into account, as well as the logistical equipments assigned them, it becomes apparent that NATO faces an opponent with support forces sufficient to maintain major groups of combat troops in the field for extended periods.

TROOPS OF CIVIL DEFENSE

Many analysts of Soviet military affairs ignore the Soviet Troops of Civil Defense when considering military capabilities. These troops are under the control of the

---

[19] See A. I. Romashko, *Voyennyye Stroiteli Na Stroykakh Moskvy (Military Builders on the Construction of Moscow)* (Moscow: Voyenizdat, 1972).

[20] Sokolovskiy, *Soviet Military Strategy*, p. 328.

[21] Marshal I. Kh. Bagramyan, "The Rear Services of Our Troops," *Yest' Stat' v Stroy (To Be in Formation)* (Moscow: Young Guards Publishing House, 1967), p. 78.

Soviet Chief of Civil Defense, who also is a Deputy Minister of Defense. Judging from the number of senior officers assigned to this activity, the total troop strength must number in tens of thousands.[22] The Chief of Civil Defense has his own military school (see below p. 88).

After 1967, when the Soviet leadership recognized that their antiballistic missile system would be ineffective against the MIRV, renewed emphasis was given to the Soviet civil defense program. Since the signing of SALT I, Marshal Grechko and other Soviet spokesmen have stressed that the Troops of Civil Defense are of major strategic significance.[23] The fact that Warsaw Pact forces are outfitted for chemical, bacteriological, and nuclear warfare already has been noted. If the population of the Soviet Union is prepared for the possibility of a general nuclear war, and its armed forces prepared to fight in a nuclear environment, it would appear that the Soviet leadership may be in a favorable position to dictate nuclear terms to an opponent who has neither its armed forces nor population so prepared.

TROOPS OF THE KGB AND MVD

Additionally, neither the troops of the MVD (Ministry of Internal Affairs) nor the troops of the KGB (Committee of State Security) can be disregarded when realistically considering the military capabilities of the Soviet Union. Both the MVD and KGB troops perform military and paramilitary tasks within the Soviet zone of interior, permitting the maximum numbers of forces under the Ministry of Defense to be deployed outside Soviet borders.

KGB troops, armed with tanks, armored personnel carriers, and other weapons similar to those found in the Ground Forces, are deployed essentially as ground troops along the entire Soviet border. KGB coast guard troops even have their own ships. It is the KGB Border Guards, and not troops under Marshal Grechko's Ministry of Defense, that frequently have skirmished with the Chinese along the Sino-Soviet border. Names of the dead from the 1969 Battle of Damanskiy Island are listed on a plaque in the officer's club in Khabarovsk—and all were in the KGB.

INCREASED SOVIET MILITARY MANPOWER
ESTIMATES AND RESERVE FORCES

Total manpower in the Soviet armed forces numbers between 4,500,000 and 6,000,000. In February 1975 the U.S. Secretary of Defense estimated Soviet

[22] James T. Reitz, "Selected Aspects of the Soviet Civil Defense Program," Washington, D.C., Strategic Studies Center, Stanford Research Institute, SRI Project 3275, 18 October 1974.
[23] Grechko, *Vooruzhennyye Sily Sovetskovo Gosudarstva.* See p. 108 in the 1974 edition and p. 115 in the 1975 edition.

military manpower strengths of 4,200,000 with the caveat that "there are a number of individuals assigned to supply research and training elements for whom we have not yet accounted."[24]

The 1973–1974 *Military Balance* had placed Soviet armed force strengths at 3,425,000. In 1974–1975 the same publication upped the figure to 3,525,000.[25] A few analysts in the summer of 1974 had called attention to the fact that published estimates of Soviet manpower strengths had failed to account for many of the Soviet support services.[26] It was somewhat overdue when ex-Secretary of Defense Schlesinger, as noted above, increased the estimate of the Soviet military forces by over 700,000 to 4,200,000.

This increase has had repercussions. As one columnist observed: "The conventional wisdom in NATO military circles has been that the Soviet Union would try for a quick knockout in any attack on Western Europe and that a moderate-sized Russian support force supports a blitzkrieg thesis.[27] The increased estimate of the size of the Soviet support forces does not eliminate the possibility of the Soviets using a blitzkrieg strategy against NATO; it does, however, indicate that if such a strategy fails, the Soviets have the option of continuing a conventional war or going nuclear.

Assumptions about Soviet military power seldom take into account the asymmetry in numbers and types of reserve forces in the United States and the Soviet Union. Combat-ready reserves for each service in the United States probably could be numbered in the tens or hundreds of thousands. Combat reserves in the Soviet Union are numbered in the millions.

In the United States the armed forces are manned on the basis of voluntary enlistments. Armed forces in the Soviet Union are maintained through universal military service, which has been in continuous existence since 1939. It is estimated that less than 20 percent of Soviet youth are excused from their military obligation. Only a very small percentage of the youth in the United States are ever exposed to military training.

By 1967 the number of eighteen-year-old youths in the Soviet Union eligible for military service passed the 2,000,000 mark. This required changes in the conscription law, which at the time prescribed a minimum of three years of service. Considering that only a small percentage are excused from military training, the number of conscripts alone in the Soviet Armed Forces would exceed 5,000,000 if the three-year service period were continued. Marshal

[24] James R. Schlesinger, *Statement to the Congress of the FY 1976 and Transition Budgets, FY 1977 Authorized Request and FY 1976–1080 Defense Programs,* Washington, D.C., the Pentagon, mimeograph, 5 February 1975, p. 8.

[25] See *The Military Balance 1974–1975* (London: The International Institute for Strategic Studies, 1974), p. 8.

[26] L. Edgar Prina, "U.S. Raises Estimate of Red Army," *San Diego Union,* 20 October 1974.

[27] Ibid.

Sokolovskiy had observed in *Military Strategy* that "the shorter the period of service in the army, the greater the number of men with military training discharged each year into the reserve."[28] The 1967 law on Universal Military Service reduced the length of training to two years, except for certain categories of personnel who would remain in service for three years. To compensate for the shortened training time, premilitary training was augmented.

By the mid-1970s, approximately 2,250,000[29] males in the Soviet Union were available each year for military service. Assuming that 80 percent complete their military obligation, then as many as 1,800,000 are "discharged into the reserves" annually. Each remains in the first category of reserves until age thirty-five, the second category until age forty-five, and the third until age fifty. Within a five-year period as many as 9,000,000 trained military personnel are discharged into the reserves and available for mobilization, if required.

Keeping track of the location and training status of this huge number of reserve military personnel is a major task. The work is accomplished primarily through the "military commissariat" offices—an agency that is almost completely unknown in the United States. The Moscow telephone directory lists the locations of thirty-five military commissariat offices in that city alone. Judging from the size of these facilities, each must house a staff of between fifteen and thirty military personnel. Throughout the Soviet Union, in cities, towns, and rural areas, similar military commissariat offices may be observed. Numbers of personnel assigned to this activity alone must run into the tens of thousands.

Military commissariat offices have major responsibilities for ensuring that youth receive their prescribed "pre–call-up" military training, and that servicemen, when they have been "discharged into the reserves," are at a known location. The same offices also keep track of the training each reservist receives.

Tasks of military commissariats are not confined just to keeping track of personnel. They must also know what equipment in their geographic area have military utility. These include bicycles, motorbikes, automobiles, trucks, skis, tractors, and certain radios. Special instructions are issued to show how basic farm machinery may be best used for military purposes.

How reserve forces are utilized is well described in *The Great Maneuvers,* published in 1974. One chapter is devoted to a discussion of the "1968 *Tyl* (rear services) 'Neman' exercises." According to the scenario, "the 'West' carried out the aggression, utilizing nuclear weapons. The 'East' counterattacked, overcoming the results of the nuclear attack." During the course of the exercises "reserves and auto transport were drawn in from the national economy." Pipelines were extended up to the front areas across rivers and through forests. These support functions, in great part, were accomplished by reserve personnel

---

[28] Sokolovskiy, *Soviet Military Strategy,* p. 309.
[29] Feshbach, "Population," p. 68.

who "yesterday were civilians—in kilkhozes, sovkhozes, communal industries—today, are experienced soldiers."[30]

The author of this book gives thanks to the workers and to all individuals in plants and factories for the use of their equipment. And specific thanks are also given to the military commissariats, who made the rapid mobilization possible. This maneuver, exercising the *tyl*, "was conducted in the first half of August 1968, over a broad area, encompassing the western area of RSFSR, the Ukraine, Belorussia and Lithuania," and extended into Poland and East Germany.[31] The maneuvers culminated just prior to the invasion of Czechoslovakia on 20 August 1968.

As noted in the 1968 Neman maneuvers, planning for mobilization is not confined to personnel. Deliberate efforts are made to standardize military and civilian equipment, whenever possible. A majority of the newer trucks and other vehicles used in civilian industry throughout the Soviet Union bear a triangle on the bumper or on the body indicating mobilization readiness. Military inspectors are assigned to check trucks as well as other vehicles to ensure that required maintenance standards are met. These inspectors are charged with making certain that the vehicles are ready for call-up at any time. The Soviet capability for rapid mobilization of both men and equipment is not matched in the West. However, this capability is so little known that it is generally ignored when the NATO-Warsaw Pact balance is being considered.

TRAINING AND EDUCATION

Specific data concerning the education and training of Soviet officer personnel might increase the accuracy of Western estimates of Soviet capabilities.[32] Most of the younger Soviet officers are products of military and higher military schools. These schools resemble, in a number of ways, West Point, Annapolis, and the Air Force Academy in the United States; Cranwell and Sandhurst in the United Kingdom; and St. Cyr in France. Entrance ages are from seventeen to twenty-two. The majority of the Soviet schools have four-year courses, a few still are three-year, and more and more are increasing course length from four to five years. Graduates receive commissions with their degrees.

How good are these schools, and what standards are expected? Exact details of the course work are not available. However, a survey of sample entrance examinations[33] indicates that the cadet beginning his first-year work is expected

---

[30] Gol'tsev, *Bol'shiye Manevry,* p. 60.

[31] Ibid., p. 59.

[32] Data for this section come from a monograph by Harriet Fast Scott, "The Soviet Military Educational System," unpublished, part of which appeared in "Educating the Soviet Officer Corps," *Air Force Magazine* (March 1975), pp. 57–60.

[33] See, for example, I. A. Kamkov, *Dlya Takh, Kto Khochet Uchit'sya v Voyennykj*

to be on approximately the same level as the West Point cadet. In particular, basic sciences are stressed.

Among the differences between the training of cadets in military academies in the United States and military schools in the Soviet Union, the degree of specialization is perhaps the most paramount. A cadet at West Point, for example, is expected to graduate as a generalist, supposedly able to enter any one of the branches of the U.S. Army. As Table 1 indicates, the situation in the Soviet Union is much different. Each arm or branch with the Soviet Ground Forces has its own schools. There are also specialized schools for other arms and branches, some of which are not a part of any Soviet service.

In the 141 military and higher military Soviet schools identified, the average length of the course of study is four years, and entry ages are seventeen to twenty-two. Size of graduating classes varies between 250 and 450. Many of the schools have impressive buildings and grounds. With but one or two exceptions, all appear to be commanded by general officers or admirals.

Table 1 identifies eighty-seven military and higher military schools that provide officers for the five Soviet military services. Table 2 lists forty-six other schools under the Ministry of Defense. Table 3 shows the number of military KGB's Border Guard and the troops of the MVD.

These 141 schools do not provide all the inputs into the Soviet officer corps. A number of Soviet universities give training that appears to approximate that offered in reserve-officer training courses in the United States. Most of the officer inputs from universities are in the support and logistical area.

The type and number of Soviet schools in specialized fields may indicate, to some degree, the importance attached to specific areas and may suggest possible trends. For example, the most recent addition to the school complex in the first half of the 1970s was the opening of a new chemical defense school at Tambov, the addition of which provides a total of three higher military schools to train and educate for chemical warfare.

Selected officers in the Soviet armed forces later attend some seventeen "academies," which are approximate equivalents of the war colleges and staff colleges in the United States and Great Britain. Generally these academies also provide specialized training and education for a specific service or branch. For example, Troops of National Air Defense has two "academies" for officer education. Course length appears to be from two to three years, although the Zhukovskiy Military Air Engineering Academy has a five-year course.

Commandants of Soviet academies are, by law, the equivalent of military district commanders in rank. Also, by Soviet law, heads of departments in the academies are general officers. Prestige of the commandants of these academies

---

Uchilishchakh i Adademiyakhi (For Those Who Wish to Study in Military Schools and Academies) (Moscow: Voyenizdat, 1968).

tion are in a process of constant evolution. The same applies to tactical concepts, which are being affected by military events that have taken place both in Southeast Asia and the Middle East. In these two areas, Soviet military equipment has been widely used, although few, if any, Soviet forces actually have been engaged.

One of the most rapid and visible changes to take place in Soviet weapons deployments can be traced to the 1967 Israeli successes in destroying Egyptian aircraft on the ground. In 1964, Soviet military aircraft were parked wing tip to wing tip on airfields in western USSR, such as at Kiev and Riga. By 1970 aircraft were in hangerettes, which could be destroyed only by a direct hit.

Thus far, there does not appear to be anything so dramatic and visible concerning possible lessons from the 1973 Mideast October War. A survey of Soviet military journals[34] and *Red Star,* the official newspaper of the Soviet Ministry of Defense, for eighteen months after that conflict, however, does point to a number of probable lessons. Some of these are certain to impact on tactics and equipment used by the Warsaw Pact forces.

In any possible NATO-Warsaw Pact conflict, Soviet tanks would play a major role. Soviet analysts gave considerable attention to tank engagements in the 1973 Mideast War and concluded that tanks remain the primary offensive weapon on the battlefield. In defense, the motorized rifleman (infantryman) requires guided antitank weapons. One of the major Soviet writers, quoting "Western military specialists," asserts that "guided antitank missiles gave to the infantry that which it had never had: the probability of destroying tanks with one shot, before the tank could use its own weapons against the infantry."[35]

Care is taken by Soviet spokesmen, however, to ensure that the apparent success of the antitank guided missile in the 1973 Mideast War will not cause tankers to lose faith in their equipment. For example:

> An abundance of antitank means (weapons) undoubtedly does not exclude successful actions of tanks on the battlefield. A well-trained and coordinated crew can successfully engage in combat with antitank means. In close cooperation with infantry, artillery, helicopters and aviation, tanks are able to successfully solve tasks placed before them, in combined-arms battle.[36]

---

[34] Journals were as follows: (1)*Voyennyy Vestnik (Military Herald),* (2) *Vestnik Protivovozdushnoy Oborony (Herald of PVO),* (3) *Aviatsiya i Kosmonavtika (Aviation and Cosmonautics),* (4) *Morskoy Sbornik (Naval Collections),* (5) *Tyl i Snabzheniye Vooruzhennykh Sil (The Rear and Supply of the Soviet Armed Forces),* (8) *Voyenno-Istoricheskiy Zhurnal (The Military History Journal),* (9) *Voyennyye Znaniya (Military Knowledge),* (10) *Sovetskiy Voin (The Soviet Soldier),* (11) *Znamenosets (Banner Carrier).*

[35] Colonel N. Nikitin, "New Developments in the Struggle With Tanks," *Zanamenosets,* May 1974, p. 38.

[36] Ibid., p. 39.

The overall tenor of the discussion concerning tanks is that more will be needed on the battlefield. It is asserted that some "military theorists in the West" insist that additional quantities of tanks be allocated "to the composition of the NATO groups of forces." Admiration is expressed for the U.S. "tri-cap" divisions, in which are organized "large units of tanks, mechanized light infantry, and helicopter fire to support them."[37] In the mid-1970s it was found that the Soviets were increasing the number of tanks allocated to both tank and infantry divisions.

Considerable attention has been given by Soviet writers to air actions in the 1973 Mideast War, but conclusions concerning the effectiveness and role of air are stated in very cautious terms. In general, air battles of Southeast Asia and the Middle East are treated in the same articles. In one case the author provided detailed tactics, noting that "regardless of the type and speed characteristics of the aircraft, the best maneuverability in battle was assured in the narrow range of speed at Mach 0.8."[38] He concluded his article with a claim that great attention is being given in the West "to questions of supporting air defense means which they see as the greatest danger to their own aircraft."[39] There can be little doubt but that the Soviet air leaders themselves are concerned with the same problem.

Soviet airmen have been told that 80 percent of the Israeli aircraft were downed by ground air defenses. They have not been told, however, that practically all the Arab aircraft lost in that war were destroyed in air-to-air combat in which Israeli aircraft losses were extremely light. All members of the Soviet Air Forces, as well as the Troops of National Air Defense, also have been made aware of the smart bombs used by the U.S. Air Force and U.S. Navy in Southeast Asia. Guidance systems are explained in detail, including their operational use. The continued and matter-of-fact discussions of these weapons in the Soviet military press indicate that the Soviet military leadership fully recognized their capability. To what degree the Soviets might be producing and developing smart bombs of their own is not known.

It is known, however, that the Soviets now are developing and deploying two new aircraft, the Flogger and Fencer, which are somewhat similar to the F-4 and F-111, respectively, in bomb-carrying capability and range. Aircraft such as these can carry the electronics equipment, penetration aids, and smart bombs themselves. Therefore, if the Soviet Air Force and air elements of the Soviet Navy do not have this new generation of bombs at present, they almost certainly will have them in the latter half of the 1970s.

Helicopters and airborne troops are given an unusual amount of attention by

[37] Ibid. Also see Colonel N. Nikitin and Colonel S. Petrov, "Israeli Aggression in October, 1973," *Voyenno-Istoricheskiy Zhurnal*, November 1974, p. 88.
[38] M. Shelekhov, "Aviation Tactics in the War in Southeast Asia and in the Near East," *Vestnik Protivovozdushnoy Oborony,* June 1974, p. 51.
[39] Ibid., p. 52

Soviet military analysts. After October 1973, helicopters often were discussed in articles that primarily were concerned with the 1973 Mideast War, despite the somewhat limited use of helicopters in that conflict. A NATO experiment, in which helicopters were matched against tanks, appears to have made an impression. Ground-to-air missiles from tanks "shot down" fourteen helicopters, "but fire-support helicopters 'destroyed' 167 tanks."[40]

Offensive capabilities of helicopters also appear as a major concern to Soviet planners. As one Soviet explains this interest:

> It is not an accident that we have looked in such detail at the flight characteristics of the helicopters in the imperialist countries; their arms and proposed tactical combat procedures against assault landing forces. This knowledge is needed by every officer, sergeant and sailor in the airborne forces.[41]

In 1967, the *Military Herald,* the monthly journal of the Soviet Ground Forces, carried three articles about helicopters and airborne troops. In 1972 only two such articles were published, although in that year the specific articles were placed under a special heading in the index. The following year the number of articles under this heading had increased to nineteen and to twenty-one in 1974! It is of possible significance here that on 23 May 1975, *Red Star* announced the opening of a new course for pilot training, but with major differences from courses previously known. This new course is for *praporshchikov* (warrant officers) and lasts but two years. All other known pilot courses run from three to four years, and graduates are commissioned as lieutenants, with wings and degrees. Warrant officers taking this two-year course must serve a minimum of five years after completion. It is hypothesized here that this course is to train warrant officers as pilots for the growing fleet of Soviet helicopters.

The attention focused in the Soviet military press on helicopters and airborne troops is not necessarily an indication of interest only in enhancing conventional war-fighting capabilities. A primary justification for airborne forces is that they could be dropped ahead of attacking groups and seize or destroy nuclear stockpiles. Judging from the Soviet press, helicopters and airborne troops would have even greater utility in nuclear war than in a conflict in which only conventional weapons were used.

CONCLUSIONS

This review of Soviet military doctrine, strategy, and tactical concepts, as well as organization and training, does not show any sudden shift in the military posture

---

[40] Nikitin, "New Developments in the Struggle With Tanks," p. 38.

[41] General Lieutenant P. Chaplygin and Colonel Y. Rodnikovskiy, "If Helicopters Attack the Assault Landing Force," *Voyennyy Vestnik,* October 1974, p. 53.

of the Warsaw Pact forces. New technology, combined with lessons from Southeast Asia and the Middle East, will bring about new emphases in weapons developments and modifications of tactics. There will be a continuing effort to upgrade conventional military capabilities.

But nuclear "sufficiency" still remains the primary concern of Soviet planners. As stated so clearly by Soviet political-military spokesmen, "the Soviet military doctrine requires that the Armed Forces, the country, the whole Soviet people be prepared for the eventuality of a nuclear-rocket war."[42] This doctrinal tenet is manifested in the structure of the Soviet armed forces and in the growing militarization of the Soviet Union as a whole. Being prepared for the worst possible threat—world nuclear war—the Soviet leadership has the option of selecting military actions at lower levels of conflict, if desired.

With respect to NATO, the Soviet armed forces remain structured and equipped for either nuclear or nonnuclear war. Soviet tanks, armored personnel carriers, and other equipment are prepared for the possible use of biological-chemical-nuclear weapons. The Soviet leadership appears to take seriously the possibility of a nuclear conflict, which the United States or the other nations of NATO may not.

Soviet military strategy stresses the necessity of first eliminating the nuclear means of an opponent, regardless of whether the war is nuclear or nonnuclear. Writings emphasize the role of airborne forces in this task. The great attention given to helicopters probably is due, in major part, to the possible use of this vehicle in transporting personnel into areas where an opponent's nuclear stockpiles are located.

Tanks, in the view of Soviet theoreticians, are well suited for going through contaminated areas, destroying any remaining opposition after a nuclear strike. Although the importance of guided antitank weapons is acknowledged, there is no indication that the role of the tank has been lowered significantly.

Soviet spokesmen are very cautious with respect to the impact of surface-to-air missiles against aircraft. Their writers give the percentage of Israeli aircraft destroyed by ground air defenses, but without elaboration. No mention has been made of the ratio of Israeli-Arab aircraft destroyed in air combat. In a rather factual way, air superiority is stated as being a continuing requirement.

New aircraft in the Soviet inventory, such as the Flogger and Fencer, appear well suited either for conventional or nuclear war. They provide an increased capability for interdiction deep in an opponent's rear area. They also can be expected to be provided with the latest weaponry and penetration devices. It is improbable that NATO will retain its monopoly on smart bombs.

The greatest change in the Soviet military posture that impacts on NATO actually is not a change as such, insofar as Soviet tactical concepts are con-

[42] S. S. Lototskiy, ed., *The Soviet Army* (Moscow: Progress Publishers, 1971), p. 333.

cerned. Secretary Schlesinger's February 1975 statement that the Soviet armed forces contain 4,200,000 personnel, plus an undisclosed number of additional men in support areas, has upset many theories and demolished planning of what NATO's own posture should be. A number of studies recommending specific policies for NATO have been based on the belief that Warsaw Pact forces did not have sufficient logistical support to fight a sustained conventional war. Reappraisals are in order.

Reevaluations of Soviet military manpower strengths probably have had repercussions in MFR negotiations. Introduction of additional tanks into Soviet infantry and tank divisions in the Warsaw Pact area during MFR discussions has altered some perceptions regarding the value of negotiations on arms limitations with the Soviet Union. Even should the Soviet leadership agree to mutual force reductions by 1977 or later, the relative strengths of Warsaw Pact versus NATO forces would be considerably greater than when the negotiations were initiated.

Although basic doctrine and strategy in the Soviet armed forces have remained relatively the same since 1962, changes have taken place in Soviet tactical concepts. The Soviet leadership now has military forces that have dual capability, able to fight in a nuclear environment or on a conventional battlefield. Continued buildup of these forces will not likely be restrained by negotiations either on strategic nuclear weapons, tactical weapons, or conventional forces.

Recent Developments in the Soviet Navy

Lawrence L. Whetten

BACKGROUND

Since the time of Catherine the Great, Russian naval policy has been relatively consistent, in part because of the critical problems of defending four disparate seas by four self-sufficient fleets. Thus for roughly 175 years Russia has maintained the world's third- or fourth-largest navy, yet until recently it never became a leading naval power. This failure was because Russia had no direct access to strategic oceans, the scale of its defensive commitments consumed excessive resources, and its leaders did not understand the use of sea power. Russia's most decisive naval victories were over Turkish and Arab fleets, and its most vainglorious defeat was inflicted by the third-rate Japanese Navy. Today, however, the USSR possesses the world's largest and most modern surface navy and the largest underseas force, a powerful naval air arm, the largest and most modern fishing and oceanographic fleets, one of the largest and fastest growing merchant fleets and one of the most advanced shipbuilding industries in operation.

The Russian Navy demonstrated a high degree of technological ingenuity, being the first to introduce high explosive shells, torpedoes, and aircraft into operations. Yet during World War I, the Russian Navy did not distinguish itself, and the Soviets inherited a legacy of malcontent within the ranks and only one battleship, employed as a floating battery, eight destroyers, and some smaller coastal craft. After the Russian Revolution, reserve and derelict warships were refitted, and, by 1924, the order of battle consisted of three battleships, five cruisers, twenty-four destroyers, eighteen submarines, and smaller craft. The Soviets then launched their own naval construction production program by building eight new shipyards to supplement the tsarist yards (some were as far inland as Gorky, 200 miles east of Moscow, where the components were constructed and floated along rivers for assembly at home ports). The Soviets were able to obtain submarine plans from Germany under the July 1926 Soviet-German naval agreement. They also salvaged and returned to service a British submarine sunk off Kronstadt. With these aids, the Soviets constructed their first natively designed submarine by 1932; in 1934 they laid down the first Kirov-class heavy cruiser. The third Five-Year Plan, announced in April 1937, provided for construction of a "big ship" surface navy, consisting of battleships, heavy cruisers, and, at the end of the plan, even aircraft carriers. The consequences of the Spanish civil war convinced Stalin of the vulnerability of the Soviet overseas operations to interdiction by superior naval forces, and, by 1938–1940, new classes of battleships and heavy cruisers were begun (after Moscow had failed to acquire battleship blueprints from the United States and had purchased abroad only the unfinished heavy cruiser *Lutzow* from Germany). But by the time of the German attack, the Soviet Navy consisted of only three pre-World War I battleships, eight old and two new cruisers, sixty-six destroyers (half new), and the world's largest underseas fleet of 218 submarines.[1]

The performance of the Soviet Navy during World War II was in many cases worse than in World War I.[2] The principal exception was in riverine warfare where armed river flotillas made major contributions to land operations. The main reason for the nadir in Soviet naval operations was that they were subordinated to army field commanders and were directed to support land battles—indeed, a total of 440,000 navy men served as ground troops during the war.[3] Nonetheless, ship losses were heavy. By 1945 there were few Soviet ships larger than destroyers and submarines in service; only the thirty to fifty submarines lost were replaced by the construction of fifty-two boats during the war. But as war booty, the USSR received the unfinished German carrier *Graf*

---

[1] On the contending schools of strategy and naval construction policy during this period see Robert Waring Herrick, *Soviet Naval Strategy* (Annapolis: U.S. Naval Institute, 1968); Michael MccGwire, ed., *Soviet Naval Developments* (New York: Praeger, 1973); Admiral S. E. Zakharov, ed., *Istoriya Voyenno Morslsoye Iskusstva (A History of the Art of Naval Warfare)* (Moscow: Voyenizat, 1969); and Admiral N. G. Kuznetsov, *Nakanune (On the Eve)* (Moscow: Voyenizat, 1966).

[2] *The Soviet Russians as Opponents at Sea,* vol. 3, Historical Division, U.S. Army Europe; and Donald W. White, *A History of Russian and Soviet Sea Power* (New York: Macmillan, 1974).

[3] Norman Polmar, *Soviet Naval Power* (New York: Crane, Russak, 1973), p. 16.

Zepplin, an Italian battleship, a German and an Italian light cruiser, ten German, Japanese, and Italian destroyers, more than twenty escort vessels, two Italian and more than ten German submarines, plus the lease of a British battleship and a U.S. cruiser. (Soviet ineptitude resulted in the sinking of the carrier, the burning out of the German cruiser, and the loss of at least one submarine.)

BUILDUP OF SOVIET CAPABILITIES

The acquisition of the foreign warships was a major solace for the USSR; it postponed the urgency of decisions on naval strategy and construction policy until the economy could be reconstituted. By the time the economic recovery was underway, the Soviet Navy had been able to digest the lessons of World War II, had analyzed the naval application of the new dimension of nuclear power, had assessed the nature and durability of the threat posed by the United States in the cold war environment, and could make modest claims on newly available resources. By the late 1940s, the Soviets began construction of a modified version of the most advanced German submarine, the U-2511, which they had received as booty. By 1957, 235 units of this W-class submarine had been completed; the production peaked at almost ninety boats per year. During 1950–1958 the Soviets constructed submarines in two other classes, Q and Z, and reached a total strength of 475 boats. Between 1951 and 1954, fourteen cruisers of the Sverdlov class were completed and seventy-five Skory class destroyers were commissioned during roughly the same period—followed by the larger, better armed Kotlin class. By the late 1950s, the Navy had a strength of ninety-five postwar destroyers and forty older vessels in this category.

The commissioning of the Sverdlov cruisers indicated that Soviet naval policy had turned a corner. The Soviet Navy's mission was no longer exclusively the defense of home waters. At 19,000 tons, with twelve main six-inch guns, it had the endurance and firepower to serve as a raider on the high seas during wartime, as had the German *Admiral Graf Spee, Scharnhorst,* and *Bismarck* during World War II. Likewise the Z- and W-class diesel-powered submarines had the range to cover the North Atlantic in an interdiction role (the numbers alone severely complicated Western defenses). Thus the Soviet Navy was constructing a fleet capable of at least threatening to venture onto the high seas and was, thereby, forcing the opponent to commit excessive resources to its own defensive missions.

The effectiveness of the cruisers and submarines in their respective roles was not entirely convincing. After Stalin's death, the naval mission and policy was vigorously debated. Admiral Kuznetsov personified Stalin's hopes of constructing a blue-water fleet and in January 1956 was replaced by Sergi Gorshkov as naval commander-in-chief. Gorshkov disagreed with the conventional wisdom that naval parity required matching an opponent ship for ship and gun for gun.

He maintained that there were few universal axioms in naval science and that each sea power should capitalize on its respective advantages and exploit the opponent's liabilities. Rather than launch an exhaustive construction program to "catch and surpass" the United States in capital ships, the Soviet Navy adopted a policy of building relatively smaller, less expensive warships armed with surface-to-surface and surface-to-air missiles as the main firepower, resulting in significant economies. Gorshkov made the following reductions: (1) total naval strength from 800,000 personnel in 1955 to about 500,000 today; (2) marines from 100,000 to approximately 15,000; (3) naval aircraft holdings from 4,000 to 1,200; (4) surface combatants from 300 to 223; and (5) submarine strength from 475 to 312.

As the trend toward missiles progressed almost fifty W-class submarines were fitted with the SSN-3 450-mile-range antiship cruise missile, and the Z-class with the SSN-4 350-mile-range cruise missile. (Both missiles require mid-course guidance by either aircraft or submarines to within ten miles proximity of the target.) Fast coastal patrol boats were equipped with short-range SSN-2 missiles and in 1959 the first Soviet nuclear attack N-class submarine was commissioned. By 1960, the Soviet Union was producing both nuclear attack (N-class) and diesel attack (F- and R-class), nuclear cruise-missile (E-class) and diesel cruise-missile (J-class), and ncluear ballistic-missle (H-class) and diesel ballistic-missle (G-class) submarines. (The ballistic-missile submarines were eventually converted to carry the 650-mile range SSN-5.)[4] In the late 1950s, ten Kildin and Krupny destroyers were also fitted with SSN-3 cruise missiles. In addition, medium-range Badger bombers of the naval air arm were equipped with the air-to-surface AS-1 Kennel missile, with a range of fifty-five miles. By the end of the decade, the conversion to missiles and the development of nuclear-powered submarines had been largely accomplished.

There were a variety of reasons for this rather dramatic policy change. First was the requirement to expand the Soviet naval defensive perimeter far enough to sea to allow attack of U.S. carriers before they could launch nuclear-armed aircraft—the mission of the destroyers and the Badgers. Second, to offset Soviet deficiencies in both ICBMs and long-range bombers, the ballistic missiles on board submarines were designed to increase the nuclear threat along the periphery of the United States. Finally, to improve the efficiency of the sea-lane interdiction mission, nuclear attack submarines were constructed.

This policy itself was soon modified by the decision to construct larger and more powerful "ship-killing" surface combatants. The keel of the first Kynda-class cruiser was laid in June 1960 and commissioned only two years later, followed by the Kashin-class missile frigate. The Kynda is armed with eight reloadable SSN-3 launchers and twin SAN-1 SAM missile launchers. The Kashin

[4] Ibid.

is equipped with two twin SAN-1 launchers. This combination was a powerful new addition, giving the fleet the best air protection yet and far more battle endurance. But after producing only four units, the Kynda class was superseded by the Kresta series, reflecting an entirely new strategy.

Four Kresta-I cruisers were constructed before the first improved Kresta-II was completed in 1969. The latter is armed with eight launchers for the thirty-mile-range cruise missile—a surface-skimming missile with a speed of Mach 1.2, auto-pilot, and infra-red terminal guidance. It also has two twin SAN-3 SAM launchers and improved ASW and electronic equipment, plus conventional guns, torpedoes, and a helicopter. At least seven ships of series II have been completed. Yet in 1973 a larger and more self-sufficient cruiser, the Kara class, became operational. At 10,000 tons, it is equipped with eight SSN-10 launchers, two twin SAN-3 launchers, and two twin SAN-4 SAMs. With its guns, torpedoes, and ASW rocket launchers, it is a veritable "pocket battleship." Its appearance was accompanied by the commissioning of the similarly armed Krivak-class guided-missile destroyer.

The fitting of the SAN-3 and SAN-4 indicated the high degree of confidence the Soviets have in the missile, accompanied by guns, in providing adequate fleet air protection. The naval cruise missile targeted against the launch platforms of U.S. naval air remains the first line of fleet air defense. This faith in the missile-gun mix has not changed despite the construction of aircraft carriers. Soviet concern with U.S. carriers is attested to by the development of the SSN-3, a 400+ nm cruise missile with apparently both mid-course correction and terminal guidance. More important, the installation of the short-range, high-performance SSN-10 indicates that the Soviet Navy is no longer content with accepting the risks of engaging warships at 400-mile-ranges. It is clearly equipping itself to operate in the same politically and militarily important waters formerly regarded as exclusive U.S. domains. "Presence and confrontation, rather than long-range strategic defense is the role of the Kresta II"[5] and the follow-on surface combatants.

Since 1967 several other developments reinforced this assessment. Two helicopter carriers have been constructed with the primary role of area ASW defense and marine helo-borne landing operations. Each carries a complement of twenty helicopters and assorted ASW gear. In 1975, the first of two aircraft carriers became operational. Two more carriers are reportedly under construction. It is believed to have a complement of forty helicopters for ASW defense and a small number of vertical take-off (VTOL) aircraft for fleet air protection and limited shore support (in the latter role Soviet VTOL aircraft can deliver only an estimated 1,000 pounds of ordnance).

On the strategic side of naval developments, the Soviets commissioned

[5] Ibid., p. 45.

during the latter stages of SALT I, the most lethal submarine yet—the D-class submarine equipped with the 4,200-mile-range SSN-8—the second version has sixteen launchers and is believed to be MIRV*ed*. This boat can fire against many U.S. cities while still in home waters, seriously complicating Western ASW defenses. Additionally, the Soviet Blinder and Backfire bombers are now assigned to the naval air arm; the latter has an unrefueled range of 3,000 miles and is reportedly equipped with the Mach-3, 300-mile-range AS-6 air-to-surface missile. The Soviets are likely to expand their force of nuclear submarines up to the level permitted by SALT I, that is, 62 boats "modern" with 950 missiles (they also can be expected to increase the size of their advanced bomber fleet, unless constrained by SALT II).

No survey of Soviet naval capabilities could be complete without a summary of present maritime activities. After World War II, the Soviet merchant fleet was the largest it had been in this century, with 507 ships totaling 2.7 million tons. But this included many Finnish and German vessels taken as reparations and 102 U.S. ships. Thus it was a heterogeneous fleet with uneven performance. Not until 1953 was the first oceangoing vessel produced in a Soviet shipyard. The Soviets relied heavily on foreign purchases to augment their merchantmen, and by 1958, despite the retirement of old vessels and the return of others, their carrying capacity had doubled over that of 1945. In 1958, it ranked twelfth among the world's fleets, and seventh ten years later. In 1973 it had 2,140 ships totaling 15.4 million tons (the United States had 680 at 13.9 million tons). Soviet planning calls for a fleet of 20 million tons by 1980—the present fleet carries about half of its foreign trade, while only 5 percent of U.S. trade is carried in American bottoms. (It should be noted that nearly 3,000 ships flying "flags of convenience" are owned largely by American companies, but they are not automatically at U.S. disposal during local crises or international emergencies. On the other hand, Soviet vessels in Western waters may become hostages if Moscow seeks surprise in military contingencies.)

The Soviet research and intelligence vessels number about 150 "legitimate" and 50 naval units. The total is double the rest of the world's combined assets in this category, providing the Soviet Union with scientific information about oceanography, naval intelligence, and maritime problems in waters throughout the world. Likewise, the USSR has the world's largest and most advanced fishing fleet, consisting of 4,000 oceangoing vessels and about 15,000 coastal craft. In 1970, the Soviet catch was nearly four times that of the United States and now amounts to roughly one-third of world's total catch.

These auxiliary maritime activities have grown even faster than those of the Soviet Navy and provide valuable support for naval operations. Merchant tankers frequently substitute for naval oilers; naval officers are routinely assigned to the merchant fleet; all Soviet vessels have secondary intelligence-gathering responsibilities, generating a worldwide collection effort; and finally, the maritime experience accrued at all levels of oceangoing operations affords valuable training opportunities.

This transformation from a land-oriented bear to a whale adept in many seas has left many Western analysts torn between alarmism and skepticism about the real value of the Soviet naval buildup. It has been so meteoric that it has often been regarded as also mercurial. Both the fleets and individual units remain untested in combat situations, raising doubts about their general proficiency under stress. Training exercises and operational contingencies provide the only evidence available.

EXERCISE OKEAN-70

On 14 April 1970, Moscow announced the beginning of the largest and longest naval exercise in Soviet history. Over 200 ships and 500 aircraft were involved (103 ships in the North Atlantic and Barents Sea, 15 in the Philippine and Japanese seas, 18 in the Indian Ocean, and 45 in the Mediterranean). In the Norwegian Sea alone there were 10 missile-equipped warships and 30 submarines. Bomber and reconnaissance aircraft conducted over 400 sorties. Entitled Okean-70, the exercise included all aspects of naval operations: amphibious landings, simulated ballistic-missile firings, coordinated maneuvers by vessels from all three Western-based fleets, gunnery training, and screening exercises by missile-armed fast patrol boats in the Norwegian Sea. The main purpose of the exercise, however, was to test simultaneous communications on a global scale. (Later Norwegian Defense Minister Gunnar Hellesen complained that the USSR had sufficient naval strength in the North Atlantic to attack from an exercise posture, with Baltic and Northern Fleet warships already at sea, anywhere along the entire Norwegian coast.)[6]

After the exercise, many of the Soviet vessels proceeded to more distant waters either for port calls or for establishing a permanent naval presence. One group went to the Cape Verde Islands and then to ports in West Africa, where the USSR has maintained routine combat patrols ever since. With target-acquisition data from submarines or reconnaissance aircraft now permanently operating from Conakry, Guinea, a patrol of SSN-3-equipped warships could engage vessels either entering Gibraltar or in the South Atlantic. (The patrol has also played the minor political functions of gaining the release of two Soviet fishing vessels from Ghana and deterring Portugese-sponsored attacks against Guinea.)

Another flotilla called at Mauritius, where in July 1970 the Soviets leased limited docking facilities. Yet another contingent visited ports around the Indian

---

[6] *Proceedings U.S. Naval Institute,* May 1971, p. 348; see also B. C. Cuthbertson, "The Significance of the Northern Gap," *Journal of the Royal United Services Institute,* June 1972, pp. 45–48.

Ocean littoral, providing the basis for a continuous naval presence. Earlier, in March 1968, the Soviets had taken the first steps toward establishing a permanent presence in the Indian Ocean by deploying a cruiser, a missile-equipped destroyer, an ASW escort and support vessels on the longest series of port calls in Soviet naval history, calling at ten ports in eight countries, including in India, Pakistan, South Yemen, Somalia, and Iraq. In 1970, twenty-nine Soviet naval vessels cruised the Indian Ocean, and, in 1971, eighteen entered these waters, including several nuclear or conventional submarines, ten combatants, and several support vessels. By 1972, Soviet naval units had paid over fifty visits to ports of sixteen littoral countries. The Soviets had negotiated commercial harbor facilities in Singapore and in Aden, and a $144,000 fuel tank farm at Mauritius. Moscow also had provided harbor improvement assistance for South Yemen, Yemen, Somalia, Egypt, Malagasy, Iraq, and India. Many of these facilities are compatable with Soviet naval repair requirements. To date, however, Moscow has concluded formal basing rights only at Berbera, Somalia. Soviet units routinely use anchorages for economic and political reasons at Socotra off the Arabian coast, in the Seychelles Islands and Chagos Archipelago. Soviet warships now deploying into these waters have been elevated to the distinction of the Soviet Indian Ocean Squadron, following, in part, the expanded Soviet commercial interests in this region.

The Soviet fishing fleet is the largest in these waters, yielding a 2-million-ton catch annually, or one-third of the USSR's total catch and larger than that of the combined littoral fleets. In November 1971, the USSR started a passenger-ship service in South Asian waters, with charter service between Singapore and Australia. Moreover, it is estimated that the USSR has as many as 100 merchant vessels in the Indian Ocean on any single day, many transporting Arab oil. Indeed, in 1971, more than 500 Soviet merchantmen called at Singapore. Finally, Soviet trade turnover with Indian Ocean countries increased from 275 million rubles in 1959 to 766 million in 1967 and 1,060 million in 1970, that is, a 12–13 percent annual increase. These figures represent only 5 percent of the USSR's total foreign trade and only a fraction of its own commerce between the Black Sea and the Far East (200,000 tons in 1967—before the Suez Canal was closed—versus 24 million tons by rail).[7] Nonetheless, these fishing and mercantile interests in the Indian Ocean have made the USSR an important regional power, faced with the classical problem of providing adequate protection.

On the one hand, the merchantmen have become valuable hostages for the USSR's good behavior and, thereby, have compounded its security issue. On the other hand, the Soviets have approached the question of protection from several directions: (1) providing arms aid and technical assistance, primarily to

---

[7] See the citation of official Soviet statistics in Geoffrey Jukes, *Indian Ocean and Soviet Naval Policy,* Adelphi Papers, no. 87 (May 1972).

Iraq, Somalia, and India; (2) signing Friendship Treaties with India and Iraq, "aligning" their mutual interests against presumed national threats; (3) attempting to organize the region into an anti-Chinese security pact that would both contain Chinese interests and elevate the USSR to the status of the dominant regional protector; (4) establishing a permanent naval presence visible to all littoral states and rival naval powers; and (5) capitalizing on the reopening of the Suez Canal, which makes it the closest naval power to the region.

A more important priority for Soviet naval interests in the Indian Ocean has been the use of naval power in great-power influence competition. When the Indian Ocean Squadron had to be supplied from Vladivostok, 6,000 miles from the Persian Gulf, it experienced obvious constraints. The opening of the Suez Canal cuts the distance roughly in half, although Black Sea shipping is now vulnerable to land-based interdiction at the Dardanelles, the Aegean Islands, and the Suez Canal. Nonetheless, the USSR could conceivably have more ships on-station in these waters faster than could the United States which would have to deploy carriers either from the Pacific Fleet or 11,000 miles from Virginia around the Cape of Africa. With this relatively rapid reinforcement capability and the vast basing complex at Berbera, the Soviet Navy has a highly durable presence and is itself in a position to interdict the Red Sea or the Persian Gulf.

The Soviet naval presence in the Mediterranean assumed a permanent posture in 1964 and has now been awarded the distinction of full fleet status—the Fifth. Operations expanded from 650 ship-days in 1964 to 20,000 in 1970. The number of ships varies from forty to seventy and reached a peak of ninety-eight during the 1967 October War. It is a balanced force of nuclear and conventional submarines from the Northern Fleet and surface combatants, amphibious craft, and auxiliary vessels from the Black Sea Fleet. Soon after the 1973 June War, the Soviets received extensive harbor facilities at Port Said, Alexandria, and Latakia and later were granted basing rights for TU-16 and MIG-25 reconnaissance aircraft. After October 1967, Soviet vessels maintained a permanent presence in the Egyptian ports as a deterrent against further Israeli attacks. But since the July 1972 expulsion of the Soviet Advisory Mission from Egypt, the use of Egyptian and naval and air facilities has been sharply curtailed, forcing the Mediterranean Fleet to rely increasingly on the Syrian facilities at Latakia.

During Exercise Okean-70, the Soviet Mediterranean Fleet was slightly augmented and increased its vigilance of the two U.S. carrier and the Marine landing task groups and monitored various choke points. Soviet naval aircraft conducted numerous reconnaissance flights against U.S. vessels. These activities again emphasized that the highest regional priority for the USSR is the naval parity with the United States. Protection of localized interests was not exercised during the operation. After the exercise terminated, the Soviet vessels returned to routine training, largely at anchorages near the various choke points, or sailed to home ports.

The Soviets' attempt to establish a permanent naval presence in the Caribbean after Okean-70 was foiled. The first large-scale naval visit after 1962 occurred in June 1969 when one nuclear and two conventional submarines and a tender departed the Northern Fleet, and a missile cruiser, missile frigate, and missile destroyer departed the Black Sea. The underseas and surface components rendezvoused off the Azores, and the force of nine vessels then steamed into the Caribbean, the first Russian squadron to visit the Western Hemisphere since the American Civil War. The squadron conducted exercises and paid port calls in Cuba for a month.

Cuba played an important role in Okean-70. It served as a refueling base for Soviet TU-20 Bear long-range naval reconnaissance aircraft. During the Okean-70 a total of six sorties were flown 5,000 miles nonstop over the Atlantic to Cuba and provided target acquisition data and inflight control for SSN-3- and SSN-4-equipped warships. This was the most successful effort yet observed in coordinating air, surface, and underseas missile launchings against multiple targets.

After the exercise, a Kresta missile cruiser, a destroyer, a nuclear cruise-missile submarine, two conventional attack submarines, and a submarine tender entered the Caribbean and steamed at one point to within fifty miles of the Mississippi coast. A series of Cuban port calls followed, including Havana and Cienfuegos on the southern coast.

In September 1970, a third squadron was sent to Cuba, consisting of a missile cruiser, a missile destroyer, a submarine tender, an oiler, and an LST loaded with two barges to support nuclear submarines. An additional force later arrived, including a ballistic-missile submarine. It was widely believed that the Soviets were constructing a naval base at Cienfuegos for servicing nuclear submarines. A base so close to the U.S. coast, especially the vulnerable Gulf Coast, would reduce by at least fourteen days the cruising time to arrive on-station and in practice would acually increase the total submarine inventory. The United States could not allow the Soviets to establish a precedent by constructing a forward base, but recognized that the Soviets might react strongly against U.S. forward base systems at SALT.

Clearly this was an unacceptable threat to the United States, and the issue was resolved only at a meeting between Foreign Minister Gromyko and President Nixon. On 17 November, the State Department announced that an understanding had been reached whereby Cuban ports or facilities would not be used for nuclear submarine bases or other strategic offensive-weapons systems. It did not preclude, however, the normal servicing of Soviet vessels not carrying strategic offensive weapons in Cuban ports. Nonetheless, Moscow has not attempted since then to establish a permanent presence even of less objectional warships.

Two other aspects of Okean-70 warrant mentioning. Moscow did not use the opportunity to stake out anchorages or waters in which to demonstrate a permanent presence in the West Pacific. Rather it sought to illustrate that it could operate a large force as far south as the Philippine Sea with considerable endurance. This was the best evidence yet that the Soviets had mastered the complicated logistical problems of adequate storage and underway replenishment for sustained operations. The Soviet Navy must now be credited with the capability to operate in sufficiently large forces to mount limited interventions for sustained periods in the West and Southwest Pacific.

Finally it should be noted that the primary mission of the Baltic Fleet is no longer the augmentation of the Northern Fleet. Several warships transited the Danish Straits to join the exercise in the North Atlantic. But this was probably more for interfleet training purposes for the remote eventuality that the Soviets could assemble an optimum force and then attack from an exercise posture. Short of such good fortune, the Baltic Fleet is primarily responsible for performing naval missions in support of the ground forces during a nonnuclear conflict, conducting naval training activities, and performing sea trials of the products of the Baltic naval yards. Thus, the Baltic Fleet has become the smallest and most locally oriented of the four home fleets.

OKEAN-75

Worldwide naval exercises on the Soviet scale are costly and less effective than the realistic testing the U.S. Navy experienced during frequent contingencies from Cuba to Southeast Asia. The USSR refrained from conducting another global naval exercise for five years, undoubtedly for economic reasons. Okean-75 was held in April 1975, in roughly the same dimensions of unit participation as Okean-70, but with substantially improved concepts of operations and physical capabilities.[8]

Okean-75 was reportedly conducted in four phases. The first phase began on roughly 14 April with the customary positioning of reconnaissance elements and the actual launching of weather, surface, and satellite reconnaissance sorties over the waters of major concern: Barents Sea, northern, middle, and southeastern Atlantic, Mediterranean Sea, Indian Ocean, and Sea of Japan. According to observations by monitoring NATO vessels, phase two opened two days later by concerted in-area and open-ocean ASW operations conducted by patrol and strike aircraft, probably in conjunction with hunter-killer submarines. Clearly, phase two was intended to neutralize any opposition to the deployment of major surface forces through the Norwegian Sea into the North Atlantic and through the Sea of Japan into the North Pacific. Phase three on 18 and 19 April involved an intensification of ASW operations in all theaters of operations and the launching of anticarrier strikes by naval bomber aircraft.

Phase four began on 20 April when opposing forces became engaged in

[8] See, for example, the 1975–1976 edition of *Jane's Fighting Ships of the World*. See also Robert G. Weinland, "The State and Future of Soviet Naval Forces in the North Atlantic," Mimeograph, October 1975; George R. Lindsey, "The Future of Anti-Submarine Warfare and Its Impact on Naval Activities in the Region," Mimeograph, October 1975;

continuous sea areas in the North Atlantic and North Pacific. During this phase an extensive air-defense exercise against simulated carrier aircraft was conducted in the Norwegian Sea. Reconnaissance was continued and probably provided both target-acquisition data and inflight control for the live launching of several SSN-3 missiles. Nuclear strikes were launched by bomber aircraft as the aggressor force moved toward the Norwegian and Japanese seas. When the exercise terminated on 22–23 April, virtually all participating units returned to home ports for exercise critiques rather than attempt to establish new precedents for permanent presence in various waters as occurred following Okean-70.

The most extensive portion of the exercise was conducted in the Norwegian and Barents seas. Apparently during phase two a force of older-class, SSN-3-equipped cruisers and attack submarines penetrated into the Norwegian Sea in the direction of the Faeroe Islands gap. In phase three this force reversed course and posed as an aggressor force against a force of Kresta-class cruisers supported by land-based aircraft in a simulated close-in fighting engagement. During this phase, amphibious operations were conducted on the Kola Peninsula, air strikes were launched, air-defense activities were conducted, and SSM's were launched, thus exercising the full spectrum of Soviet naval capabilities. The phasing and composition of the cruiser task forces suggest that the Soviets plan initial penetrations into the North Atlantic with long-range SSN-3 attack and raider submarines and surface combatants. The breakthrough is to be exploited by more modern, faster, SSN-10-armed warships for proximity engagements.

Operations in the Mediterranean were on a relatively small scale, with most vessels probably participating only in the communications portion of the exercise. A SAM destroyer and a cruise-missile-equipped submarine simulated an attack on the U.S. carrier *Forrestal*, and a Kara-class cruiser entered the Mediterranean via Gibraltar, probably to conduct ASW operations and test Soviet reconnaissance capabilities at this choke point. The reason for these relatively minor activities is that over the past decade, the Soviet and NATO navies have repeatedly exercised against each other and on several occasions conducted live contingencies operations.

Operations were more extensive in the Pacific Ocean, with four major task groups participating in the exercise. As in Okean-70, one group consisting of Kashin-class frigates and escort vessels with no cruise missiles, deployed into the Philippine Sea, which suggests that it may have been simulating a close-in intervention assignment. The breakthrough to the open ocean was conducted by two separate task groups equipped with cruise missiles (Kresta-II), which then simulated aggressor forces. One amphibious group deployed into the Sea of Japan, simulating a landing operation. The amphibious groups were then the target of a combined air and surface attack, including live cruise-missile firings.

---

and John K. Beling, "New Elements in the Naval Environment of the North Atlantic," Mimeograph, October 1975.

Medium bombers simulated nuclear strikes and Bear reconnaissance aircraft apparently provided the customary target data and inflight control for the SSN-3 missiles. The bulk of the intercepting task group, however, consisted of older-class warships providing primarily SAM air protection and conventional fire-power. There did not appear to be an air-defense exercise conducted by land-based aircraft, primarily because the operations against surface force were apparently conducted east of the Kuriles.

Activities in the middle and southern Atlantic consisted of operations independent of developments in the North Atlantic. Two relatively small Krivak-class destroyer groups were formed. The southernmost consisted of the routine West African coastal patrol that moved north of the Cape Verde Islands, off the Spanish Sahara, with the apparent mission of interdicting northbound surface shipping into the Mediterranean and European waters with its SSN-10 cruise missiles and conducting ASW operations against NATO defensive activities. The second task group may have been composed of surface combatants from the Mediterranean and Baltic Fleets. It operated west of the Bay of Biscay with the probable mission of using SSN-10s to interdict surface shipping transiting the English Channel or southbound to the Mediterranean.

The exercise in the Indian Ocean was not as extensive as those conducted in other waters. The number of vessels was not an all-time high, and the principal emphasis seems to have been on command and control procedures and capabilities rather than on unit performance and fleet coordination. The flagship was a Sverdlov-class cruiser that served as the control center linking IL-38 May ASW aircraft, TU-95 Bear reconnaissance aircraft, and surveillance satellites with Berbera and Moscow and deployed ships. There were no strike aircraft involved and no known missile firings, indicating that no nuclear phase was conducted in this theater during the exercise. Operations during the exercise indicated that the training objectives were to conduct wide-ranging surface surveillance and to establish a defensive ASW perimeter that would permit limited sea-space control for a limited period of time.

Several generalizations can be made about the concepts of operations observed in Okean-75. According to qualified observers, the Soviet naval air arm demonstrated a high degree of flexibility by transferring reconnaissance and strike aircraft from one theater to another as air-support requirements changed. Such mobility permits maximum concentration of air resources to counter anticipated or actual battle requirements and yet allows the aircraft to return to home bases as needed, all without creating logistical dislocations. Second, there was apparently close coordination in target selection between strike aircraft and inflight control of cruise missiles. If true, this would require highly centralized command and control procedures and excellent communications between the command center and the various strike units.

Third, during the air-defense exercise, TU-126 Moss aircraft, the equivalent of the U.S. airborne warning and control aircraft (AWAC), apparently coordinated vectoring of interceptors from the naval air arm and the national air defense forces (PVO) that may have been specifically deployed to forward bases to augment over-water interception. Again, if verified, such operations would suggest that the AWAC aircraft are indeed verstatile and able to control several types of aircraft and that some PVO units may have received specialized low-level over-water interception training, not associated with B-52 penetrations, to augment naval air in an exclusively interfleet fighting contingency.

These observations suggest that Soviet naval air has been able to maximize its centralized geographical advantages by concentrating air assets anywhere along its periphery as the threat requires and to augment these movements with selected regular air force units if necessary. Both defensive, reconnaissance, strike, and ASW aircraft, however, are still constrained by range limitations that will not be easily overcome even with two operational aircraft carriers. Long-range air operations over noncontiguous oceans will remain dependent upon overseas bases, as presently utilized in Havana, Cuba, Conakry in Guinea, and Berbera in Somalia, and overflight rights from CENTO members.

In surface operations, Okean-75 demonstrated that the Soviet Navy has the capability of attacking opposing forces at over-the-horizon ranges, conducting landing operations, engaging in ASW and limited sea-control activities, and operating at extended distances from home ports for political or limited-intervention purposes. Deployment patterns of the various classes of ships revealed a rationalized assignment of capabilities to missions.

For some time, conventional wisdom has concluded that Soviet naval-construction policy has placed the highest priority on firepower, speed, electronics, endurance, and crew comfort—almost the reverse of U.S. priorities. As a result, the latest Soviet warships are more compact, faster, and carry a greater assortment of weapons than their U.S. counterparts. But the Soviet SSN missiles and torpedoes do not have a reload capability (only the four aging Kynda-class cruisers can be reloaded with a second salvo), indicating that many classes were designed for a sea-denial role: first strikes and quick dispersal before any task force approaches within striking range of the USSR. Deployments in Okean-75 tended to confirm this supposition: older SAN equipped warships with land-based tactical air protection remained in contiguous seas and attacked aggressor forces in conjunction with strike aircraft and submarines at extended range. The Kara, Kresta-II, and Krivak classes, equipped with the short-range SSN-10, operated on the open ocean and at substantial distances from the security of contiguous seas. These deployments suggest that the parameters of the primary mission of sea denial have been greatly expanded, seriously complicating Western defenses.

Although sea denial remains the primary mission against the U.S. and NATO navies, the development and deployment of the SSN-10 indicates that the Soviets anticipate its additional employment in other roles: close-in fighting with secondary naval forces, sea-lane interdiction with nuclear warheads, or sea-raider operations with conventional armaments. Okean-75 demonstrated that the Soviet Navy is equipping and training for a wider spectrum of naval contingencies than previously estimated.[9]

OPERATIONAL EXPERIENCE—THE OCTOBER WAR

This perception of Soviet concepts of naval operations based on massive training exercises has been reinforced by observations of actual Soviet naval contingencies in the Mediterranean Sea and Indian Ocean. Soviet naval operations during the Mideast October War demonstrated a high degree of seamanship at all levels. Moscow was surprised by the outbreak of hostilities, having no more than seventy-two hours warning. Three ships actually returned to the Black Sea on 5 October, leaving less than twenty surface combatants. Within three weeks twenty more combatants were deployed from the Black Sea Fleet (bringing the total naval ships to ninety-eight as opposed to sixty-five for the United States). A major sealift operation also was conducted, delivering before 25 October ten times more total cargo tonnage to the Arabs than the United States did to Israel. During the war, the Soviet Navy initiated four major fleet movements: (1) it withdrew all vessels from the Egyptian combat zone; (2) it stationed screening forces at all choke points—that is, the straits of Gibraltar, Messina, Sicily, and the Aegean Sea; (3) it mounted a major sea-control operation to protect the sea-lanes from the Dardanelles to Syria after Israel unexpectedly attacked Soviet vessels in Latakia; and (4) it deployed key combatants into positions from which the three U.S. carrier task groups south of Crete could be threatened by a multidimensional (air and sea), simultaneous, omnidirectional attack.

These operations revealed professionalism, deliberation, and precision in a series of unanticipated contingencies that can now be expected to characterize future Soviet naval behavior. They also reflected the most likely thrust of Soviet war plans for the Mediterranean theater. Regardless of the source of tensions and the political developments ashore, the Soviets' highest priority will be to deter or preemptively strike key U.S. warships. The second priority will be to assure egress for friendly vessels and to block ingress or passage of hostile warships at the various choke points. A third mission will be to protect Soviet national interests in the region, by sea-control operations or physical intervention if necessary. Only when these requirements have been satisfied will the localized needs of client states be met (the airlift and sealift to Syria began only on 10

[9] See the comparative study of U.S.-Soviet capabilities release August 1975 by the Naval Ship Engineering Center. Hyattsville, Maryland.

October, after the other deployments were achieved or underway and the material for the lift could be assembled).

OPERATIONS IN THE INDIAN OCEAN

The only operational experience available relating to Soviet contingencies in the Indian Ocean occurred during the 1971 Indo-Pakistani crisis. Britain was in the process of withdrawing its last task force from the region, consisting of the carrier *Eagle,* the commando carrier *Albion,* and six escorts east of the Suez Canal, which remained scattered among East African ports. The Soviet naval presence was composed of a non-SSM-equipped destroyer, an F-class conventional attack submarine, a minesweeper, and a tank-landing ship. Normal six-month rotations introduced a SAM-equipped destroyer and a minesweeper, while existing units were detained. This was an insignificant force that the Soviets augmented by dispatching a Kynda SSM cruiser, a SSM submarine, and a SAM destroyer from Vladivostok four days after the outbreak of hostilities on 3 December.

The United States had no major warships in the Indian Ocean when war began, but on 6 December it formed a task force from units in the Gulf of Tonkin and held it off Singapore on 10 December. The task force consisted of the carrier *Enterprise* and helicopter carrier *Tripoli*, three guided-missile escorts, four destroyers, and a nuclear attack submarine. It arrived in the Indian Ocean on 14 December.

On 12 December, the Soviets sent a second task group from the Pacific Fleet consisting of a Kresta SSM cruiser, a Kashin SAM destroyer, and two submarines, one SSM equipped. The first Soviet group did not reach the Indian Ocean until three days after the American carrier task force and two days after the end of the war. The distances were simply too long to readily offset the disadvantages of being tactically surprised in the Indian Ocean.

McConnell and Kelly have pointed out that the American purpose in mounting an awesome show of force was not humanitarianism or refugee evacuation—all refugees had departed by commercial airlines by 12 December.[10] It was an attempt to back up Washington's ban on arms deliveries to the belligerents and to register its disapproval of aggression that dismembered a friendly nation. It was also designed to impress the Chinese during the forthcoming summit conference with the virility of the defense of U.S. regional interests. It was hoped that such a strong presence would calm the anxieties of other littoral states who were witnessing the indifference of the former colonial powers to open aggression in a region they had only several years earlier fought vigorously

---

[10] J. M. McConnell and Anne M. Kelly, "Super-Power Naval Diplomacy: Lessons of the Indo-Pakistani Crisis 1971," *Survival,* November–December 1973.

to defend. Finally it was intended to underscore U.S. disapproval of Soviet complicity through its recently signed Friendship Treaty with India that apparently gave New Delhi the confidence it needed to attack.

While events of the mainland occupied the United States, the Soviets were concerned mainly with American naval deployments. When the Soviets' second group arrived in the Indian Ocean on 24 December, eight days after the war ended, a scattered but sizable flotilla had been assembled, consisting of one conventional destroyer, three SAM destroyers, two conventional attack submarines, two SSM conventional submarines, one Kynda SSN cruiser, one Kresta SSM cruiser, and a tank-landing ship. This force did not have sufficient strength or flexibility to perform either an intervention or interdiction role against determined opposition. It did, however, have an impressive collection of possibly twenty-four SSM launchers and twelve SAM launchers, which were clearly intended to counter the *Enterprise* task force. Because the U.S. force was deliberately held at Singapore and did not arrive in the Andaman Sea until the day before the fighting ended, there was little likelihood of American intervention—unless the war continued in the west. Aware of this disposition, the Soviets' main purpose was apparently to mount a counterdemonstration, but against the U.S. "intrusion," not against the mainland belligerents.

Several generalizations can be drawn from this type of analysis. A central objective for both powers is to employ its naval power as an extension of its political interests in the Indian Ocean, to be used in conjunction with other levers of influence. For nearly a decade there has been growing concern by many littoral states that the Indian Ocean was again becoming an arena for great-power rivalry and possible hegemony detrimental to their respective regional ambitions. Discussions about the new "imperialism," the propulsion of the Indian Ocean into the cold war, most frequently start by assigning responsibility for which navy entered first, thereby forcing the rival to respond in kind. The Indians usually blame the Americans for allegedly deploying Polaris submarines into the Arabian Sea. But this claim should have been buried in 1972 when articles by Robert Weinland[11] and Geoffrey Jukes[12] pointed out that there was no cost-effective reason for deploying submarines over 11,000 miles to be on-station for low-priority targets, when higher-priority targets could be struck after only 1,000–3,000-mile cruises. Moreover, when the Soviets made their first sustained deployments in 1968 and 1969, they were ships with maximum endurance but very poor and obsolete ASW capabilities. It was clear from the equipment aboard the aging cruisers and destroyers and from the training conducted in these waters that their mission was political not anti-Polaris. Thus,

[11] R. G. Weinland, "The Changing Mission of the Soviet Navy," *Survival,* May–June 1972.
[12] Geoffrey Jukes, *Indian Ocean and Soviet Naval Policy.*

there is yet to be released any firm evidence that the United States used the Indian Ocean for offensive purposes that compelled the Soviets to respond with defensive deployments. (It is entirely plausible, however, that *today* the United States might disperse several Poseidon submarines, with missile ranges nearly double those of the Polaris A-1, into the southern Indian Ocean, not the Arabian Sea. Such dispersals would severely strain the Soviet capabilities in waters where ASW conditions are less favorable for the defense. It should be noted that such dispersals are designed primarily to ensure unit survivability, not to pose a constant menace to the USSR.)

The issue of great-power naval "racing" in the Indian Ocean, however, has recently taken on more realistic attributes with the signing of Friendship Treaties, mentioned earlier, between the USSR, India, and Iraq, and the construction of the most elaborate Soviet naval and air facilities outside the Warsaw Pact countries at Berbera, Somalia. As the most expensive investment of its kind, it was intentionally built by the Soviets for their own requirements for which they apparently retain some legal jurisdiction; therefore, it is a bona fide military base. Ex-Secretary Schlesinger told the Senate Armed Services Committee[13] that it consists of harbor naval repair and storage facilities, permanent barracks ashore, operational air-defense missiles and guns, surface-to-surface cruise missiles with ranges that cover all the approaches to the Red Sea, accompanied by storage and repair facilities. It also has billeting and training areas for a sizable ground combat force, plus aircraft hangars and two 15,000-foot runways that can accommodate the heaviest Soviet transports. The base also has an extensive antenna farm for direct communication with Moscow, reconnaissance satellites, ships at sea, and possibly submerged submarines. (To improve communications and surveillance accuracies, the Soviets have reportedly requested use of the former American base at Cam Ranh Bay, Vietnam.) A facility of this size could serve as the home port for the expanding Soviet Indian Ocean Squadron, including the 40,000-ton Kiev-class carriers when they become fully operational.

The Berbera base far exceeds the modest U.S. modifications planned for Diego Garcia, which according to ex-Secretary Schlesinger, are intended merely to provide local support for a task force whose home port is at Subic Bay in the Philippines, 7,000 miles away. Such disparities in basing rights often foster alarmist claims that the naval balance has shifted in the Soviets' favor. But there are also countervailing asymmetrics in force postures that must be considered. First, the United States has a more versatile weapons mix, especially in tactical aircraft, that affords it greater flexibility in initiating contingencies. Second, the USSR is more vulnerable to air and sea access into this theater. The presence of a large permanent force will require guaranteed passage through the Dardanelles

---

[13] Statement by ex-Defense Secretary James Schlesinger before the Senate Armed Services Committee, 10 June 1975.

and Suez Canal, plus uninhibited aircraft overflight rights from Turkey, Iran, or Pakistan. In the event of some level of nuclear exchange, Soviet forces in the Indian Ocean would become hostages of much smaller monitoring forces. Third, the United States has allies and friendly states with assets in the region, that is, France, Britain, Australia, and South Africa, that may be drawn upon; the USSR has few. Finally, the United States can use the Indian Ocean for strategic purposes by striking the USSR with SLBMs. The USSR cannot attack American interests from the Indian Ocean in any comparable manner.

The logic derived from these disparities is that they can be offset only by mutual accord or by a sizable increase in the Soviets' permanent naval presence. The gravest danger in the reopening of the Suez Canal, making the USSR the closest naval power to the Indian Ocean, is that U.S. political interests in the region will remain relatively static and immune to rival "racing." Furthermore, because of the relatively low U.S. interests in the region, it is more susceptible either to a natural or negotiated arms ceiling—until then, the "racing" pace will be set by the Soviets. In this situation, the Soviet naval buildup should also be assessed in a purely regional context, that is, in terms of the implications of Soviet naval expansion for littoral states.

AUGMENTATION OF SOVIET NAVAL MISSIONS

As implied throughout this chapter, there are several techniques for comparing strengths and intentions for naval forces: (1) comparisons of technical capabilities, and accounting for perceived discrepancies and justification for appropriate countervailing systems; (2) observations of actual naval operations and exercises and appraisals of auxiliary support derived from other maritime activities; and (3) rational deductions of the most probable missions, based on assessments in the first two categories. Earlier portions of this paper attempted to make these estimates for Soviet naval intentions against its primary threat: the United States and NATO. It is more difficult to calculate objectives and missions in theaters of lesser importance to vital Soviet national interests, such as the Indian Ocean.

A variety of analytical techniques may be used to determine the purpose of a permanent Soviet naval presence in out-of-area waters. First there are numerous potential missions for naval operations, such as political intervention, military intervention and counterintervention, sea-lane interdiction and raiding, sea-space denial, sea control, strategic offense and defense, and establishment and recognition of naval parity. Although there are obvious overlaps between some missions, in general the optimum execution of each mission requires different classes of ships that are variously equipped. Multipurpose equipping has been employed as a compromise for reasons of economics and flexibility, but it has not been possible to produce single units that can effectively cover even most of the possible missions.

Second, the type of countries to be influenced by naval power also varies widely. The target country might be individual littoral states, possibly with distinctive maritime features, such as the control of international waterways. Or the target might be a group of littoral states with the potential of organizing effective political opposition or collective military resistance to offensive incursions. An additional target might be the commercial interests of third parties not physically represented in the region by naval power, such as British-New Zealand trade or Japanese-Middle Eastern oil imports. A final target might be the rival great power itself, whereby the goal of gaining rival recognition of naval parity might necessitate at least the demonstrable use of force within the region. The maritime geography of each littoral state is critical in determining its vulnerability to naval influence and the type of naval force required to ensure durable results. The range of reciprocal actions open to littoral states or third parties may also influence the choice of target countries and the instruments of power.[14]

Third, it is conceivable that the USSR might construct a variety of political and military purposes for asserting its naval influence that are broader in scope than the simpler motives of formulating the means for influencing other countries on immediate or localized issues. For example, the Soviets might argue that a naval presence is imperative for the military defense of its stated global national interests. That is, a squadron should be conceived of as an in-place military force with sufficient flexibility to react to a variety of contingencies envisioned in long-range Soviet political plans for regional developments, for example, the gradual recession of Western interests and the rise of pro-Soviet governments. Likewise, the demonstrative use of power might be envisioned as a possible method of precluding unwanted regional polarization or of inducing cooperation, as in the case of Chinese incursions and Soviet attempts to promote an Asian Security Pact. Finally, the manifestation of naval parity with a seemingly disinterested great-power rival might be programmed as an integral part of a grand design to manipulate influence among relatively vulnerable states, requiring in-place forces while imparting acceptable risks of a great-power confrontation.

Thus, naval power can be used for a wide range of purposes, but it is the most transitory of all the forms of military coercion. Gunboat diplomacy is only as effective as the gunboat. When the ship sails away, its impact may be largely abated. Success in limited naval operations requires that warships of the right size be at the right place at the right time—that seldom happens.[15] For best effect, naval power must be integrated with the ground and air forces into

---

[14] See Edward N. Luttwak, *The Political Uses of Sea Power* (Baltimore: John Hopkins University Press, 1974), for a discussion of the "theory of naval suasion."

[15] James Cable, *Gunboat Diplomacy* (London: Chatto and Windus, 1971).

combined operations. The isolation of naval operations in the Indian Ocean remains one of the most severe constraints on Soviet options in the region, a limitation that will not be easily overcome by the deployment of two carriers, several cruisers, and a battalion of naval infantry.

In view of both operational experience and the rationalization of capabilities it appears that the primary naval mission of the Soviet Navy in out-of-area waters, such as the Indian Ocean, will remain the deterrence or defeat of the U.S. naval threat, such as it is or might be at any given time. Yet while deterrence is the highest priority, greater significance is likely to be attached to the political objectives aimed at local targets and long-range political-military options that might ultimately benefit Soviet state interests.

CONCLUSIONS

While there is no doubt that the USSR has succeeded in constructing a blue-water navy, its purposes and future orientation is the subject of extensive debate and conjecture. Its overall naval policy indicates that some missions have been favored and others neglected. The highest priority has been given to the design and construction of a large number of smaller surface combatants and aircraft that can be used and employed in a preemptive nuclear strike for the defense of waters contiguous to the USSR. Equally high interest has been demonstrated in the construction of ballistic-missile submarines that serve as a credible second-strike capability against the United States. Lesser, but still important, attention has been paid to the production of nuclear attack and cruise-missile submarines and larger surface warships for the interdiction of sea-lanes and raiding missions. The lowest priority has been granted to intervention capabilities. The differing importance of these priorities is reinforced by operational patterns where ship deployments vary from sea to sea. As a result, important weaknesses persist in fleet balance that are likely to serve as constraints on contemporary Soviet options and may indicate the future development of its naval policy.

Submarine propulsion and ASW technologies are believed to lag behind those of the United States. Ship design has produced vessels with limited endurance both in range and sustained combat at sea. The lack of access to the strategic oceans means the Soviet Navy may have to fight its way into distant waters for the conduct of its secondary missions or rely on overseas bases. In the past, the Soviets have sought bases primarily for economic and political reasons; they are unlikely to place much stock in the future in the military utility of foreign bases under wartime conditions. Yet a persistent area of neglect has been in the production of modern support vessels for sustained out-of-area operations. Intervention forces remain the weakest component of the Soviet Navy. The Soviets' total amphibious capability is less than one-fifth that of the United States and is scattered among the five fleets. The addition of two VTOL carriers will increase tactical air protection but will not substantially improve the shore-bombardment capability—the fleet will remain dependent upon the aging Sverdlov-class gun cruisers for this support.

For the Soviet Union to develop the forces necessary to exert positive control of out-of-area seas and to project its power more effectively overseas, it will have to meet several prerequisites; (1) development of new classes of surface warships; (2) acquisition of a sea-based fixed-wing aircraft capability; (3) construction of larger and more capable assault forces; (4) expansion of the Soviet Navy's land-based infrastructure; and (5) development of logistics forces capable of providing support on the high seas in a hostile environment.[16] Short of making these basic improvements, the Soviets' overseas war-fighting capabilities will be severely restricted to limited naval actions. (The needed improvements will have to be made against the backdrop of a new surge in U.S. naval procurement. Shipbuilding funds alone tripled in 1974 over 1969 and are currently 50 percent higher than the 1962–1969 average.)

Yet since roughly 1967, the Soviets have recognized and emphasized the political value of naval forces deployed permanently in distant waters.[17] They have attempted to demonstrate that these forces restrict the flexibility of the rival great power, deter aggressive actions by enemies of their clients, protect Soviet political interests abroad, and promote good will. It would certainly be imprudent to argue that the Soviet Navy has become purely a political instrument for the projection of national interests abroad, even though this is undoubtedly a prime task during peacetime. But the Soviet Navy has progressed through a maturation process after decades of domination by continental interests and army priorities. The gravest danger about the future course of Soviet naval development is that the favored status and momentum in research and production experienced since 1967 will be sustained and, in turn, will inject greater risk taking into Soviet foreign-policy options.

[16] Barry M. Blechman, *The Changing Soviet Navy* (Washington, D.C.: Brookings Institution, 1973), p. 33; see also Robert G. Weinland, *The Changing Mission Structure of the Soviet Navy,* Professional Paper 80, Center of Naval Analyses, Washington, D.C., 1971.
[17] See the entire series by Admiral S. G. Gorshkov, "Navies in War and Peace," *Morskoi Sbornik,* February 1972–February 1973.

Soviet Theatre-Warfare Capability: Doctrines, Deployments, and Capabilities

John Erickson

Though it has now been with us for well nigh thirty years, 1945 being the date of its massive irruption into, and extensive emplacement within, Eastern Europe, the Soviet army and an attendant European "theatre capability" has received remarkably little sustained public examination as a subject in itself. There is, of course, the fact that this Soviet presence has become altogether a commonplace of the European scene: Memories of that rampage in 1945 have long since faded and the *frisson de terreur* induced by the Soviet invasion of Czechoslovakia in 1968 was not long sustained. Admittedly the term "theater capability" has little of the dramatic ring of the "missile buildup" or the excitation brought on by the bristling ships of the Soviet Navy's "expansion." Thus bemused or benumed, this present European society might well meet its own doom not with T. S. Eliot's celebrated whimper but simply with a yawn. Nor has official cliché promoted either purposeful analysis or even simple historical understanding. Terms such as "the deployed threat" are trundled out—but just how is this threat deployed and for what purpose? Soviet "superiority" is constantly emphasized, yet (even presupposing for a moment the existence of that superiority) how has it come about that the Soviet Union, disbursing less than NATO in the way of human and budgetary resources, attained such an advantage? By way of dispiriting paradox, if apathy is encouraged, reforming zeal is constrained. The plans of those who would reorganize or refurbish NATO are also vitiated by a lack of convincing knowledge of Soviet military organization and theater capability. Strategic generalization may be intellectually satisfying, possibly aesthetically pleasing, but it is hard to sustain them without an up-to-date grasp of Soviet developments—unless one discounts the enemy, even down to the more mundane items of his equipment. *Aviation Week and Space Technology*, in a recent appraisal of the lessons of the October 1973 Mideast War, spelled out the terms of this cautionary tale:

> We think that every citizen in Western Europe and this country [the United States] should take a penetrating look at what happened to Israel as a result of major technical surprise in October, 1973.[1]

Talk of "postural cores" may be all very well, but it was Soviet mechanized bridging capability and night warfare devices, among other things, that did the damage in the Middle East, much as they might work the same effect in Europe.

There is, therefore, something of a prima facie case for investigating the Soviet provision for a theater-warfare capability in Europe, viewed not least from a variety of perspectives. From the outset, in the immediate postwar period, this capability developed as an unusual amalgam. The vastly extended frontier line, which ran far to the west of the Soviet border proper, established a buffer zone that required the protection of the Soviet army and its presence in some strength, while in the changed postwar strategic environment and the existence of the U.S. nuclear monopoly, Soviet Ground Forces in Eastern Europe embodied the prime element in the Soviet Union's "deterrent"—holding Western Europe "hostage" with the threat of overwhelming conventional force as an indirect but potent counter to American nuclear capability. The demobilization, restructuring, and reorganization of the Ground Forces at this time makes an interesting passage in the history of the Soviet armed forces and the evolution of Soviet military policy at large, even though both were constricted by the dogmatic tenets of "Stalinist military thought." But for all the artificiality of that Stalinized environment, the Soviet command was forced to make several crucial choices—reliance on the armored fighting vehicle, the tank, as the mainspring of its strike power, the concentration of building up *combat units,* and the development of a war-fighting capability, for all the limitations imposed by a war-shattered economy and an arbitrary, not to say eccentric, official military doctrine.

This "linkage" between Soviet strategic requirements and the relevance of theater-warfare capabilities has proved to be one of the most interesting ele-

---

[1] "The Shock of Technical Surprise," *Aviation Week and Space Technology,* 24 March 1975.

ments in the evolution of Soviet military theory and practice. Thanks to technological advance, the MRBM-IRBM component could latterly take over the role of holding Western Europe "hostage," while the Ground Forces advanced in the late 1950s toward something of a dual capability, nuclear and conventional. To the strength and mobility of the armored formation was added that of motorized/mechanized infantry force and a missile component was also being steadily introduced, all of this resulting in a whole new outlook, whereby mobility and operational flexibility replaced the old concepts of "active defense" followed by the counteroffensive. In the late 1950s, Soviet doctrine came to emphasize offensive operations in quite unequivocal terms, based on seizing the initiative and exploiting "the surprise factor" in both nuclear and conventional conditions.

During the Khrushchev period, this progress was visibly slowed and finally brought to a halt, as the Soviet command concentrated perforce on building up strategic nuclear forces—the Ground Forces were correspondingly reduced in rank and importance. "One-variant war" envisaged that any future general conflict would be nuclear, and it was the strategic nuclear forces that would play the primary role in achieving Soviet military and political goals. The argument, which at times was bitter, revolved round the question of what role the Ground Forces might play and how theater capabilities might be employed to achieve "the final goals of a war." Would ground operations begin simultaneously with the initial strategic strikes, or would there be some interval between those first strikes and a follow-up action in depth (most probably with airborne forces)? The introduction of nuclear weapons and tactical missiles into the Ground Forces also added further complications all their own. The relationship between strategic nuclear operations and ground theater operations was far from being clarified—would strategic strikes "open the way" for ground operations and what, in turn, would be the role of tactical missile units within the framework of these same operations? There remained also the place of purely conventional capability, with Sokolovskiy's *Voennaya Strategiya* (in both editions) acknowledging that conventional forces might be "extensively employed in both local and world wars, either independently or in conjunction with new types of weapons."

In September 1964, the Soviet Ground Forces (Soviet army)[2] were deprived of the status of an "independent high command," the post of commander-in-chief Ground Forces was suspended, and this branch of the Soviet armed forces was placed under the direct administration of the Ministry of Defense. It took three years for this phoenix to arise from the Khrushchevian ashes, a period also dominated by an intense and wide-ranging debate on Soviet military policy at

---

[2] I have used these terms interchangeably—Ground Forces/Soviet Army—except for general references to "ground forces" as such.

large, producing a decisive break with "one-variant war," the quest for genuine parity with the United States in strategic nuclear power, and the implementation of a more equitable balance between strategic nuclear and conventional forces—all in order to increase Soviet "options." The Soviet army experienced the first benefits of technological modernization, embarked on a revised manpower program (though that proved to be a mixed blessing), and reappraised its operational theories. It is essentially this form of theater capability with which we are faced at the present, based certainly on the basic framework established over some two decades (1947–1967) but with new technological and operational ramifications. Nonetheless, the basic principle of organization has remained the same—maximizing force composition by holding logistic support to a minimum, developing tactical forms that do not require an abundance of sophisticated equipment, maintaining a rapid reinforcement and mobilization system, and proceeding with the integration of tactical nuclear weapons into a *war-fighting system.*

Much of this is borne out by the evidence of large-scale exercises (even allowing for the artificiality of that environment): Dnieper in 1967 practiced this new-found conventional capability (with a wide variety of equipment), the invasion of Czechoslovakia in 1968 when exercises rolled over into an operational commitment, and Dvina, which investigated the relationship between nuclear and conventional operations (and latterly the reappraisal of that same problem), not to mention the multitude of exercises aimed at a greater integration of Soviet with non-Soviet Warsaw Pact forces (as well as integration within the non-Soviet forces). It might be argued (as indeed it will be here) that here is a genuine "theater capability" that has emerged over the past five years or so, involving modernization and doctrinal change—and completing the third of the major cycles in tactical-technical modernization, the latter phase witnessing the introduction of powerful self-propelled conventional artillery. Here we go back to those introverted debates of a decade ago, but the present emphasis on conventional artillery (as opposed to tactical missiles) may reflect Soviet conviction that under the present conditions of Soviet-American strategic "parity," conventional operations need *not* escalate automatically and speedily toward a strategic nuclear exchange.

It should be said from the outset that a basic Soviet tenet has been (and continues to be) the development of *dual capability*—both in theory and in practice. This raises at once a number of significant questions in relation to nuclear weapons and theater warfare, in this case, the European theater. The overall Soviet view is that nuclear and conventional weapons do not present an "either/or" proposition, such as those advanced in the West, but that rather it is a matter of "both/and"—nuclear weapons are an indispensable element of war-fighting capability, but it has been argued for some time that conventional weapons, important as they are in their right, can in certain instances enhance the effect of nuclear weapons. It is readily comprehensible, therefore, that there is no Soviet doctrine of "escalation" corresponding to that in the West—namely, that recourse to nuclear weapons is an act of "escalation." The Soviet view is that it is not the weapons involved but rather the nature and scope of the *political objectives* that define the scope and nature of an armed collision.

In view of the "both/and" concept, Soviet understanding of dual capability, it is not surprising that the buildup in conventional capability has been accompanied by a growth in the capability and flexibility of Soviet theater nuclear forces—a greater number of tactical nuclear weapons are now stationed forward, Frog and Scud capability has been improved, improvements in Soviet tactical aviation also imply that nuclear air strikes are a much greater likelihood, and, not least important, the new Scaleboard missile virtually trebles the range of the Scuds, thus bringing critical targets in Western Europe into range (thus diminishing the reliance on the MRBM/IRBM force). The increase in tactical nuclear missile strength is in the order of 25—30 percent (and, correspondingly, stocks of nuclear warheads must have been increased).

The really significant factor is, therefore, the emergence of a Soviet concept of theater nuclear war as a distinguishable form of engagement and operations— as opposed, that is, to the "strategic" undertaking conceived formerly as prolonging and completing the effect of nuclear strikes launched in the course of a "nuclear missile war" (general war). By the same token, it is necessary to look at what the Soviet command intends with its recent buildup of conventional forces. If anything, this represents a logical extension of dual capability, but this buildup does *not* mean an exclusively conventional option in its own right. This improved capability must be understood in the context of conducting conventional operations in *the initial phase* of a theater campaign and for *some sustained period,* though, as ever, against that constant nuclear backdrop. In essence, Soviet doctrine and operational practice continues to emphasize the importance of *combined nuclear and conventional operations.*

There is also much to suggest that the Soviet command has developed, almost tacitly, a "table of intervention-reaction" gradated in relation to several operational levels and the reaction of a potential enemy, as well as incorporating a perception of the "balance" between nuclear and conventional forces. And, as will be seen, this tends to reinforce the policy of maximizing force effectiveness by reducing the logistical load and concentrating flexible, hard-hitting, mobile strike forces, with one interesting corollary—that *movement* can itself implement and enlarge the effects of fire (and this seems to be the key to understanding the Soviet concept of fire-support, with its indifference to indirect support).

Thus, we come to the genuine *point de départ.* The organization, composition, and deployment of the Ground Forces has been a matter of continuous debate within the Soviet command. The whole process can be understood only by reference to its historical evolution. Doctrinal adjustments have been made over the same span of time, complicated by the dual capability with which the Ground Forces were invested: Important though these doctrinal enunciations have been, the actual equipment and organization "on the ground" (not to mention the evidence of exercise patterns) must also be considered, though "the ground" must also be taken to include the role of tactical air capabilities, where significant change has also recently taken place. In order to comprehend the complexity of this development and the diversity of the arguments, this paper is divided into four sections:

   1. The evolution of Soviet theater capability, the general deployment patterns, the course of the buildup 1970–1974/1975, the characteristics of organization and main equipment.
   2. Operational concepts and general doctrine, the military principles underlying theater warfare organization, main tactical forms, "maneuver and fire," the role of nuclear weapons and "combatting the enemy means of nuclear attack," tactical principles, the role of artillery, aviation, logistical support, and the "short-war" concept.
   3. Operational norms, ground operations, tactical air, combined operations, and the role of naval forces—also airborne and helicopter/assault operations.
   4. "Tables of intensity"—total preemptive capability, nuclear operations, nuclear/conventional operations, integrated force (Warsaw Pact) operations—objectives and capabilities, military goals, and military-political objectives, including the political utility of Soviet Ground Forces.

This formulation has certain advantages. It does not beg the question of "superiority," it takes account of Soviet preoccupation and commitment, and does not hang too desperately on that awkward concept of "intentions and capabilities," which can be switched at will.

THE EVOLUTION OF SOVIET
THEATER-WARFARE CAPABILITIES:
THE "DEPLOYED FORCE"

The postwar demobilization, which occupied all of three years (1945–1948), reduced the gigantic wartime tally of over 500 Soviet divisions to 175, of which about one-third (65) were retained or reorganized as armored strike forces, split between tank and mechanized divisions. In this first great adaptation to wartime experience, the mechanized division was stabilized at a strength of 12,000–13,000 men (with three mechanized regiments and two tank regiments), the reduced tank division emerged with 10,500 men (with three medium-tank regiments), and the rifle division was left with an establishment of 11,000 men (with three regiments). The basis of striking power was the tank, in which the Soviet command invested almost all its hopes. The rifle division, whose mobility was strictly limited, was about to undergo an extensive program of motorization, which brought in its wake the problem of integrating the shock power and flexibility of the tank/mechanized formations with a more mobile infantry force. For the moment, the Soviet command also retained the wartime artillery divisions (with 9,000 men, a field-gun brigade, a howitzer brigade, and a howitzer regiment and a medium-gun regiment) and the antiaircraft division. Here was the outline of "shock-power" capability and what Dr. Steven Canby pinpoints as "surgeability," or "stress upon initial hitting power" with a number of important psychological implications.[3]

Organized into "all-arms"[4] and mechanized armies, these reorganized and reconstituted divisions were deployed well forward as "Groups of Soviet Forces" in the new buffer zone formed out of the occupied states of Eastern and Central Europe (including Austria at this stage, with its own "Central Group/Soviet Forces"). Here the Soviet command committed its "all-arms" and mechanized armies, the "all-arms" army consisting of two to three corps made up of two rifle divisions and a mechanized division, while the mechanized army comprised four divisions (two tank and two mechanized). Thus, the Group of Soviet Forces/German amounted to two "all-arms" armies and no less than four mechanized armies, with a total strength of twenty-two divisions (ten mechanized, eight tank, and four rifle divisions). In Poland, the "Northern Group" maintained one tank and one mechanized division, with Rumania and Hungary each holding two mechanized divisions and Austria one rifle division—a total of twenty-nine Soviet divisions, the bulk of them the basis of a strike force that has never fallen in real strength from the level of twenty-four to twenty-six first-line divisions (a superiority of 3:1 even in those days, when the Soviet army confronted nine British, American, and French divisions all told). Behind these forces deployed forward into the Eastern and Central European staging area were as many as eighty divisions held in the western regions of the Soviet Union proper, a readily available reserve for operations in the European theater, supported in turn by a huge tank park.

This deployment pattern has persisted to the present day (save for the removal of lines of communication troops and the establishment of the Southern Group in Hungary and the Central Group in Czechoslovakia—both the result of internal policing actions within the Warsaw Pact area). It was not until the late 1950s, however, that the structure and organization of the Soviet army assumed its recognizably modern form. With the inhibition of "Stalinist military science"—and Stalin himself—removed, involving the anachronism (if not the downright fiction) of *aktivnaya oborona* and resort to the counteroffensive, Zhukov and the Soviet command could attend to effective modernization, the recog-

---

[3] See Steven Canby, *The Alliance and Europe,* Part IV, Military Doctrine and Technology, Adelphi Papers, no. 109 (London I.I.S.S., 1975), p. 20, n. 59. In this significant and original paper, Dr. Canby distinguishes between "firepower" and "shock power," with a "shock-power army" relying more on maneuver to defeat the enemy and a greater proportion of *direct firepower,* the very themes underlined by Colonel Savkin (see note 21).

[4] *Obshchevoiskovyi,* meaning "all-arms," or "combined arms."

nition of the importance of surprise, and the need for real mobility, though not at the sacrifice of "shock power." Indeed, both were to be combined in a reorganization that attempted to integrate the tank forces with "mechanized/ motorized infantry." The unwieldy mechanized division gave way to the more compact tank division and the rifle division now redesignated the "motor-rifle division"—thus bringing back the tank army into the order battle (consisting initially of three to four tank divisions), and the "all-arms" army with two to three motor-rifle divisions and a tank division. Heavy-tank divisions, which had formed a part of the mechanized army, were to be withdrawn from formations and assigned as independent tank battle groups at the disposal of Front commanders. As for the tactical missile component, which was already making its appearance, Marshal Zhukov's reorganization called for missiles to replace the heavy guns at army and division level and, by the same token, the "antiaircraft division" was stripped out in favor of mobile brigades of surface-to-air missiles.

These changes, which added appreciably to the "shock power" and mobility of the Ground Forces, were accomplished against a background of *manpower reduction* in the Soviet armed forces at large. They also reflected the unequivocal shift to offensivism, based on seizing the initiative and exploiting the surprise factor: the Ground Forces (like the navy and tactical air units) would in the event of war strike as far and as fast as possible against the enemy, committing him to "close battle" in conditions of Soviet choosing and thus denying him the opportunity to utilize nuclear weapons at will and also at the same time moving Soviet combat forces out of the hinterland regions threatened by nuclear bombardment, thereby preserving a war-fighting capability. Marshal Zhukov was abruptly removed from the scene before these plans took effect, but Malinovskii continued the program, cutting the Ground Forces total strength to 140 divisions and deploying the new-style tank armies, as well as introducing the motor-rifle division. The corps had by now vanished, the division became the basic tactical entity, and the regiment given growing self-sufficiency. Advancing technology, combined with Khrushchev's strategic "new look" unveiled at the beginning of 1960, contributed nonetheless to obscuring the future of the Ground Forces and the requirement for theater-level operations. The role of holding Europe "hostage," assigned initially to the Soviet army, now began to pass to the MRBM/ IRBM missile units (which came under the command of the freshly minted Strategic Rocket Forces). With the first tactical missiles coming into service with the Ground Forces, the role of tactical aviation (together with conventional artillery) came in for a certain amount of anguished scrutiny, but this "in-house" argument paled into insignificance against the drastic downgrading of traditional arms that Khrushchev envisaged through his reliance on strategic systems and the concept of the short, spasm war.

The disappearance of Khrushchev in October 1964 and the subsequent revamping of Soviet military policies brought literally a new lease on life for the Ground Forces in the mid-1960s, beginning with limited experiments with a

ron service—the SU-19 (Fencer)[8] VG aircraft designed specifically for close-support, the improved MIG-21 SMT and the MIG-23 fighter-bomber variant (four ordnance pylons and the GP-9 gunpod with twin-barrel GSH-23 cannon), also the SU-20 modified VG aircraft, complementing the counterair role but adding to the ground-attack capability.[9]

Even on this cursory inspection, Soviet forces in the European theater have been given a substantial "face-lift," increasing their firepower, flexibility, and mobility. It is worth noticing also that many of the new weapons are the products of the developments of the mid- or late 1960s, being presently brought into front-line service, while it is reasonable to suppose that the tried and tested T-54/PT-76 combination (the basis of a whole family of vehicles and trans-porters) will be replaced by the new T-70/BMP-76-type vehicles. Meanwhile a *genuine* dual capability has come into being and with it an "independent conventional option."[10] Having looked at the development of capability, it re-mains now to look at the doctrinal assumptions and operational/tactical prac-tices underlying these developments.

GENERAL DOCTRINE AND OPERATIONAL CONCEPTS

In the evolution of a Soviet theater-warfare capability, both theory and practice alike have undergone a steady transformation. Traditional military doctrine (though retaining its essentials) has been substantially modified, whereas on the ground itself selectively has been applied to the principle of mass on the battlefield. The result, in brief, has been the development of a very singular concept of the blitzkrieg (though Soviet military theorists would vehemently disavow that attribution and would point, correctly enough, to the amplification of earlier theories of *glubokii boi,* "operations in depth," albeit with a great

[8] The SU-19 VG is an all-weather close-support/ground-attack aircraft, capable of under-flying NATO early-warning systems and making deep penetrations at very low altitudes, thanks to significant advances in Soviet radar technology: this lo-lo-lo mode may account for Soviet aircraft in camouflage configuration.

[9] *Ordinance:* As yet no "smart" (PGM) weapons have appeared on the Soviet side, but with this new equipment and enhanced capability the *Frontovaya aviatsiva* would seem to be a prime candidate for air-delivery of such weapons, in view of their enhanced role in theater operations and the move away from ground-delivered (missile) systems. Such a move would have considerable implications for NATO's air defense. *RPVs:* Possibly one reconnais-sance drone based on the AS-5 (Kelt).

[10] See G. Isserson, "Razvite teorii Sovetskogo operativnogo iskusstva v 30-e gody," *Voenno-istoricheskii Zhurnal,* no. 1 (1965), pp. 36–61: this important article repays the closest study, as does *Voprosy Tatktiki v Sovetskikh Voennykh Trudakh (1917–1940 gg.)* (Moscow: Voyenizdat, 1970), especially the introduction pp. 13–25 and pp. 70–100 (Isserson, Tukhachevskii and Frunze Academy study on offensive/defensive operations). Also relevant here is General Eike Middeldorf, *Taktik im Russlandfeldzug Erfahrungen und Folgerungen* (Darmstadt: E. S. Mittler & Sohn, 1956).

additive of mobility and flexibility).[11] In the postwar context, Soviet doctrine has certainly established forward deployment in the Central European *place d'armes* as an axiom, if only to hold the buffer zone against any potential military threat developing against the Soviet Union proper. It could be said that the "local adversary" concept is also built into this notion, though that contingency has now faded appreciably. While this is largely a defensive notion, in an offensive context, forward deployment is seen logically as a means of acquiring a staging area and the jumping-off ground for the "all-arms" theater capability, which would be exercised in an all-out high-speed offensive—a principle held to be viable under conditions of both nuclear and conventional warfare.

The organization, structure, and deployment of Soviet theater forces bears out these strictures. The profile of the Ground Forces, which are being continuously improved, is that of a highly mobile strike force, with powerful armored and motor-rifle (rather mechanized) elements and with nuclear (or chemical) weapons organic down to division. These strike forces, supported by battlefield missiles, are also supported by powerful conventional artillery as well as rocket launchers and heavy mortars: mobile air-defense systems are organic in regiment strength in Soviet armies; antitank defense exists throughout down to battalion level; engineering capacity is related to high-speed assault river crossings and overcoming extensive obstacles or ravaged ground (fire, nuclear demolitions, flooding). Perhaps the most distinctive feature, however, is the logistics arrangement, which is drastically *centralized*,[12] particularly in maintenance and replacement—the "tail" has been chopped in order to provide a greater number of combat units and to provide support where it is most needed. (This same centralization principle—which is a major derivative of wartime experience—is also applied to the conduct of air operations in both the offensive and defensive mode. In sum, it embodies the belief that resources can be best administered in this fashion, even if the price is inflexibility at lower levels.)

Against this background of continuous and overt preparation for all-out offensive operations, it would appear that there is some major inconsistency with Soviet claims that their purposes and deployment in the European theater

[11] This problem of the continuity (at least in Soviet perception) of prewar, wartime, and postwar doctrine really deserves much closer examination. It can also be assisted by reappraising military-historical works, which are often attempts at a form of "operations research"—accomplished officially by a complete statistical/operational analysis of all tank/rifle/aviation armies and divisions in wartime operations, as well as a comparable analysis of German operational experience.

[12] The first, and indeed one of the best examples of this centralizing practice was Marshal Voronov's innovation in 1941 of stripping out divisional artillery, setting up a "High Command artillery reserve," grouping available guns on threatened sectors and resorting to direct fire, over "open sights." This was also necessitated by the loss of trained gun crews.

are essentially defensive. It is the capability for *preemption* that blurs what might otherwise be a straightforward distinction between "offensive" and "defensive" postures: Soviet theater forces must provide and preserve that capability to seize the initiative and launch a preemptive counterforce blow against NATO forces with the place, time, and strength all of Soviet choosing. It is, in Mr. Malcolm Mackintosh's succinct phrase, the ability to "strike first in the last resort," that is, when "the interests of Socialism" are imminently threatened (or appear to be so threatened). In a rare moment of some frankness, General Boleslaw Chocha (head of the General Staff Academy of the Polish armed forces—LWP) intimated that in any "local" conflict in Europe, the use of tactical nuclear weapons was certainly possible but by no means inevitable—but should there be a dire threat to "the interests of Socialism," then "moderation" must be virtually counted out, even if such a decision (emanating in Moscow and not from the military commanders in the field) would not be made "without due consideration."[13] In the light of this requirement, it is consistent that the Soviet command should proclaim its defensive deployment and design in the European theater, yet proceed vigorously to modernize its theater forces, to fit them out for offensive operations in both the nuclear and conventional mode, to lay down the basis for a *rapid deployment* into an offensive posture, and simultaneously to train these forces intensively for offensive operations. It also explains the Soviet insistence on retaining a *relative superiority* (as opposed to that massive superiority necessary for a great conquering drive to the English Channel). This principle will be applied in the field as well as being pursued in the negotiating processes of the MBR talks.

If this might be called "received doctrine," the formalizing of its various phases has occasioned no small amount of astringent argument as well as sheer ambivalence. To encapsulate much of this, the first specific concepts for operating in a nuclear environment were enunciated in the late 1950s, with great stress laid on the principle of mobility and the high-speed offensive. Here that cardinal Soviet doctrinal tenet of the primacy of the offensive was given a new lease on life—the consequence of nuclear weapons on the battlefield gave greater urgency to "closing" with the enemy, thus denying him the chance to loose his own nuclear weapons. And for the first time the notion of heavy battlefield loss was admitted, requiring rapid replacement of divisions and the creation of substantial reserves. Here again, wartime experience and postwar requirement were merged in somewhat abrupt fashion. More important, however, was the issue of the "long war" versus the "short war," round which much of the debate in the Khrushchev period turned. The Khrushchev mode involved committing the Ground Forces to the rapid exploitation and follow-up of nuclear strikes at the expense of conventional capability and the sparse support that Soviet divisions

---

[13] See *Polityka* (Warsaw), 16 February 1973.

even then enjoined. In the post-Khrushchev phase the emphasis on the seizure of the initiative and high-speed penetration into the depth of the whole theater remained understandably intact, though now the issue was joined over the nuclear/conventional relationship.

Some adjustments were made in the direction of improving conventional capability in the mid-1960s, including the addition of a motor-rifle division to a tank division to give greater flexibility, the increase in conventional artillery, and some adjustments to the logistics system (on the fuel and ammunition side). Meanwhile, the protagonists of an improved tactical nuclear war-fighting capability pressed their case; those in favor of increasing conventional capability used the novel argument that nuclear weapons of themselves enhanced the significance of *conventional* weapons. By way of compromise (if that is the right term) the "superiority norms" of World War II have been applied to both nuclear and conventional capabilities (though it is worth noting that the standard textbook *Taktika,* published in 1966, treated only nuclear operations).[14] Recently, while improving their capability for tactical nuclear warfare, Soviet theater forces have also been prepared more effectively to wage a short, intensive, conventional campaign. The ambiguities, however, remain. For example, Soviet military doctrine places unambiguous stress on the value of surprise and deception as an indispensable means in seizing the initiative, yet also demands a given preponderance in force and adequate reserves (the accumulation of which might well dispel any "surprise"). Equally, there seems to be a large gap between the guarded admissions of the feasibility of conventional operations even on some scale and the possible "limited" use of tactical nuclear weapons without automatic escalation to general war, as opposed to the view that any large-scale military collision in the heart of Europe would inevitably become "uncontrollable." Perhaps the most significant shift has been the provision for conducting conventional operations *in the initial phase* and for a sustained period—in other words, the recognition of an "independent conventional option." (No doubt this was the burden of the recent "military-scientific conference" of the Ground Forces commanders convened in January 1975—the terse summary does at least indicate that conventional capability was reviewed, as was the experience of the major maneuvers, going back to Dnieper.)[15]

For all the conditions of potential operations—general nuclear war, tactical nuclear war, and conventional warfare—the essence of Soviet operational theory

[14] See Major General V. G. Reznichenko, ed., *Taktika* (Moscow: Voyenizdat, 1966), Series "Biblioteka ofitsera."

[15] See under "Voenno-nauchnye Konferentsii," in *Voennyi Vestnik,* no. 1 (1975), pp. 8–9: specific papers cited were Colonel General Dragunskii on maneuver and Lieutenant General V. G. Reznichenko on the tactics of airborne troops. Marshal Peredel'skii's study section considered the problems of increasing the effectiveness of firepower.

and practice is (to use a colloquialism) "to get in and under, fast."[16] In the case of general war, this would almost certainly mean massive preemption; in the other two contingencies, surprise and extensive deception would be exploited to the full, though no doubt the military command would press for a form of preemption. Thus, in general outline and for all contingencies, the pattern of Soviet operations in the central region would assume the dimensions of offensive action—even preemption—with great superiority of "all arms" operating along several axes.[17] The aim of offensive operations is to breach enemy defenses in order to launch tank formations into the deep rear. Under conditions of tactical nuclear warfare, formations are assigned *wide sectors,* in which they maneuver on *narrower* attack frontages, again with the object of breaching enemy defenses and selecting favorable axes for advance. "Shock power" is concentrated in the first echelon, whereas the second echelon is committed without halting the first—companies attack in a single echelon without a reserve, but all formations and units deploy an *antitank reserve.*

Under nuclear conditions, after the mass initial nuclear strike (with air- and ground-delivery), Soviet formations are committed to an advance of 100 kilometers in a twenty-four-hour period. Under conventional conditions, this advance rate has been adjusted to some 70 kilometers. Soviet operational methods lay principal stress on:

1. Attacks "off the march" (without prior concentration), movement with open flanks and along divergent axes.
2. The rapid crossing of rivers and water obstacles.
3. Airborne landings and helicopter-assault units committed ahead of the advance to seize river crossings, road routes, and other objectives.
4. Good cross-country performance for all vehicles (though advances along roads reduce logistical requirements, and many Soviet vehicles still possess only limited off-road performance).
5. Tight control of movement and effective traffic discipline.

Formations will move in tactical groupings and will be prepared for rapid deployment into combat operations. Night movement is generally favored (and night fighting is extensively practiced in the Soviet Ground Forces), or move-

---

[16] The course at the Frunze Military Academy is divided into two parts: (1) NATO and its capabilities; (2) Soviet offensive and defensive responses.

[17] See A. A. Sidorenko, *The Offensive (A Soviet View)* translated and published by the U.S. Air Force in *Soviet Military Thought* (Washington, D.C.: Government Printing Office, 1973); also Army General P. A. Kurochkin, ed., *Obshchevoiskovaya Armiya v Nastuplenii* (Moscow: Voyenizdat, 1966). The Kurochkin work is an analysis of wartime operational experience and, as such, is singularly relevant in view of the present Soviet preoccupation with a conventional mode of operations, while Sidorenko is the embodiment of the nuclear blitzkrieg.

ment under conditions of poor visibility, conducted with radio silence save for reconnaissance reporting and broadcast warnings of nuclear, chemical, and air attack.

The "meeting engagement" (*vstrechnyi boi*), which can be very extensive in scale, will be a normal form of action, while attacking "off the march" will help Soviet forces to retain the initiative. A "Front offensive" (army group level) is designed to breach enemy defenses and open the way for a tank army to be launched into the enemy's deep rear. Such an offensive will normally include all deployed armies in *the first echelon,* with only divisions held in immediate reserve and where the tank army operates along the axis of the "main thrust" (*glavnoe napravlenie*). In the event of heavy enemy resistance, "all-arms armies" will proceed to breach these defenses and the tank army is then committed as a second echelon. If a tank army (or tank division) is committed in the first echelon, then neighboring formations will also commit their tank division (or tank regiment) in their own first echelon in order to maximize the thrust.

The motor-rifle division will normally attack with its three regiments in the first echelon (with the tank regiment also committed in this attack echelon); similarly, the tank division attacks with up to three regiments in its first echelon, and with its motor-rifle regiment simultaneously committed to neutralize possible resistance. In this mode, motor-rifle regiments attack without decentralized tank support, and the tank regiments in turn attack without decentralized infantry support. At *regimental level,* two battalions will attack in the first echelon—in this instance, the tank battalion operates *by companies* with motor-rifle units. On a wide front, motor-rifle and tank battalions attack in linear style (line abreast), with three companies forward and a platoon in reserve; tank and motor-rifle companies attack as a single echelon, with no reserve. In an attack with tanks and infantry mounted in APCs, the tanks operate at intervals of 100–150 yards; with infantry dismounted, the tanks will be up to 200 yards apart, but in the absence of infantry support, Soviet tanks operate at intervals of 50–100 yards. These linear tactics are designed to commit the maximum number of battalions/companies in combat situations and to bring Soviet forces into the "hugging" contact prescribed much earlier.

Soviet doctrine delineates several standard forms of attack: the "meeting engagement" and the "rapid attack"—on encountering prepared defenses—and attack "off the march" which varies in strength from company to regiment. (If an immediate attack "off the march" is not possible, then an assembly/concentration area will be temporarily occupied, and the assault will be deployed from there.) Soviet riflemen will normally attack mounted in APCs, furnishing covering fire on the move with their APC-mounted weapons and through the firing ports. Dismounted attacks will be made against prepared positions or those that have survived intact after nuclear/chemical bombardment; rifle companies dismount at a distance of some 500 yards from their objective and proceed to the attack utilizing cover or screened by smoke, with APCs supporting the assault with their on-board weapons.

The initial nuclear fire-plan is obviously of commanding importance, but Soviet doctrine has also come to regard *movement itself* as a means of exploiting fire, whether nuclear or conventional—a Soviet innovation, in a sense. (It should be added quickly that the conventional fire-plan may also include chemical weapons.)[18] Large-scale direct fire is required only during the breakthrough phase, which must involve an intensive engagement, but otherwise indirect fire support is employed. Although the artillery may be well forward during any approach, during an attack "off the march" it is possible (indeed likely) that not all the available artillery could be utilized. It will be interesting to see how these artillery/assault tactics are modified in the light of the introduction of the new SP-gun battalions, which will increase direct fire support and will be able to reinforce artillery support for attacks "off the march."

Night fighting is both heavily emphasized and much practiced in the Soviet army, if only to maintain the momentum of the twenty-four hour battle. Motor-rifle troops take the first echelon usually in such operations and attack mounted in their APCs, though the second echelon at divisional level is not normally committed before daylight. Night attacks may also be launched *without* fire preparation, and (as might be expected) artillery is more than usually decentralized. With the same objective of maintaining the pace and momentum of the offensive, divisions will also form "forward" (*peredovoi*) combat groups ranging in size from battalion to regiment, designed to strike ahead and secure important tactical points, such as river crossings and other objectives. These same "forward" combat groups can also be used to support helicopter-assault landings already launched, formed from a motor-rifle battalion and committed to a "tactical airborne assault."[19] Airborne troops proper are to be committed on a large-scale and also in a specialized role as forward reconnaissance/sabotage groups (*reidoviki*), as opposed to the even more specialized "raider/commando" groups, trained in free-fall parachuting, demolition, and forward reconnaissance roles (the *vysotniki*). Warsaw Pact non-Soviet forces also maintain their own specialist paracommando groups, such as the *"Willi Sänger"* battalion of the NVA, the Czechoslovak brigade, or elements of Polish Sixth Airborne Division.

In sum, the object of any Soviet attack—nuclear or conventional—is to achieve a rapid breakthrough and to accomplish the destruction of the enemy's tactical and operational reserves, as well as simultaneously "combatting the means of the enemy's nuclear delivery." *Speed* is the key to success, for this

---

[18] Chemical weapons are also included in the nuclear fire-plan.

[19] On the *peredovoi batal'on* and its importance, see a recent article by Army General I. G. Pavlovskii (commander-in-chief, Ground Forces), "Vboyakh za Rodinu," *Izvestiya*, 13 March 1975. This is a very useful summary of Soviet tactics 1941–1945 and their contemporary relevance.

can also contribute to preventing any organized retreat. The initial fire-plan, is obviously of great importance. The nuclear fire-plan, involving the first mass strike, is planned by the highest command echelon (that is, "Front" HQ), whereas army echelons (in conjunction with "Front") will plan strikes of lesser scale and to a lesser depth in order to effect "operational-tactical success" (for example, an assault on a defended river-line). At *divisional level,* nuclear strikes may be planned with those launchers available to division and effective within its own divisional boundaries, with release required from army level; launchers will also be held ready to fire against targets of opportunity. (The nuclear fire-plan is also coordinated with the air sortie plan—with a current situation where the majority of warheads are delivered by ground missiles, though this could change appreciably in the near future.) The chemical fire-plan (which is presently conceived as part of an overall nuclear fire-plan) involves missiles, aircraft, and conventional artillery for means of delivery and is designed to implement surprise by *sudden concentration.*

As for *conventional artillery*—growing in number and increasing in capability—the bulk at "Front" and army level is usually committed to the first echelon, whereas at divisional level, organic (and assigned) artillery is committed to the assault regiments, such artillery being used for *direct* fire-support to assist the battalions. The overall fire-plan (involving guns, RLs, and heavy mortars) will call for fire lasting from fifteen to thirty minutes, with artillery deployed well forward and even advanced ahead of the main body to support an impending assault. A large proportion of Soviet artillery has antitank capability, while antitank guns as such can be used to provide indirect fire-support, not to mention tank guns, which can also be used for further indirect fire. When used in this role (that is, in the second echelon at divisional level) tank fire is classed as "additional artillery" and is designed to engage enemy artillery targets up to the first 5,000 meters of any advance.[20]

---

[20] There are, of course, many variants of fire-plans: a "nuclear fire-plan" could prescribe first strikes by tactical aircraft, artillery fire, and, in the last minutes of that fire, the use of tactical nuclear weapons—a number of them air-bursted—against prescribed targets, though excluding forward positions in order not to hit advancing Soviet armor. Soviet sources admit this difficulty in targeting. Conventional attack only would mean fire directed largely against link points and positions, with long-range artillery and tactical air support concentrating on inhibiting enemy movement.

Again, a number of estimates can be made of gun densities per kilometer, as well as the expenditure of nuclear warheads. Artillery concentration in a nuclear attack would probably be in the order of 100 guns and heavy mortars per kilometer with up to forty-five tanks (that is, 10,000 rounds expended), while in a conventional attack that gun density would be virtually doubled, reaching at least 180 and doubling the volume of fire (20,000 rounds). Soviet military studies naturally point up the problems associated with *target distribution,* including damage to point and area targets and equally the efficacy of reconnaissance. A certain amount of target acquisition is preplanned, while Soviet target acquisition means extend to some 500 miles from FEBA, consisting of photo-reconnaissance aircraft (day and

Much of this has received extensive analysis on the part of Soviet military specialists, ranging from tactical minutiae to the wider principles governing the operations of ground troops. One of the best examples of this is the work of Colonel Savkin,[21] who has asked some awkward but fundamental questions about the planning and conduct of operations: although great lip-service is paid to "mobility," he asks, what *is* "mobility" and how does simple movement differ from effective maneuver?[22] Colonel Savkin argues that carrying out all the labored stages of an encirclement operation is a waste of true "mobility," in that elimination of enemy forces could be accomplished finally by using tactical nuclear weapons. Thus, real "mobility" is essentially accomplishing "the assigned task with maximum effect" and "maneuver" is part of this (though again not to be confused with mobility as simple movement). In passing, it is worth recording that Colonel Savkin's study is concerned almost exclusively with arguing the case for the surprise employment of massed tactical nuclear strikes on a narrow front—followed by swift penetration in depth by armored forces in conjunction with large-scale airborne landings in the deep rear: *quod erat demonstrandum.*

Though not properly a component of "operational doctrine," the problem of *command and control,* as well as anticipated military performance, is so integral a part of Soviet preoccupation with respect to theater warfare that it can scarcely be omitted here. To sum this up as briefly as possible, Soviet concern is concentrated at the extreme ends of the spectrum—efficacy at the highest level with its supercentralization and efficiency (*effektivnost'*) at the very lowest, at subunit level. First, let us consider the aspect of the "supercentralized" direction of theater operations. Here again there is a close relationship with wartime experience, for the General Staff "model" with its *predstavitelii* ("representatives") sent into the field may well have recommended itself to the Soviet command as the way in which to control theater operations (which correspond to multi-Front operations of World War II). Certainly, it cannot be assumed that the administrative apparatus of GSFG will "command" Soviet divisions in war operations—rather the actual command apparatus is a General Staff "command-in-being" organization, highly centralized and responsible for both operational planning and execution. (By the same token, the Warsaw Pact as such is not a war-waging organization in the operational sense, but rather an administrative and training apparatus for peacetime purposes; it is worth noting here that

---

night), emplaced agents, deep penetration patrols (up to 200 miles), army reconnaissance groups up to 50 miles, radar surveillance, intercept/monitoring, and microwave radiometry. Targets of opportunity are assigned to tactical aircraft in the first instance, though ground-delivered weapons are also committed in part to this task.

[21] Lecturer in tactics/operational theory, Frunze Military Academy.

[22] See Colonel V. Ye. Savkin, "Manevr v Boyu," *Voennyi Vestnik,* no. 4 (1972), pp. 22–27: see also the rejoinder to Colonel Savkin, *Voennyi Vestnik,* no. 8 (1972), pp. 30–33.

during the invasion of Czechoslovakia *operational* command passed to the commander-in-chief, Soviet Ground Forces). *Upravlenie voiskami* ("troop control") is very much a Soviet preoccupation, both in theory and practice, whereas the problem is vastly complicated by difficulties encountered at the *subunit level*.[23] Here, for all the theory, "effectiveness" faltered badly and has needed much repair. There seems to be greater confidence in cohesion and "effectiveness" at the regiment/division level (even at battalion), but the small combat entity, whose role is increasingly crucial, has proved to be the source of multiple worries—what, for example, is the basis of subunit cohesion, how effective is training, how should logistics units be broken down into smaller subunits, how efficiently would reconnaissance be carried out . . . ? Added to this is the related factor of how the Soviet soldier will react to battlefield stress, particularly that of the nuclear battlefield, in both physical and psychological terms. The correct response to that problem obviously bears closely on training programs (for example, the degree of realism required for simulated battlefields).

Though not technically a constituent of operational concepts as such, no Soviet military authority worth his salt omits this aspect (and not merely as a ritualistic bow in the direction of official orthodoxy).[24] For all the theorizing, it is this factor—the man behind the gun—that will exercise a powerful effect on the outcome of both ground and air operations.

TYPES AND INTENSITIES OF OPERATIONS: GROUND/AIR ENGAGEMENT "NORMS"

Perhaps the most prominent feature of the Soviet military establishment, save for its visible mass, is the lack of any large-scale, protracted operational experience since 1945. Police actions internal to the Warsaw Pact (1953 and 1956) and

---

[23] Among a great body of writing, three recent publications are of significance: General S. P. Ivanov, *O Nauchnykh Osnovakh Upravleniya Voiskami* (Moscow: Voyenizdat, 1975); Colonel A. F. Shramchenko, *Voprosy Psikhologii v Upravlenii Voiskami* (Moscow: Voyenizdat, 1973); and an important historical-theoretical work, N. N. Popel' et al., *Upravlenie Voiskami v Gody Velikoi Otechestvennoi Voiny* (Moscow: Voyenizdat, 1974).

[24] On the contrary, the literature is ferocious and polemical. Not surprisingly, Colonel Savkin also applies his concept of true mobility to troop control, though he is but one of many specialists who insist on examining troop-control methods and its extension into training practices. This is an army without substantial or sustained combat experience—and the same applies to the tactical air forces. One of the current campaigns is to improve the quality and efficiency of Soviet staff work, as well as involving the staff in the training program. I have translated the term *effektivnost* as both efficiency and effectiveness, but perhaps it should be understood in the wider context of "performance."

Quite the best definition of what the Soviet command is aiming at is supplied by the late General Beaufre in his *Strategy for Tomorrow* (New York: SRI, 1974) when he speaks of "agility" (p. 29), which he defines as "the combination of mobility and the reaction capacities: information, decision, transmission of orders, execution." Both Colonel Savkin and the authors of *Ideya, Algoritm, Reshenie* (Moscow: Voyenizdat, 1972) would agree with that formulation.

to that side—all other conditions *being equal*—which acts more aggressively and captures "the decisive initiative."[28] Finally, there is unequivocal emphasis on the short highly intensive war—"prolonged combat operations have passed irretrievably into history and have instead been replaced by highly mobile operations." (For organizational charts see Figures 4—8.)

It is axiomatic, therefore, that the Soviet command intends to wage and *to win* a European campaign at all levels of conflict, assuming in all instances a "short war." This raises the question at once that present "peacetime" Soviet deployment, which is administratively and politically convenient, would not correspond to an operational order of battle: for example, the "Groups of Forces" facade would collapse at once and be replaced by operational combat groupings, with a limited number of non-Soviet Warsaw Pact formations in the first echelon.[29] What Colonel Savkin seems to be saying is that under certain conditions a "standing start" offensive would mean numerical (manpower) parity, or that counterstrikes by an opponent would soon result in manpower parities and that a number of major Soviet formations would have to fight on with "limited numbers" brought on by breakthrough loss, though deception might help to offset this disparity.[30]

Soviet concepts of theater operations envisage both great depth and initial high intensity of combat. The basic notion is to overwhelm an opponent in a Soviet version of the blitzkrieg, concentrating on narrow sectors of a front in order to shatter the defenses and then move in strength into the rear and deep rear. Should only one or two major breakthroughs be required because of the weakness or lack of depth of enemy defenses, then this would be indubitably a "short war"; in the face of stronger defenses, a series of breakthrough operations might well be required. In any event, according to the Soviet view, the logistical requirement is not great—with the breakthrough accomplished, armored thrusts contributing to the total disorganization of the enemy would not need major artillery or logistics support, while the "statistical incidence" of heavy break-

---

Voyenizdat prefaces publication of Savkin with a note to the effect that these publications represent "the personal point of view of the author" and wherein certain theses are "open to debate," See Colonel V. Ye. Savkin, "Cherty Sovremennogo Boya," *Voennyi Vestnik*, no. 3 (1974), pp. 24—28.

[28] I discussed this problem of tactical-operational surprise at length with Marshal Koniev and was rebuked for my "fantasies" ("*tol'ko poeziya*") by the marshal. I was not sure whether this referred to my status as an ex-infantry sergeant or my incompetence as a mere professor. Nonetheless, surprise and deception play an important part in Soviet operational thinking and I took the marshal's strictures. (These encounters with Soviet senior commanders have been set down in my contributions to Field Marshal Sir Michael Carver's forthcoming study on modern commanders.)

[29] In late March 1975, secret major military exercises—involving Soviet, NVA, and Polish units with a combined strength of several divisions—took place in the DDR. These exercises prescribed a rapid thrust of the Cottbus/Dresden forces along a *northwest* axis.

[30] Savkin, "Cherty Sovremennogo Boya."

through fighting is so infrequent as not to call for extensive logistical preparation for such eventualities. Such a concept also accepts having first-echelon formations "ground down," to be replaced by other formations *en bloc* in order to maintain the tempo and speed of the offensive.

A "Front operation" (and a full theater operation would mean the coordination of possibly several "Fronts") would reach to a depth of 500–600 miles—in this instance, that is to say that the Rhine and the Netherlands are some two to three days drive from the German border in the west and north. This also presupposes that under conditions of major threat (or presumed threat), preemption will have been generally authorized, with the MRBM/IRBM missile component brought to bear on European secondary nuclear power bases (the British Polaris, for example), ports, early-warning systems, and with the Soviet Navy also committed to the domination of European coastal waters, including a preemptive act to secure its egress points.[31] A Soviet "Front" (comprising several armies) would hold a sector of some 200 miles, with an anticipated depth of its operations reaching to 500 miles or so. An individual Soviet army (tank or motor rifle) would hold a front of up to 80 miles, with an attack frontage of up to 30 miles and with its immediate objective set at a depth of 30 miles, with its further objective fixed at a distance of a maximum of 50–60 miles. Divisional sectors run to a maximum of 20 miles, with attack frontages set at 9–10 miles, immediate objectives at 10–20 miles, and further objectives up to 30–40 miles. A Soviet regiment is committed across an attack frontage of 3 miles with its immediate objective set at a depth of up to 8 miles. Army and divisional operational depths reach up to 150 miles and 50 miles, respectively. As for subunits, a tank company with 10 tanks can be deployed along a 700–800 meter front, whereas a two-company battalion will occupy an attack frontage of 1,700 meters, and a full battalion (with a tank company in reserve) 2,000 meters. As Colonel Savkin points out, the present depth of penetration of *a battalion* can reach 2 kilometers (as opposed to 0.5 kilometers in World War II).[32]

In any major assault on the central sector, the Soviet command can deploy up to 200 battalion-sized combat groups, supported by well over 6,000 tanks and some 4,000 APCs. As for the use of nuclear weapons, their use comes under three headings: the initial *mass strike, group strikes,* and *single strikes.* To take an attack frontage of 60 miles (2 × 30) for two armies mounting the main thrust, and including Frog, Scud, and Scaleboard missiles, the depth of this bombardment would reach from 65 to 350 kilometers (Frog-7, Scud-B, and

[31] See Whetten "Recent Developments in the Soviet Navy," on Soviet naval policy and deployment (pp. 95–116 in this volume).

[32] Savkin, "Cherty Sovremennogo Boya." See also Colonel V. Ye. Savkin, *Osnovnye Printsipy Operativnogo Iskusstva i Taktiki* (Moscow: Voyenizdat, 1972), pp. 265–302. Translated as *The Basic Principles of Operational Art and Tactics (A Soviet View),* published under the auspices of the U.S. Air Force (Washington, D.C.: Government Printing Office, 1974), chap. 3, pp. 167–201.

Scaleboard), with the larger warheads reaching the deep rear. Assuming (not improbably) that 40 percent of the available warheads would be used in the initial mass strike (though this excludes warheads assigned to air-delivered means and also provision for targets of opportunity), across a 60-mile attack front some 35–40 warheads would be used in this first ground-delivered strike, followed by 36 (3×12) within the same sector in the ensuing 48–72-hour period, depending on the degree of resistance encountered and on Soviet target acquisition. (This scale would seem to be commensurate with available launchers and distributed warheads within the lower KT range, allowing also for the usage of air-bursted and terrain-fire weapons[33] together with the number of launchers held available for strikes against targets of opportunity. With Soviet tactical missiles, the greater the range the larger the yield—Frogs up to 25 KT, Scuds up to 50 KT, and longer-range missiles up to 500 KT—though only small-yield weapons [up to 5 KT] would presumably be used in the immediate vicinity of the FEBA.)

As for basic operational forms, these comprise *encirclement, frontal assault,* and the single "pinning" attack designed to thrust the enemy against some natural barrier or obstacle. The encirclement operation is the Soviet *pièce de résistance* (if that is not too maladroit a description), though Colonel Savkin considers that in all its technicalities it can be wasteful of time and resources. The Soviet encirclement operations consist of two main attacks launched along converging axes, designed also to shatter the main enemy defenses and irrupt into the rear. A possible area for a Soviet encirclement operation of this type and on this scale is the central region, with the Soviet command committing a conventional armored thrust across the good tank country north of Hanover and striking simultaneously for the gap south of the Harz Mountains. This presents some difficulty east of Paderborn, but once through, one segment of the Soviet forces could operate so as to cut off NATO troops located between their two thrust lines with other Soviet elements striking to the west in the direction of Dortmund and Münster. In view of the importance of the terrain factor, the obvious choice for good tank-going must be northern Germany, where a "leap-frogging operation" with amphibious forces would also be possible, striking in the direction of Schleswig-Holstein and Denmark—hence a massive armored thrust across the north German plain, basically a frontal assault. Meanwhile in the southern sector, where the going for tanks is less favorable (but by no means impossible), the Soviet command could launch a feint offensive designed to pin the American forces. There would be in all these contingencies a substantial commitment of airborne forces and up to ten battalion-sized helicopter-borne

---

[33] This highlights the point that the tactical nuclear posture on both sides is different, and obviously from the Soviet side indiscriminate terrain-fire weapons cannot be easily "limited." As early as the 1960s, Soviet commanders were voicing reservations about large-yield weapons—Soviet weapons are intended to blast "passages" and to disrupt the rear.

assaults—all engaged in the seizure of important tactical objectives (though perhaps not on a scale to cause general disruption of the NATO rear, as is sometimes conjectured).

It goes without saying that a "theater operation" of this magnitude would call for powerful forces (of which the Soviet command demonstrably disposes, though not perhaps without some reinforcement). As for non-Soviet Warsaw Pact forces, the relatively few "earmarked" first-echelon divisions would also be engaged, even if not committed to independent roles (as, for example, using a Polish division in the northerly Baltic coast strike). Non-Soviet formations would no doubt be kept within combined battle groups and would inevitably be "corseted" by Soviet units. In the context of a short war of high intensity, the flanks would assume less importance, save for further feints to engage or tie down NATO forces and for high-speed action to secure Soviet passage and egress. The concentrations of forces-in-being on the Northern Flank are impressive and are supported by rapid reinforcement facilities. The strong forces in the Kola Peninsula, including an amphibious contingent, could be speedily reinforced thanks to improvements in road and rail links; the newer large-size runways permit a rapid buildup of airborne forces. Within ten days the Soviet command could have a force of twelve to fourteen divisions at its disposal in this area, complemented by the ability to transport some ten divisions through the Baltic. Due to terrain difficulties and the disparate nature of possible objectives, operations in this subtheater may develop rather more slowly after the first acts of seizure. It is worth noting the Swedish military opinion that holds that the Soviet command could mount a simultaneous multithrust invasion of Sweden while making a major effort elsewhere in Europe.[34] (By the same token, Soviet forces could be used to establish operating facilities, including air and naval bases, in Yugoslavia and thus bring Southern Flank forces into a much more advantageous situation, though this is to simplify all political factors out of existence in such a scenario.)

Such high-intensity operations on the ground would be supported—possibly preceded—by large-scale air activity, a picture now complicated by the improvement and expansion in Soviet tactical air power in the European theater. With the introduction of the SU-19 (Fencer) VG fighter-bomber, the Soviet Air Force has brought the first postwar aircraft designed for close support into squadron service.[35] The MIG-23 (Flogger) is also in front-line service in Europe, together

---

[34] See General Synnergren, commander-in-chief, Swedish armed forces, "Military Policy and Armed Forces, Situation and Tendencies in 1975." Mimeograph.

[35] Though the SU-7 and the MIG-21 are employed in ground-attack roles, they are derivatives of aircraft designed originally for quite different purposes. The SU-7 is currently employed as the standard ground-attack fighter, but it possessed in the beginning a certain commonality with the SU-11 all-weather interceptor, with similar fuselage and tail assembly. The initial model was designated the SU-7B, improved as the SU-7BM: the SU-7BMK was

with new gunship/assault helicopters (MI-24s). The Fencer, with its low-level penetration capability, presents a threat all its own to NATO defenses, getting under the early-warning system. Though suppression of the opposing strike force is still a major task devolving on the Soviet Air Force, the numerical and qualitative improvements in mobile air defense—conventional and missile weaponry—has "released" a number of aircraft from a purely defensive role for other offensive missions—the Soviet intention with its tactical mobile air defense has been to achieve the progressive saturation of air spaces from very low to high altitudes—SA-4s, SA-6s, SA-7s, and SA-9s. It is still an article of faith (at least in formal doctrine) that the Soviet Air Force should fight for and maintain air superiority, but the newer types of aircraft coming into service indicate a greater interest in, and capability for, direct intervention on the battlefield with their own tactical support aircraft (the SU-20 Fitter quasi-VG aircraft, for example, which is an attempt to "stretch" the capability of the SU-7)—as well as improving the ordnance loads of these aircraft.[36]

With 900 first-line aircraft with Sixteenth Air Army (GSFG), plus strong tactical reinforcement from other groups and western districts of the Soviet Union, as well as ninety or more airfields from which to deploy in East Germany and Czechoslovakia, the Soviet Air Force is operationally well placed to mount an intensive air campaign in Europe. One of the first results in Soviet tactical air power is the increase in the capability to support a higher sortie rate for sustained operations at a longer range. Air reconnaissance has thus been improved on a "search-and-strike basis," directed largely against nuclear delivery means. Much more interesting, however, is the conduct of the air battle in its several phases. The air defense role, conducted by the PVO, is highly centralized (with the Warsaw Pact area forming an integral part of the overall Soviet PVO Strany organization) on the tested principle that such centralization facilitates speedy switching of resources for both defensive and offensive purposes. This, nonetheless, raises the question of the relationship between "tactical air" and "air defence"—that is, in the release or commitment of resources. Would PVO "release" its aircraft (unlikely in the event of an unfavorable outcome, but equally unlikely in the event of a favorable outcome)? With the advent of a

---

used extensively during the Indo-Pakistan war (1971) but demonstrated an inferior radius of action and vulnerability to groundfire. The original version of the MIG-21 was intended to be a relatively simple clear-weather point defense and air superiority aircraft: the MIG-21PFMA with additional wing pylons and drop tanks furnished some limited ground-attack capability.

[36] The SU-19 Fencer VG aircraft has a reported tactical radius of 600 miles with an ordnance load of 6,000 pounds. The SU-20 (also designated the SU-17) in its quasi-VG form offers improved short-field performance, greater load-carrying capability, and greater range— four underwing pylons, with a maximum ordnance load of 7,700 pounds for short-range missions (external stores consisting of UV-16-57 or UV-32-57 rocket pods or 550-pound or 1,100-pound bombs).

dense air-defense environment on the Soviet side, it is also necessary for the Soviet command in committing its tactical aircraft to implement a "switch on/switch off" battle, with highly accurate timing for passing through Soviet defenses, or else inextricable confusions in IFF, and so on. The danger of low-level long-range penetration has obviously much increased, but the main Soviet air mission will remain local air superiority and close air support (the latter also much improved in performance). Presumably the bulk of non-Soviet Warsaw Pact air units would be committed, as before, to the air-defense role in their local/regional environments, with the exception of a small number of specialist and ground-support squadrons. Air strength has certainly been increased of late, by as much as 25 percent per regiment. The next great change in the operational environment may be assigning the Soviet equivalent of "smart" weapons to the Soviet Air Force, though a steady increment in numbers and enlarging the ordnance load of modernized machines might make the case for "smart" weapons less compelling, save for attacks on vital point targets (warning systems, command centers, nuclear dumps).

In the absence of comparable political scenarios (or political actuality itself), there is inevitably an element of military metaphysics in this manner of looking at Soviet capabilities for theater warfare. Nonetheless, what is both plain and consistent is the general concordance between "doctrine" and the buildup on the ground—both envisaging high-intensity, high-speed operations. In the case of general war, this would mean preemption and widespread initial use of nuclear weapons (including the IRBM/MRBM arsenal of 600 or so launchers), in this contingency to "clear" the European theater of hostile nuclear capability and forces, with the eventuality of breaching traditional neutralities and overriding the status of the neutralized states (Finland and Austria). In addition, the Soviet Air Force would go for air control of Western Europe, and the naval forces would perforce seek domination of European coastal waters, as well as securing the "preemptive access" of Soviet surface and subsurface attack units. But then this would be Armageddon in all its unimaginable horrors. In all other circumstances, save for the Soviet Union and the "interests of Socialism" being or about to be *in extremis,* then the case for caution rather than any reckless preemption would seem to hold good, certainly on the crucial central sector. Any major operation at the center would reduce flank operations to feints or limited but time-urgent tasks to seize operationally important "bits" of territory, access points, or installations (air fields, early-warning sites, and so on).

Much also depends on the Soviet command's appraisal of NATO's capabilities. Suffice it to say at this juncture that they seem convinced (and plan on the basis) of the efficacy of the guarantee of the integrity of NATO's territory, thus ruling out "probes" (for nothing is to be "probed") and the military equivalent of a smash-and-grab raid. Equally, the premeditated all-out assault to take over Europe by out-and-out military conquest seems to be presently a remote contingency (if only because the requisite massive superiority has not been assembled, and, in any event, this act of outright war might well result in the obliteration of those resources—human, industrial, and economic—that the Soviet leadership proposed to enlist and acquire). Nonetheless, this kind of perception of utility and parity could change, and that speedily, under two sets of circumstances: (1) the change in the qualitative balance[37] (in which there are presently several trade-offs—"smart" weapons on the NATO side, improved antiair defense of the Warsaw Pact side, and so on) and (2) further weakening in the level of defense effort on the part of the NATO powers, with a consequent perceptible shift in "the balance," which is as much a matter of will as being able to make early identification of the main thrust and also to inflict a heavy rate of attrition on attacking armor. Under such circumstances the emergence of a "low-risk option"—exercised with conventional force—might well become reality and substantially affect Soviet military planning.[38]

MILITARY OBJECTIVES AND POLITICAL GOALS

In the first (and last resort) Soviet Ground Forces and the related extensive theater-warfare capability exist to implement the defensive purposes and commitments of the Soviet Union. If there is to our eyes a certain paradox here (precisely in terms of the steady buildup in offensive capability), from the Soviet point of view there is both consistency and logic—namely, the capacity to carry through that essential preemption in pursuit of the "last-ditch" defense of the "interests of Socialism," or at the very least making effective provision for the fulfillment of "defense interests" in any major crisis situation. This would certainly explain the Soviet pursuit of *relative superiority,* with the newly emerged proviso that such superiority might well pertain almost exclusively to "armament norms" rather than simple manpower. In addition, general-purpose

---

[37] "In the past, we counted on the superior quality of Western weapons, equipment, and technology to offset the decided advantage the Warsaw Pact enjoyed in quantity. That time is now past. The hard fact is that the Warsaw Pact has achieved *near qualitative parity* with the West in general-purpose weapons and equipment." *United States Military Posture for FY 1976.* General George S. Brown, chairman JCS, Senate Armed Services Committee, 1976, p. 67.

[38] The burden of this paper is that the Soviet Ground Forces (and related theater capability) are now embarked on an interesting "learning curve" all their own. Here I must record my gratitude to the commandant and officers of the RAF Staff College for the opportunity to examine this thesis and for the exchange in a seminar from which I learned more than I contributed. As for Soviet estimates of their own capability, in the absence of any established methodological guide, there is nothing for it but a plunge into base subjectivism. My own estimate after exchanging views with Soviet officers is that in quite sober fashion they put their chances at about 60:40, they are much concerned with *effektivnost,* they are skeptical—along with non-Soviet Warsaw Pact officers—about automated command and control but also understand the "learning curve" process.

forces have been developed in order to facilitate the control of the Europe-Asia landmass, including possible participation in limited conflicts—and here we are speaking as much of the political utility of the enlarged Ground Forces as their military efficiency. There is, finally, one comcomitant of the "relative-superiority" doctrine that must be recognized—it brings with it a "high visibility" of Soviet military power within the European theater, and that has produced significant indirect political results, one of which has been to maximize the strategic position of the Soviet Union as the one *indigenous* European super-power.

Two principles are also connected within this European emplacement. The first is the requirement to secure the defense of the Warsaw Pact area and thereby to buttress Soviet hegemony within its own security area (after all, Soviet forces provide some 60 percent of the military effectiveness of the Warsaw Pact, a marked contrast with the percentage contribution of the United States to NATO's ground/air force effectiveness). The second is the provision to wage and *to win* a European campaign conducted at all levels of conflict, where "winning" means less than the physical conquest of Europe and more the effective disarming and disintegration of NATO, particularly its nuclear capabilities, ranging from prolonging and completing the effects of a full-scale strategic strike in the initial stage of any major conflict to a more "limited" action in which the enemy forces are destroyed and the most important political, administrative, and economic centers are occupied in the shortest possible time. In any event, the requirement is for a rapid breakthrough into the depth of enemy defenses and for the fastest penetration in a short war of high intensity. Conventional weapons may be employed at the outset, and the use of conventional weapons may be sustained, but there is always the shadow of the use of tactical nuclear weapons, and these, if committed, would result in rapid escalation. Thus, there is every reason to make provision for the maximum deployment of conventional forces.

Though the critical decision must be enforced on the central sector, there are plausible threats that the Soviet Union can implement on the flanks, once again by sheer "visibility" of force and presence, as well as through the emergence of "third-party" conflicts. Although there is a military case for expanding the Soviet military perimeter, and an act of "unintended expansion" might be set afoot (if only because the Soviet Union, like others, is sometimes the prisoner of events), the conjunction of political pressure and military infiltration can produce some of the desired results—such as exploiting the first break in Western European solidarity since 1949 brought on by events in Portugal and Soviet requests for refueling facilities (which contributes to expanding the military perimeter). There is also one contingency that looms steadily larger—and is presently the occasion of a bitter verbal dispute involving Grechko and

Yakubovskii[39] —and that is the "case" of Yugoslavia, which might promote direct Soviet intervention or intervention by proxy (Bulgaria being the prime candidate), all under the guise of "proletarian internationalism," which is a carefully worked out doctrine and is undergoing consistent elaboration. Yugoslavia could well fall within the ambit of a "third-party" conflict.

This is to say, in sum, that the Soviet leadership (military and political) will press for the maintenance of relative superiority in "armament norms" in any negotiation over force reductions in the European theater: Such superiority will *not* involve a buildup for outright aggression, but it could provide the means to implement "unintended expansion," even through the very visibility of such a force complement. (I would also add the proviso that the outcome is unpredictable if NATO defense levels fall below a given level of effectiveness and operational fitness.) Equally, the qualitative balance is no longer a factor unilaterally in the favor of NATO. If the Soviet command has to fight, it will fight to win, in a ferocious display of military Darwinism. Here I agree with Dr. Colin Gray's prescription of a certain desperation in the Soviet situation, not out of a comparison of NATO-Warsaw Pact resources but a sense of driving Soviet soldiers to war. Meanwhile, that "learning curve" will climb steadily, and we shall have to wait upon what discoveries the Soviet command makes for itself, sliding slowly from out of their nuclear shell (into which quite a few commanders would like to creep back, with all that security of the nuclear womb).

Nevertheless, once engaged on operations, the Soviet army will fight in all its varying degrees of efficiency—including the tramps, *brodyachaya Rossiya*[40] at large—to win. There is no other alternative but to win—or go under—in one particularly dramatic Soviet scenario. Yet such winning might be otherwise accomplished simply by the possession and persistent display of preponderant force, in which the political utility of the Soviet theater forces is every whit as important as brute military capability.[41]

---

[39] See the recent exchanges—polemics—in Marshal Tito's rejection of the *Rude Pravo* articles by the Marshal Grechko and Marshal Yakubovskii on the wartime liberation of Yugoslavia. See SWB (BBC Monitoring Service) 25/3–65/4.75.

[40] This is Trotsky's vibrant phrase about "vagabond Russia," which he himself set to fight for the Revolution, and which managed to win.

[41] The capability for "relatively prolonged conventional operations" has been recently improved by increasing manpower strength in both the GSFG tank and motor-rifle division (from 9,000 to 11,000 and from 10,500 to 13,500 respectively); divisional artillery has also been strengthened (from 36 to 54 towed guns in a tank division and from 105 to 144 guns in a motor-rifle division); the number of multiple rocket launcher tubes has risen from 200 to 720; the new 122-mm and 152-mm SP guns have been introduced as divisional artillery, with a new radar vehicle to control their fire. The most striking change, however, is the dramatic increase in the *tank strength of the motor-rifle division,* which has risen by 41.4% from 188 to 266 (thus making it only some 59 tanks short of a Soviet tank division as such) and which has been brought about by increasing the tank strength in tank battal-

ions organic to motor-rifle regiments and adding an independent tank battalion to the division (supplying a further 45 tanks).

Under these new provisions a motor-rifle company has been attached to each tank regiment, with a rifle (infantry) element added to the "forward detachments" of tank units. The net result of these changes in organization and establishments has been (i) to eliminate the vulnerability of Soviet attacking columns, (ii) to increase the number of guns available for the artillery preparation and (iii) to remedy the shortage of infantry on the main axis or axes of advance.

Meanwhile the heavy helicopter assault units have been growing, with over 130 assault helicopters now deployed with the capability of lifting some 17 assault battalions. Stocks for conventional operations amount to more than one month's *ammunition supply* and two weeks of POL from Soviet-held stocks in GSFG without relying on East German strategic stocks.

The Soviet Threat to Western Europe: An Example of Theater-War Capabilities

Lothar Ruehl

The security of Western Europe and its defense against a military threat by massive Soviet power has been in the center of strategic thinking and planning ever since the end of World War II. Throughout this period, the evaluation of this assumed threat, however, has proved difficult. The issue of Soviet intentions and the degree of probability of a major war have clouded perceptions and discussions of what might be termed the objective factor in the equation: Soviet military capabilities versus Western capabilities in Europe. The issue of "warning time," or of the evidence offered by preparations for a major attack against the defenses of Western Europe before the actual outset of war, has further complicated the assessment of the active threat as opposed to a latent but permanent risk of military aggression. Finally the peripheral problems of "flank attacks" against the NATO countries separated from the bulk of continental Western Europe by geography, "Northern Flank threat" against Norway and "Southern Flank threat" against Greece and Turkey, have helped to confuse the picture. The addition of a "security threat" in the Mediterranean both by Soviet forces and various combinations of Soviet and Arab actions have further compounded the problem. In his contribution to this volume, John Erickson has reduced the scope of analysis to the military realities of the European situation and dealt with the central issue: "Soviet Theater-Warfare Capability." Once this core problem has been correctly analyzed, all the other assumptions can be put into proper perspective.

THE ISSUE OF THEATER WAR
ON THE CONTINENT OF EUROPE

In their communique of 23 May 1975, the ministers of defense of NATO nations stated that they had received additional information about recent increases in the military posture of the Warsaw Pact. This statement referred to the secret report made by the NATO Military Committee and to an assessment by SACEUR indicating that since the end of 1973 the ongoing effort to further improve the equipment, training, and combat readiness of the Soviet armed forces in particular and the Warsaw Pact forces in general had reached an alarming pace and scope. The unanimous conclusion of the military staff of NATO was that for the first time an indication of qualitative superiority of Soviet forces in Europe over NATO forces had become apparent. If this trend were to continue, a definite change in the military balance to the advantage of the Warsaw Pact would be evident within three to five years. The military committee, however, did not make public this last conclusion. It decided to examine the advisability of publishing the salient facts exposed in the report at some later date in order to warn governments and the general public against the emerging risk of a real Soviet military superiority over NATO in Europe.

The facts on which this assessment is based concern all categories of military equipment, all components of the Soviet Ground and Air Forces in Eastern and Central Europe, including apparently those in the northwestern and western parts of the USSR itself. Particular emphasis was placed in Brussels on indications: (1) that Soviet armored forces have been reinforced both in numerical strength and in technical combat quality, operational capability, and support; (2) that the new armored personnel carrier (APC) BMP-76 PB with a 73-mm smooth-bore gun with armor-piercing heat rounds is being massively introduced to equip the mechanized infantry divisions—a weapon without equal at this time in the infantry of NATO nations; (3) that the new 122-mm self-propelled (SP) assault gun and the 152-mm M-1973 gun mounted on a tracked chassis are being issued to the armored units; (4) that the distribution of new tactical ground-to-air missiles SA-6 and SA-9 (an improved model of the SA-7 and mounted on a BRDM-2 vehicle) is in full swing; and (5) that the introduction of more efficient bridging and river-crossing equipments and of new antiarmor missiles and guns is being pursued on a large scale.

According to NATO intelligence the Soviet armored divisions are in the process of being reinforced with one additional tank battalion of 49 tanks each. An armored division until recently was composed of 310 tanks (3 tank regiments with 93 tanks each, adding up to 279, plus one tank battalion in the motor-rifle regiment of the division with 31 tanks, bringing the total to 310). To field 40 more battle tanks indicates that the Soviet armored division will be for the first time stronger in the number of battle tanks (350) than the U.S. or German armored division of NATO standards, with 270 battle tanks for the German Panzerdivision, plus 54 lighter reconnaissance tanks—324 tanks in all. The organization of the German Panzer division is being modified in favor of smaller-sized units (the number of tanks in the overall forces will remain the same).

The Soviet motor-rifle divisions are being reinforced by an additional tank battalion with 31 tanks and one SP assault artillery battalion to replace the truck-towed pieces. These changes together with the introduction of the BMP APC armed with the 73-mm gun—in itself a combination of a light SP assault gun, an APC fighting vehicle, and an antitank weapon—give more offensive fire-power and thrust to these light combat units.

The exchange of the older T-55 main battle tanks for the modern T-62 is almost complete in the Soviet divisions in Germany and the USSR. The T-55s have, however, not been withdrawn. They remain in additional cadre tank company units or in depots and are being maintained in a state of operational readiness. According to West German sources, there should be between 1,000 and 1,500 T-55s in the Soviet deployment area in Central Europe, unless some Arab armies had been resupplied with a limited number of tanks from this reserve.

All this corroborates John Erickson's data and basic assumptions concerning a sustained effort to build up the offensive strength of the Soviet and Warsaw Pact Ground Forces in Eastern and Central Europe in confrontation with NATO. Since 1968–1969 the Soviet theater forces in Eastern and Central Europe have been reinforced by an overall increase in tank strength of about 30 percent, in divisional artillery holdings of about 50 percent, and by an increase of about 25 percent in tactical aircraft. The increase in aircraft is upgraded in value by the introduction of more modern types of aircraft such as the MIG-23 and the SU-20 VG fighter-bomber, a MIG-23 fighter-bomber variant, and the improved version of the MIG-21. These new aircraft are entering service slowly, however, and there seems not to be any particular effort to speed up their introduction.

The first question that arises concerns the time frame of this buildup of offensive strength: Is it a beginning or is it an ongoing effort that will level off at some point in the near future? Will the T-62 be replaced in the next decade by the T-70 in equivalent numbers and would the T-62s then remain in a forward readiness reserve position with the front-line forces in Central Europe? Since the opening of the Vienna negotiations on force reductions in the center of Europe between members of the Warsaw Pact and NATO in the spring of 1973, NATO intelligence has observed an increase of about 10 percent in personnel strength in the in-place Soviet forces, which may or may not be significant for further developments and changes in organization of combat forces. The Soviet command has also begun to organize replacements of personnel serving with the forces in Germany in an exercise operation, using air transport to bring in within a few days about 40,000 men from the Soviet Union and fly out the returning (home-bound) soldiers. This kind of exercise provides experience in swift forward deployment of troops without heavy equipment by air. It gives added significance to the forward storing of tanks and artillery pieces held in reserve for possible reinforcement of a second attack echelon.

This second question concerns the use and usefulness of this buildup of offensive strength facing NATO on the continent of Europe. In terms of gross statistics, NATO forces outnumber Warsaw Pact forces on the continent of Europe by roughly 100,000 men under arms at present and in a peacetime posture: NATO fields on this count 1,170,000 men excluding French and Portuguese forces and British and U.S. forces not physically present on the continent and in the Mediterranean for NATO use in the defense of Europe. Although Turkish forces in Asian Turkey and all Greek forces are included, British forces in Britain and all French forces, as well as U.S. rotation forces and other U.S. forces earmarked for use in Europe but stationed in North America, are not counted. If French forces in Germany were included, NATO total strength would go up by some 55,000 men to 1,225,000. If all French forces in France were added, another 450,000 would bring the NATO total in Europe to about 1,675,000. If the British forces in Britain were added (Britain being part of Europe geographically on the same account as Norway or Greece and more so than Turkey) about 280,000 more troops could be counted for a total of 1,955,000 men serving in NATO armed forces in Europe.

The Warsaw Pact fields only about 1,065,000 men in peacetime, including about 200,000 Soviet soldiers in the three Western military districts of the USSR. If all but the Portuguese forces of NATO countries in Europe were counted against the Warsaw Pact total, the numerical superiority of NATO forces would amount to about 875,000 men under arms in Europe. Such a difference in personnel strength is considerable, if not decisive. The numerical comparison shows that NATO at least is not in a position of utter weakness and that there are means to compensate for superior fighting strength and quantities of combat equipment on the Warsaw Pact side, in particular the Soviet ground and tactical air forces deployed in Europe. This compensation value should, however, not be overrated. As John Erickson has demonstrated, the Soviet military organization gets more fighting power out of a given number of men at divisional strength: 18 battalions for some 11,500 men against 12 battalions in the U.S. division for 16,300 men, both mechanized infantry. (The German performance is so far much better on this account than the American, as ex-Secretary of Defense Schlesinger noted in late 1974 after a visit to U.S. and German troops.) Nonetheless, with an overall increase of some 120,000 men since 1971, the Warsaw Pact forces in Europe now seem to have reached the planned manpower level for the missions assigned to them.

The buildup in recent years has enabled the Soviet Union to field about 200 battalion-sized battle groups with an available tank strength of 8,700, supported by some 1,750 tactical combat aircraft in Central Europe. The entire Warsaw Pact force amounts to 43 divisions, with 31 Soviet divisions. The reinforcement capability within 30 days of mobilization is generally considered to be 25 to 30 Warsaw Pact divisions as opposed to 2 to 5 NATO divisions, the latter figure being a minimum, if only for U.S. overseas reinforcement and call-up of reservists in West Germany. This general estimate credits the Soviet Union with 30 divisions ready for action in Central Europe on a war footing within 30 to 40 days, and another 50 reserve divisions to be called up in 30 to 60 days in the territory west of the Urals. The overall deployment of Soviet ground troops indicates a choice in favor of rapid and massive reinforcement of the Soviet forces in Central Europe and for the defense of the western glacis—of 167 divisions counted, only 47 are permanently deployed in the border regions against China and in Mongolia, 5 are stationed in the central USSR, and 23 in the southern territories. Thus, 92 known Soviet divisions (including 33 tank divisions) are deployed in the western USSR and Central Europe—61 in the USSR (of which 22 are tank divisions) and 31 in Europe west of the Soviet borders (with 10 tank divisions). All of the divisions committed to the Warsaw Pact are in first-category readiness as are some of those in the western and eastern USSR. Is this a "theater-warfare capability" sufficient to wage a major attack against NATO in Western Europe? Soviet doctrine, organization, force structures, and deployment of forces all point to an emphasis in this direction; Erickson's conclusion is that the Soviets seek "shock power" for "blitzkrieg" with an "independent conventional option" in order to destroy the NATO defense and occupy large parts of Western Europe.

But can such a mission be carried out by the forces available to the Soviet Warsaw Pact command *without substantial reinforcement* from the western USSR and without calling up reservists in a mobilization? Could a "standing-start attack" be carried out with the necessary degree of efficiency and sustainted thrust? Could it be done without first use of nuclear arms, at least atomic battlefield weapons? Would it be possible to continue the offensive in the face of stiff resistance and nuclear arms delivered on the attacking Warsaw Pact forces?

Soviet training doctrine looks upon NATO forces as being well armed and capable of offering sustained resistance, fighting with heavy arms and in prepared defenses in depth. If so, how could the shock power and the momentum of the thrust of Soviet assault forces break through the defense? This assumption and the question it poses lead on to the decisive question at issue in this discussion: Has the Soviet Union enough "striking force" for a blitzkrieg attack across Germany along two or three main axes toward the Rhine and the English Channel in order to bring the war to a rapid decision? In other words: Are Soviet doctrine and training programs, as they have become known and are apparently practiced, in harmony with the means available? Or are they based on ideal assumptions, with the reality not allowing their use for the desired end? This is not idle speculation, because much of Western assumption of Soviet capabilities and military aims in war is based on the reading of Soviet military programs and doctrinal works.

In any event, Soviet military power, while predominant on the Continent vis-à-vis NATO forces in Western Europe, may not be sufficient to win an all-out war against NATO without nuclear weapons. Although Soviet war doctrine seems to rely on nuclear arms to force victory over NATO forces, there is obvious reluctance to conceive of war as a nuclear exchange from the start in order to force a decision to Soviet advantage. Therefore, Soviet planning for war must necessarily be ambiguous: An independent conventional capability for theater warfare without nuclear weapons, on the one hand; a nuclear strike capability, on the other, to assure ultimate victory on the European theater.

An "independent" conventional option, however, makes no sense if it is only the initial strategy at the outset of war. To be truly independent as a strategy for conquest or for defense, such an option must be carried through to the final decision. If it cannot be, then its success would be dependent on superior nuclear power to intervene at the critical moment—that is, to remedy the shortcomings or failures of the initial operations. A theater war escalating from conventional operations into nuclear exchange (even on the level of nuclear battlefield weapons without use of heavier long-range tactical nuclear arms) would not be determined by an "independent conventional capability." It would be decided in the end either by tactical nuclear arms used in a limited theater nuclear war or else by the effects of further escalation into the selective use of strategic nuclear arms—which means into limited nuclear war. The conventional option within the limits of a theater of operations, such as the continent of Europe, would only serve as a prologue on the stage. There would be no strategic independence, no effective control of escalation with the power necessary to pursue limited war short of use of the more devastating nuclear arms. (The case of NATO's strategy of "flexible response" is different inasmuch as it provides for the use [and even first use] of nuclear arms as soon as necessary to counter attacking forces. Escalation is part of that strategy.)

The same rationale holds for the "dual-capability" concept, both conventional and tactical nuclear capabilities for attack forces. The term "dual capability" is vague and ambiguous. It does not distinguish between the two entirely different operational and psychological-political environments created by the two alternatives. The use of nuclear arms, however limited and selective, causes a change of the nature of war; it escalates the war into a new dimension of risks, possibilities, and reactions. There would be no smooth continuation from a conventional to a limited nuclear war in any theater, least that of Europe. The use of nuclear battlefield weapons cannot be considered to be a mere continuation of conventional artillery barrage or bombing. The shock of being plunged into a nuclear exchange and environment on the battlefield would cause reactions and conditions for fighting not experienced in all the training programs, doctrinal discussions, and military exercises in peacetime. It would create psychological imponderables for the conduct of war.

For this reason alone, no military doctrine can assume rational and controlled behavior of combat units, command authorities, and individuals, however forceful the persuasion of propaganda, indoctrination, training, and sanctions by disciplinarian action or sheer terror. One might argue, then, that the theory of "dual" warfare may remain entirely without foundation in reality; as others might argue, on the contrary, that such "dual capability" could be translated into actual combat behavior by training, indoctrination, and discipline. There is no way of knowing until war breaks out and orders are given, shocks experienced, and losses suffered.

However, the fact that since 1967 Soviet commanders and author have admitted the possibility of conventional theater warfare without immediate escalation into nuclear exchange means that there is at least a theoretical option for war without nuclear arms in Europe. NATO planning, since 1961 at the latest (practically since 1957) has considered this possibility and tried to adapt to this contingency of conventional theater warfare in Europe.

According to Soviet doctrine and explanations by Western military experts, the Soviet military leadership does not conceive either of an all-out war of aggression, unprovoked and started by surprise after careful preparation, or of limited probing actions beyond the borderline between the two alliances. This leaves the analysis of Soviet plans and intentions, as well as capabilities, without much choice for reasonable explanations of Soviet armament efforts and forces deployment in Europe.

There is, of course, the convenient case of "preemption," that is, the preemptive strike against a menacing danger to the security of the Soviet Union itself or that of the East European Warsaw Pact area. This explanation does not carry Soviet war doctrine and defensive or offensive postures in Central Europe beyond the line of departure: If there were such a menace, then preemptive action would indeed be necessary. The same argument is being used by NATO doctrine, not for "preemption," the war being defined as aggression by the presumptive adversary, that is, the Soviet Union, but for the *casus belli* and the initial operational situation of the "defense of Europe." Here lies the problem of "forward defense."

But this assumption of the outbreak of a major war in Europe by aggression of the opponent—or aggressive behavior representing an immediate threat—is but a rationalization of the ideological and moral necessity to wage only a "defensive war." It does not enlighten us on the conditions and possible circumstances leading to war or creating the contingencies for the implementation of a war-fighting strategy.

If no enemy has to be preempted, no actual attack to be resisted, what then would be the purpose and the use of Soviet and Warsaw Pact forces in Central Europe, deployed in a forward posture with an "offensive structure" and an "independent conventional-warfare capability" as well as "dual-strike capabilities" for a "blitzkrieg option," based on a doctrine for fighting and winning a war in Europe? The answer is that unless the entire doctrine is purely rhetorical, the purpose must be the offensive for an all-out war of conquest. This conquest may be limited to obtaining the control of the situation as opposed to occupation of all or most of the territory of Western Europe. For such a victory, a "war-fighting potential" with the appropriate but limited means may be created according to force-goal possibilities and assumptions concerning the requirements for a limited theater war.

But in any case, the goal of this victory would have to be reached in a European campaign against the resistance offered by NATO. Victory, according to Soviet military doctrine, would have to be achieved at all levels of conflict, with or without nuclear arms, by energetic pursuit and the commitment of all available forces. Because, according to Soviet assumptions, NATO resistance would be stiff, an offensive war even limited to the objective of the *control* of the European theater of operation would need all the Soviet and Warsaw Pact forces in Eastern and Central Europe, including those ready in the western USSR. The consequence for Soviet force-goal thinking and war planning is to create a sufficient superiority of strike forces and support for a sustained all-out offensive.

This superiority in strike force and shock power does not seem to exist in Europe at the present time, nor has it ever really existed, according to all NATO commanders and U.S. secretaries of defense. John Erickson has come to the conclusion that the Soviet Union continues the effort to build up "relative" superiority over NATO forces in Europe but does not seem to pursue the goal of massive superiority required for a massive and swift thrust through Germany and the Netherlands to the Rhine and the English Channel. On the other hand, it is not being assumed that the Soviet armed forces would be committed to fight a defensive holding operation against NATO, nor to execute a swift raid into NATO territory to seize some positions or values as bargaining pieces, and then negotiate an advantageous compromise.

If there is no overwhelming superiority for an all-out attack to conquer most or all of Western Europe or at least to win control over the situation on the Continent, if at the same time escalation into nuclear war is to be prevented by a rapid decision and the war therefore to be kept short, then surely the present Soviet and Warsaw Pact war-fighting capabilities and conventional options for a theater war in Europe are not sufficient to win a short and limited war for control of Europe as long as NATO remains intact and ready for defense. If a "standing attack" without considerable reinforcements from the east for a clean sweep through Germany is considered unlikely with the present Warsaw Pact force levels in Central Europe, then the entire Soviet and Warsaw Pact military posture in Europe does not make sense in terms of a "theater-warfare capability" with an "independent conventional option" for an offensive strike concept.

If this is so and if the Soviet military doctrine is accurately interpreted, then it is doubtful that the Soviet Union enjoys the predominant power position for preemptive strikes to coerce Western Europe and to win a major European campaign against NATO. In the last resort then, the Soviet Union, for all its military power, does not have the capability to coerce countries protected by NATO and cannot pose a credible challenge in a crisis unless it relies on the threat of nuclear attack. Nuclear attack would bring about an uncontrollable situation and a confrontation with American nuclear power as long as the U.S. commitment for Europe holds and U.S. forces are present in the theater. One might argue then that Soviet and Warsaw Pact force levels and conventional capabilities in Europe are inadequate for all reasonable purposes against NATO as it stands at present, the risk of any aggressive action being too great, both in itself for operational reasons and because of the escalatory process into nuclear exchange.

OTHER USES OF MILITARY POWER IN EUROPE

What remains then of the possible usefulness of the "relative superiority" of Soviet and Warsaw Pact forces in Europe over NATO? This question remains unanswered. A general suggestion, however, may be offered by political reasoning: The high profile of Soviet military power casts a threatening or at least an impressive shadow over Europe. This perceived superiority of Soviet military power and readiness to strike is supposed to grant indirect benefits and political gains. It has maximized the advantageous strategic position of the USSR in Europe and fortified the glacis west of the Soviet borders including the political control over Eastern Europe. It is difficult to judge the precise merits inherent in this position. Generally it is thought in the West that the massed military power of the USSR in Europe far exceeds the requirements for both strategic defense and political control over Eastern Europe. This may be so, but it is arbitrary to distinguish between the "necessary" minimum of forces for such purposes and "excess power." To be effective, internal dissuasive power needs to be overwhelming. The margin of security is always defined by worst-case assumptions. The Soviet idea of security is by all standards maximalist in the demands for guarantees and assurances. Beyond the Warsaw Pact borders, Soviet policy is designed to exercise influence through political and military power.

There is little doubt that the diplomatic leverage and political influence of the Soviet Union in Western Europe are not entirely or even primarily due to détente and the promise of fruitful cooperation in trade and industry. When the French president, for example, affirms in public (21 May 1975, in Paris) that the problem of a West European defense organization could not usefully be approached because of "understandable Soviet fears" that such a new military grouping might threaten or create military pressure against the Soviet Union, it indicates the measure of appeasement that is inspired by Soviet policies. Such superior power or "perceived superiority" creates in other nations the readiness to comply with the demands of that great power and discourages adverse policies. One can argue the finer point whether this is a "coercion" or "persuasion" or simply "influence." One cannot deny the effectiveness of the Soviet protest in Paris and elsewhere. Here lies the problem of "finlandization of Western Europe."

Although the USSR may not have the power to move massively against the present NATO defenses, it can demonstrate readiness and determination to threaten, intervene, or preempt with military force. One example was the forward deployment of reinforced Soviet armies, flanked by Warsaw Pact forces, during the summer crisis of 1961, leading to the construction of the Berlin Wall and the open threat to use the massed military force if the Western allies tried to force their way to Berlin across East German territory. Another case in point was the 1968 military intervention in Czechoslovakia and the forward deployment of strong ground forces in the southwestern USSR coupled with the concentration of Bulgarian, Hungarian, and Soviet forces in Hungary close to the Rumanian border. This demonstration of force was directed against Rumania and indirectly also against Yugoslavia. It was perceived as such in Bucharest and Belgrade, and President Johnson publicly warned the Soviet Union at that time "not to unleash the hounds of war" by threatening other European countries. The most recent example is the readiness for use of alerted airborne troops (up to 50,000 men) in the southwestern USSR and tactical combat aircraft in Bulgaria at the height of the October War in 1973 for operational deployment in the Middle East, regarded by Secretaries Kissinger and Schlesinger as an actual threat to the security of Israel and the interests of the United States.

SOVIET MILITARY POWER
AND EUROPEAN SECURITY NEGOTIATIONS

These demonstrations of military force in political conflicts by the Soviet Union show that the problem is real. They are in the general background of the diplomatic negotiations on security and mutual force reductions in Europe. They also relate to the bargaining power in such a negotiation as well as the possibility of using arms and forces, force levels and modes of deployment, for political purposes within international security structures. This particular use is offered by their quality: They are elements and component parts of political construction, pieces of architecture, as can be seen in arms-control policies.

This last variant is clearly shown by the Soviet draft for an agreement on the reduction of armed forces and armaments in the central part of Europe (MFR), introduced at the Vienna conference on 8 November 1973, and still upheld in mid-1975 by all Warsaw Pact delegations. This proposal offers to reduce the present force levels of the two alliances in Poland, East Germany, Czechoslovakia on the Warsaw Pact side, in West Germany, Belgium, Luxembourg, and the Netherlands on the NATO side by roughly 17 to 17.5 percent. Formally the draft contains three consecutive and equal reductions: 20,000 men on either side within the zone under consideration in the year 1975, then from the remaining forces another 5 percent on either side in 1976, finally an additional 10 percent in 1977. The Warsaw Pact delegations did not offer any precise information on their actual force levels in Poland, East Germany, and Czechoslovakia, nor did they accept data introduced by the NATO delegations. The Soviet proposal included ground and air forces, while the NATO members excluded air forces from reductions. On this basis of counting, NATO considered that the Soviet draft would result in small reductions. According to the official NATO estimate, the Warsaw Pact forces in the area under consideration total about 925,000 men in ground troops alone, as opposed to 777,000 men on the NATO side, not counting the French forces in Germany. The difference of 148,000 men is the numerical superiority of Warsaw Pact ground forces in the central sector. NATO counts 15,500 main battle tanks on the Warsaw Pact side against 6,000 on the NATO side, a numerical tank superiority of 9,500 for the Warsaw Pact. If the Soviet draft were to be applied to both sides on the basis set forth above and to ground forces without air forces, it would result in a total reduction of about 133,000 men from NATO forces and 151,000 men from Warsaw Pact forces. NATO forces would then stand after execution of this agreement at a ground force total of 644,000 men as opposed to 774,000 men on the Warsaw Pact side. The new net difference between the two ground force totals in the agreement are, or would be, about 130,000 men, as opposed to roughly 150,000 men before reduction. The net gain in reductions would be a modification of the numerical disparity by only 20,000 men. This seems to be hardly worth the effort of negotiation and the obligations that would have to be undertaken for an agreement on troop reductions. The difference would be slightly larger if the air forces were to be brought into an agreement, but even then it would not be significant in terms of the massive military confrontation in the center of Europe (1.7 million men on both sides, excluding French forces, Hungary, and all air and naval forces in the central sector). What then would be the effect of NATO agreement with the Soviet draft proposal?

NATO introduced a proposal calling for a common ceiling of ground force levels at 700,000 men on each side in the central area. This would reduce Warsaw Pact ground forces by 225,000 men, and NATO ground forces by 77,000 men. It would produce a "balanced" posture, a criterion the Soviet side refused to admit from the start as being inconsistent with the proclaimed aim of "undiminished security" for all participants; global strategic balance would be shifted in favor of NATO. What is interesting in this context is the comparison of the U.S. and Soviet reductions according to the two opposing proposals: The NATO plan would reduce U.S. ground forces in this area by 29,000 men, the Warsaw Pact plan by 33,000 men. The difference of 4,000 U.S. soldiers can hardly be central to the controversy. Under the NATO plan Soviet ground troops (estimated at about 460,000 men in East Germany, Poland, and Czechoslovakia) would be reduced by roughly 68,000 men as the Soviet part of the total Warsaw Pact reduction. It is not clear what the Soviet reduction in ground troops would be under the Soviet plan, but it would probably be about 79,000 men (17 percent of 460,000 or about half the reduction of the entire Warsaw Pact ground forces in the area). The difference would be about 11,000 men between the NATO and the Warsaw Pact plans, again an insignificant difference. This is underlined by the fact that the NATO delegations at Vienna did not ask for balanced reductions in tanks, but only in personnel. A balanced reduction in tank strength would mean that the Warsaw Pact forces would eliminate 9,500 tanks from their inventory. This would be a real modification of the balance in the central theater and of what NATO calls "the offensive structure" of the Warsaw Pact ground forces. But it is, of course, out of the question that the Soviet Union would seriously consider such an asymmetrical reduction of armor, because Soviet military power is squarely based on armor as the main component of offensive and defensive warfare. Yet, U.S. Secretary of State Henry Kissinger told the North Atlantic Council that the NATO negotiation position held from 1973 to 1975 was "extravagant." NATO proposed that the Soviet Union withdraw one tank army, with 1,700 tanks, from Central Europe on a step to reduce the superiority in armored forces, looked upon by NATO as the backbone of the official structure of Soviet deployment.

At NATO meetings in Brussels during 1975 there was some discussion concerning a reduction of the number of tactical nuclear arms by 1,000 and the removal of some delivery systems such as tactical F-4 and tactical missiles such as Lance.

The main thrust of the Soviet draft tabled at the Vienna conference in November 1973 was for troop reductions to establish national force-level ceilings (called "subceilings" in NATO terminology) and strict controls of arms and equipment. The draft stipulated that reductions would be in the form of units of ground and air forces, including nuclear forces. Those units selected for reduction in the national forces of the seven countries within the central area would have to be dissolved, their personnel released from military service, and their arms and equipment dismantled. Simple stand-down of those units and redistribution of personnel and equipment would not be enough to comply with the agreement. Those units of the stationed forces selected for reduction would have to be withdrawn with all their arms and equipment and could not be reintroduced into that area. A list of all elements of reduction would be drawn up and added to the text of the agreement. Verification of the agreement would require, in NATO's judgment, a detailed description of the organization and equipment of the armed forces remaining in the respective national force levels. It was not clear, however, whether the Warsaw Pact countries really wanted such a far-reaching international or mutual arms-control system. This system of reductions, however, would not rule out unilateral disarmament measures through mutual example.

The national subceilings are of great importance to Soviet policy, because the Soviet negotiators reject the concept of "common ceiling" on the grounds that it would allow exchanges within the alliances between national forces. Some could be cut and others could be reinforced to make up for reductions. This argument points to the main conceptual concerns of the Soviets: (1) to promote a substantial reduction of the West German military forces; (2) to prevent reinforcement of the West German Bundeswehr; (3) to preclude the creation of a new West European collective security organization, including West European countries outside the zone of reductions, for example, Britain, France, and Italy. Thus, the arms-control system of national subceilings in Central Europe would cut across the internal boundaries of the European community and NATO; it would set West Germany and the three Benelux countries apart from their economic and military partners of a future West European confederation or federal union. The reductions, about 40 percent of the NATO total or about 50,000–55,000 men, would have to be made in the West German army (334,000 men), and possibly the air force (11,000 men). Finally the issue of nuclear arms raised by the Soviet draft would be a means of changing the organization of the distribution of tactical nuclear weapons within NATO, reducing mostly U.S. nuclear units and West German units armed with warheads under U.S. control.

On the whole, the obvious interests of Soviet policy in MFR are in reducing the means of military-political organization, common defense, and unity of action both within the present NATO system and in Western Europe, preventing a new West European defense community, and constraining national autonomy in defense and armament for the European countries concerned. The price to be paid by the Warsaw Pact in terms of force reductions, constraints, and controls would be acceptable, because Soviet forces would be withdrawn only from Central Europe—probably not dissolved nor far removed from the center of the Continent. The strength of Soviet forces in Europe, including the European USSR, and favorable geography (600 kilometers between the Soviet border and the frontier between the two parts of Germany), assure the Soviet Union that the glacis would not be weakened nor the capability to deploy Soviet forces toward the west substantially changed. The strategic position of the Soviet Union in Europe would remain unchanged, but influence would be gained via the control measures of such an agreement on the military defense organization in Western Europe, the autonomy of which would be reduced.

CONCLUSION

New arms technologies, such as precision-guided conventional and low-yield tactical nuclear arms, could complement a strategy and operational tactic of "selective and flexible options" that could change the military balance in Europe. The advantage may shift from offense to defense. Antiair and antitank weapons may overcome the shock power of attack forces and their main weapons systems such as the fighter-bomber and the tank. Electronics may curtail the basic problems of communications, control and command, targeting, reconnaissance and logistic support, particularly in a defensive position. But this is not certain. It cannot be excluded that means will be found to make equally good use of such new technologies for the offense. The technological prospects in Western Europe for reinforcing defensive forces will probably provoke new energetic Soviet efforts to compensate in every conceivable way: by increasing the quantity of arms, reinforcing combat units, changing the structure of units, introducing new equipment, and making maximum use of electronic warfare systems, as well as, of nuclear arms to shield the attack forces.

For the Soviet Union, military power is congenial with the nature of its political system: The use of force for coercion is integral. It is the instrument that has raised Soviet influence and prestige to the global power level and has compelled recognition of its equality with the United States. It is the insurance against the hostile or unmanageable environment in Asia. The economic and technical investment in arms and forces may seem unreasonably heavy to the Western mind, and further capital invested in the armed forces may be subject to the law of diminishing returns. By comparison, however, there is no other field in the Soviet economy where better returns have been made in the promotion of Soviet power, influence, and prestige, with the possible exception of space technology. Whatever may be detracted from the T-62 tank, it has bought the Soviet Union more leverage on the outside world and more constraints on the policies of opposing powers than all the agricultural machinery for harvesting crops.

The Soviet military establishment has political and police functions not only in Eastern Europe. It has educational and disciplinarian missions within Soviet society. It serves as an instrument of Soviet foreign policy, as Marshal Grechko has pointed out. It may be far in excess of what is really needed, but needs are relative to expectation and to changing phenomena. It may seem to the Soviet leadership that in troubled times three field armies too many may be a better insurance for state interests than three divisions too few when the crisis breaks. This may be a crude philosophy, but the growing sophistication of Soviet military technology and organization suggests that the military machine may be run by as highly developed and refined engineering minds as are found in the areas of management and policy making. *The quest for strategic parity* with the United States and military superiority over all immediate neighbors has been neither unreasonable nor futile. Possession of superior force does not necessarily guarantee political control of the situation nor absolute security in conflict. But it has at least one advantage: It does not depend on the goodwill and peaceful intentions of other countries, and it still leaves a government the choice not to use it for war, but as an instrument for influencing an opponent's policy. There is no question but that Europe is dominated by its existence and appearance.

The Soviet Union
and Current Multilateral
Arms Negotiations

Robert Legvold

The hopes that the Soviet Union once had for Europe's two most prominent negotiations—those concluded at the Conference on Security and Cooperation in Europe (CSCE) and those scarcely underway in the Conference on the Mutual Reduction of Forces and Armaments and Associated Measures in Central Europe (MFR)—are changing in two respects or at two levels. The first shift is more substantial than the second and more predictable. It relates to the role that Soviet leaders once hoped the CSCE and MFR discussions might play in promoting specific, relatively concrete, intermediate objectives. The other shift is more subtle than the first and of less certain consequence. It relates to the role they assigned these negotiations in promoting their basic conception of European security.

MAXIMUM HOPES: SPECIFIC OBJECTIVES

As might be expected leaders began these negotiations with reasonably far-reaching objectives. In the case of the CSCE, to judge from their approach to Basket I, they sought to do more than give a general sanction to the bilateral treaties signed earlier with the Federal Republic of Germany or rewrite these treaties as a multilateral undertaking. Rather, their proposals on the issue of the inviolability of frontiers and their opposition to the Federal Republic's counterproposals on the issue of peaceful change looked like an attempt to *extend* West German commitments by avoiding the qualifications attached to the Moscow Treaty. In short, their first maximum hope for the CSCE was that it would not only (1) give general expression to Bonn's recognition of the East European status quo and (2) involve others in a semiguarantee of Bonn's commitment, but, that it would (3) finally remove the German reunification issue as such and turn the CSCE into a peace conference.

Second, they hoped that the CSCE would substantially reinforce the spirit of détente in Europe. To get the most mileage out of the Conference for this purpose, the less elaborate it was the better. The objective was to avoid the complications of an involved discussion of Europe's basic political problems, counting on a vague, goodwilled exchange to help relax the political atmosphere. What they had in mind was what they proposed late in 1969—a conference limited to the two general topics of the mutual renunciation of the use of force or threat of its use and the expansion of trade, economic, scientific, and technical relations among European states. Their second maximum objective, therefore, was not merely to circumscribe the alternative uses to which the West would try to put the CSCE, but to use the Conference as an uncomplicated and essentially nonsubstantive boost to European détente.

MFR was a somewhat different matter. Because this was much less a Soviet project—indeed, Soviet leaders had a critical objective to pursue before they could commit everything to the pursuit of maximum objectives or gains. These, most people think, include: (1) establishing control over the evolution and growth of the Federal Republic's Bundeswehr; (2) establishing a *droit de régard* over West European efforts at defense cooperation and integration; (3) influencing the nature and timing of U.S. force withdrawals; and (4) attacking the forward-based-system (FBS) problem from another direction. Achieving these maximum objectives, of course, could be one way of denying the NATO participants their objectives in MFR, but, it was fairly evident from the start that if most of these objectives remained out of reach for the short term, Soviet leaders would still regard as their first concern the obstruction of Western proposals for reciprocal troop cuts.

Parenthetically, Soviet leaders also had a basic interest in keeping the two negotiations as separate as possible in order to get the maximum from each. From the start they resisted any linking of the two. Raising arms-control questions at the CSCE or making progress in CSCE dependent on progress in MFR threatened both the Soviet conception of the security conference and the priority assigned to it. Whatever might have been maximum Soviet objectives in MFR, these were subordinate to their maximum objectives in CSCE. In addition, they appeared to fear that the Western powers would try to exploit a link between the CSCE, where the Soviet Union's greater stake seemed to put Soviet leaders in the position of demandeur, to weaken their negotiating leverage in MFR.

MAXIMUM HOPES: BASIC CONCEPTIONS

There was, I think, a second level at which Soviet leaders had maximum hopes for Europe's negotiations and that was in the role these would play in promoting their conception of European security. What that conception might be is not so important here as the fact that Geneva and Vienna were assigned a central place in proceeding with that conception.[1]

If the Soviet conception of European security had to be compressed into two short formulas, however, I would argue that Soviet leaders first of all seek a transformation of political-military blocs in a fashion providing practical as well as psychological support for the Eastern status quo. In a phrase, they are committed to Europe's economic reunification and political division, and they would like to see NATO and the Warsaw Pact evolve in ways facilitating both. Second, Soviet leaders seek a process (or perhaps a structure to East-West relations) that helps to contain undesirable change and promote desirable change. That is, a process that retards West European integration and East European disintegration; a process that promotes change in the Atlantic Alliance and continuity in their own alliance.

But, again, I am stressing less the content of the Soviet conception of European security and more the earlier conviction that the two negotiations could contribute much to its realization. In different ways, the CSCE was important as the very epitome of their conception: Not only did it symbolize European security *as a process*—rather than a situation—but, at the outset, it promised to be the best instrument for protecting against one kind of change and promoting the other. MFR, in contrast, served best to preclude an alternative conception of European security that would focus early on redoing Europe's underlying military balance. Soviet leaders prefer to attack the problem of European security by altering the political atmosphere between East and West; they, as the beneficiaries of the present military balance, have no reason to treat its restructuring as the key to improved all-European security. In this sense, the present focus of MFR negotiations has sustained the Soviet order of priorities. To the extent that Soviet leaders were successful in pursuing their maximum objectives in MFR, it also offered another avenue for controlling one particular kind of change—that is, for impeding progress toward West European defense cooperation or, short of that, for influencing the way the Europeans, particu-

---

[1] I have speculated about the nature of that conception in "The Problem of European Security," *Problems of Communism* (January–February 1974), pp. 13–33.

larly the Germans, would compensate for a reduction in U.S. forces in Western Europe.

All of this, however, was three years ago and already a key factor to Soviet expectations was passing: East-West relations were ceasing to be the primary focus of Western foreign policies. By 1972–1973 Western leaders were more and more distracted by the problems in their own relations. More and more they were coming to see the collapse of the postwar economic order and the challenge of harmonizing relations among the industrialized capitalist states as their overriding concern. Less and less could they afford, they felt, to treat East-West relations as the most dynamic arena of international politics. Thus, even as the formal negotiations in the CSCE and MFR were being launched, the main weight of Western concern was shifting elsewhere. Today Soviet specialists recognize that their expectations of three years ago have been victimized by a shift in momentum to West-West relations and the related part of North-South relations.

As a result, it appears, there has been a double evolution in the Soviet leadership's maximum hopes for the CSCE and MFR. The first has been substantial and predictable.

THE EVOLUTION OF MAXIMUM HOPES:
SPECIFIC OBJECTIVES

It was reasonably predictable that the Soviet Union would not be lightly conceded its maximum objectives in these two negotiations. Surely from the early phases of the preparatory discussions on the CSCE, begun in November 1972, Soviet leaders could see that the West intended to put its own imprint on the Conference. Thus, the array of issues raised in the name of improving East-West cultural and human contact did more than threaten Socialism's insulation from bourgeois ideas. It also undermined the Soviet hope of turning the Conference into a simple, uncomplicated fillip to détente. Rather than a swift, simple first step toward a new multilateralism, the Conference has turned into involved three-year negotiations, and the results have evidently stirred some Soviet doubts over what the Conference serves as a first step toward. The idea of permanent follow-up machinery—which was originally designed to institutionalize the kind of CSCE the Soviet Union had in mind—takes on a different quality when the CSCE has sides to it that Soviet leaders do not care to perpetuate, sides to it that Western participants insist on highlighting in any follow-up.

Second, the Western participants, in particular the West Germans, successfully avoided Soviet efforts to remove the option of a peaceful reunification of Germany. Soviet leaders had apparently hoped that the numbers, the neutrals, and the nature of the Conference would make it difficult for Bonn to insist on the same reservations attached to the Moscow Treaty. In this they were ultimately disappointed, despite the obvious importance they attached to the objective.

Thus, the Soviet Union's maximum objectives for the CSCE were irretrievably lost. (There is some suspicion among some observers that the Soviet Union looks at a follow-up conference as a second chance, if it can be divorced from the encumbrances of the first CSCE and can be focused more along the lines that Soviet leaders had originally proposed.) In the MFR negotiations, on the other hand, the Soviet Union's maximum objectives are only momentarily foreclosed. At present, however, Soviet leaders must realize that the Western powers are not inclined to concede the Soviet approach to arms control in Central Europe. They are faced with two basic choices: (1) to yield, in part, to the other side's principles for force reductions and, therefore, in part to abandon their own or (2) to settle for a token agreement that does not seriously impinge on either side's principles, that is, that circumvents the contest of principles that the MFR negotiations have been up to this point.

My estimate is that Soviet leaders do not yet feel compelled to make that choice because they are curious to see what will happen to the Western position over the next several months. If I am not mistaken, they have a reasonably definite sequence in mind: First the CSCE must be gotten out of the way; then, or perhaps before, Brezhnev's fourth summit with the U.S. President should produce a new SALT accord; once these two events have taken place--hopefully in the way of fostering renewed Western interest in East-West détente—attention will inevitably be focused on Vienna. By this time, Soviet observers suspect, economic, congressional, or popular pressures may again be building up for force reductions in Europe. The Soviet Union, therefore, is likely to wait several months after the CSCE to see whether the Western negotiating position shows signs of softening. If it does, then Soviet leaders will be drawn toward the first choice. If it does not, then they are likely to settle for a token agreement, valuing such an agreement for its psychological impact.

However, to return to the original point, whichever of the two choices Soviet leaders select, they will not be able to deny the West the use of Vienna to deal with its internal or alliance problems by pursuing their own maximum gains—not for the near term. (A third choice, that is, letting Vienna fail, would of course deny the West its objectives but at the risk of doing damage to East-West détente, something Soviet leaders appear eager to avoid.)

THE EVOLUTION OF MAXIMUM HOPES:
BASIC CONCEPTIONS

The second evolution in the Soviet leadership's maximum hopes for European negotiations has been more subtle and of less certain consequence. This is in the role that they once assigned to conferences like the CSCE and MFR in promoting their basic conception of European security. No longer is it viewed so grandly. Neither conference has done so much as Soviet leaders had earlier hoped to favor the Soviet notion of how East and West would reconstruct their relations.

In the case of the CSCE, the most striking reflection of a change of heart is in the evolution of the Soviet attitude toward follow-up. From the beginning the CSCE was almost a personification of the Soviet conception of European security. Security being a state of mind, they implied, it can only be enhanced by gradually moving away from old attitudes of confrontation toward a greater predisposition to cooperate in mutually acceptable areas. The first step in shedding the old mentality of fear and hostility is to come to terms with the "postwar European reality" and secondly to accept a vastly expanded economic cooperation with the Socialist states. Thus, when Soviet leaders spoke about the urgent need "to build an all-European security system," they were not thinking so much of the final shape of a new security system or even of the structures that might replace the two political-military blocs whose dissolution they constantly urged. Their security system was no system at all, but a process for modifying attitudes, a process without a particular destination. In effecting this process, the CSCE was the best available mechanism. It represented the first concrete instance when states from all over Europe (and the United States) would formally turn their backs on their old hopes of seeing the postwar changes in Eastern Europe undone. It represented the most precise occasion for rallying the whole of Western Europe to the idea of East-West economic cooperation. And it represented an untested way to wean the West European states (or publics) away from the idea of special military and economic groupings.

But it was only a first step. The process that Soviet leaders called "building European security" was to be propelled by institutionalizing such multilateral and bilateral encounters. Others would follow to keep Eastern and Western leaders in contact, to keep them talking about the importance of revising East-West relations, and to prod the search for ways to preserve the momentum of East-West détente. The notion of a permanent mechanism—or institutionalized mechanism—therefore, figured prominently in the original Soviet approach to the problem of European security.

Once confronted with a CSCE different from their first hopes, however, Soviet leaders failed to go on and give this notion specific form. The interesting aspect of the Soviet (formally, the Czechoslovak) proposal for follow-up to the CSCE is that it is so elusive and vague. The Rumanians are convinced that the Soviets have been put off by the unwanted features of the CSCE, such as Basket III, and no longer care to risk a follow-up that will check into the results of their first CSCE. Nor do Soviet leaders want, according to the Rumanians, machinery permitting lesser (East) European states to restrict Soviet freedom of maneuver in East Europe by holding them responsible for their conduct in a multilateral East-West forum. Thus, say the Rumanians, Soviet leaders are far more concerned with their right of veto over follow-up meetings than they are with creating mechanisms by which they can interfere in the process of West European integration.

Even the Western powers who are less convinced that Soviet leaders no longer seek some kind of permanent machinery designed to give them access to developments within Western Europe have noticed a reduced emphasis on this problem by Soviet negotiators. Soviet representatives at the CSCE have long shown a readiness to compromise on the issue of follow-up and, because the Czechoslovak and Danish (that is, the Nine's) proposals are not all that different, the result is likely to be a slightly watered-down fusion of the two—agreement to meet in Belgrade in June 1977 to review compliance with the convention signed in July 1975 in Helsinki.

None of this is to argue that Soviet leaders have repudiated their ideal of a permanent mechanism and what it could theoretically contribute to their conception of improved European security. But whether, like the Rumanians, one believes that the Soviets are so wary of the actual potential of follow-up that they would happily see the French or other holdouts sabotage this part of the CSCE's work or, like the U.S. negotiators at Geneva, one believes that the Soviet Union is still interested in "safe" but diluted follow-up, the reality is that they have downgraded the importance of the CSCE and similar ventures in the long-term process of building European security.

The Soviet attitude toward MFR, too, reflects lesser expectations for the role of multilateral negotiations in promoting their conception of European security. Here, however, the exact evolution is more obscure. Reciprocal force reductions have never been integral to the Soviet approach to European politics, certainly not if one works with my notion of the Soviet conception of European security. Therefore, the Vienna negotiations were from the beginning of secondary importance and the temptation great on the part of Soviet leaders to value them more for the political impact they might have on the atmosphere in Europe than for opportunity they opened to whittle away at the European military balance. As stated earlier, Soviet leaders will soon face two choices in MFR: Either to compromise some of their principles of European arms control in order to draw compromises from the West or to settle for a token accord that begs the question of fundamental principles. Both choices are compatible with the Soviet tendency to stress the "politically symbolic" importance of reaching an agreement in Vienna. At the moment this is a growing tendency.

The consequences are twofold. *First*, the Soviet approach to the Vienna negotiations is more and more likely to reduce the search for agreement to the level of political effect. On the one hand, this keeps Soviet leaders interested in some kind of agreement. On the other hand, it weakens whatever limited willingness Soviet leaders had for tackling the intricate trade-offs of a substantial arms-control accord. Moreover, although it leads them to think of these negotiations as a long-term process, punctuated by periodic agreements, their concern with political effect robs this phasing of much of the potential that phasing has in the SALT context. Although at a painfully slow pace and in a frustratingly loose form, SALT has developed a basic coherence: Quantitative limitations are to open the way to qualitative limitations and then quantitative reductions or vice versa. If the genie cannot be put back into the bottle, SALT nevertheless does leave the impression for the optimistic that the two sides genuinely want to hem him in. No such commitment is evident in Europe, and the Soviet concern with political effect (they are not alone, of course) distracts them from developing one.

Second, this concern with political effect turns the conception of military détente, which Soviet spokesmen feature these days, into something increasingly diffuse and indefinite. The more they emphasize the need to reinforce "political détente" with "military détente," the vaguer they become about the content of military détente. Perhaps it will involve progress in Vienna—but not necessarily. For Soviet specialists now also talk about the virtues of creating nuclear free-zones in the Nordic countries and in the Balkans. Or they refer to the importance of arranging mutual defense-budget cuts, or sometimes to tightening up the application of the NPT to Europe. The vaguer they become about the content of military détente, the more the term appears to be political détente by another name.

Two qualifications ought to be attached to this analysis, however, and they will serve as an appropriate conclusion. First, in describing the double evolution in the Soviet Union's original hopes for the CSCE and Vienna force reduction negotiations, I have not meant to leave the impression that Soviet leaders are either disillusioned with the results of these negotiations or in the process of modifying their basic conception of European security. The CSCE, in particular, has yielded less than they had hoped but not so little that they see nothing to be pleased about. Similarly, the modification in the role that Soviet leaders reserve for multilateral negotiations in promoting their conception of European security is not the equivalent of a modification in that conception. However, as these negotiations have become less central to the Soviet conception of European security, this conception, already rather vague, has become more so.

The second qualification is closely related. Earlier I maintained that Soviet observers sense that their expectations for Europe's negotiations have been partially victimized by changes in the general political context, that is, specifically, by the shift in Western preoccupations to West-West and North-South relations. But it should be added that the tribulations of the major industrialized capitalist states responsible for this shift make it easier for Soviet leaders to accept any disappointment that they feel. It is enough these days to stand back and watch the course of events within the West. Europe's future, they realize, is not for the moment really within their control, and, under the circumstances, perhaps they are not discontent. When the context changes, then Soviet leaders may begin to develop a clearer notion of the link between Europe's negotiations and their conception of Europe's future.

Index